The Educational Messiah Complex:

American Faith in the Culturally Redemptive Power of Schooling

by

Sanford W. Reitman

THE EDUCATIONAL MESSIAH COMPLEX;
AMERICAN FAITH
IN THE CULTURALLY REDEMPTIVE POWER OF SCHOOLING
By Sanford W. Reitman

Published by **Caddo Gap Press**
915 L Street, Suite C-414
Sacramento, California 95814

Price - $19.95

ISBN 1-880192-00-4
Library of Congress Catalog Card Number 92-070299

Contents

Preface

It is with an uncommon, yet highly appropriate and understandable mixture of great pleasure and deep pain that I serve as publisher of *The Educational Messiah Complex: American Faith in the Culturally Redemptive Power of Schooling* by Sanford W. Reitman. The pleasure comes from the opportunity to share this insightful and unique contribution to educational scholarship with prospective readers; the pain is felt because Sandy Reitman died in December of 1989, shortly after completing the final revisions of this manuscript.

I anticipate that my pleasure will be shared by educational scholars and critics, as well as interested lay readers, as this volume is received, studied, reviewed, and discussed. In the pages of this book Reitman examines with great care and detail the traditions of and expectations for American education, charts the development of the phenomena which he terms "The Educational Messiah Complex," discusses a variety of historical and philosophical manifestations and interpretations of that "Complex," explains his view of the folly and inherent failure of such traditions and expectations, and offers his prescription for a more realistic and appropriate future for American education.

In this scholarship, Reitman remains true to the best traditions of the social foundations of education, as he examines historical, philosophical, sociological, political, anthropological, and economic aspects of "The Educational Messiah Complex," as well as drawing on cross-cultural comparisons with Israel. The breadth and depth of his analysis, involving a myriad of historical and contemporary references of both an educational and political nature, provide a strong foundation for his unique and challenging viewpoint.

Also intrinsic to his presentation, as it was to his teaching, is a clear and practical understanding of American public education, gained first as a teacher himself and honed by time spent in supervision, observation, and assisting preservice and inservice teachers; Sandy Reitman was not the prototypical ivory tower professor aloof from the real world of the schools. He symbolized the necessary and appropriate mix of academic grounding in the foundations of education with effective classroom understandings and performance as a teacher, and that same balance informs the analysis presented in the pages which follow. While not all who read this volume will agree with Reitman's orientation nor his ultimate conclusions, I anticipate that all will agree that this work represents a significant addition to American educational scholarship.

I further anticipate that my pain concerning publication of this volume will also be shared widely. Sandy Reitman was a leader in the social foundations of education and teacher education, both through his scholarship and teaching, as well as through his service on the Executive Council of the American Educational Studies Association (AESA) and as a member and chair of the AESA Committee on Academic Standards and Accreditation. I first came in contact with Sandy in the early 1970s, when the two of us had independently embarked on national surveys of the status and health of the educational foundations field; we then shared those findings jointly as part of the program at an AESA annual convention. From that beginning, I enjoyed two decades of association with Sandy, and I know that foundations scholars across the nation share the loss I feel over his premature death at the age of 54.

Those who were not privileged to know Sandy Reitman personally, but come now to know his scholarship and ideas through this book, will also share the pain, since he is no longer present to participate in the healthy and spirited professional dialogue which this volume is sure to engender. While the discussion will necessarily be of benefit to all who seek to understand and improve American education, the loss of a key critic and scholar from that conversation, let alone one whose ideas inform and propel the dialogue, must be felt by all involved.

While Sanford W. Reitman is no longer with us in person, I offer publication of this book as one means to assure that his scholarship, his analysis, his critical viewpoint, and, indeed, his spirit will continue to be available to the field of American education which he loved and served so well.

--**Alan H. Jones**
Publisher
Caddo Gap Press

Chapter 1

Introduction: A General Overview

The Perceived Practicality of Schooling

Pick one hundred Americans at random; ask each to explain what is wrong with the public schools today, and how they think they ought to be improved. Assume that they represent a diversity of religion, economic, occupational, and political interests, as well as ethnic orientations and lifestyles. A few are far right in social and political orientation, more are moderately conservative, still a greater number are middle-of-the-road; several are moderate liberals, and two or three harbor radically left-wing views on the direction American society ought to take. In short, they are a microcosm of American social and cultural pluralism.

Although in such a random sample answers would vary considerably, most people would probably respond that a large part of what is wrong with schools today is that teachers are all too frequently incompetent; recruit better teachers and train them more efficiently. That will go a long way toward improving the schools. That platitude transcends social class, ethnicity, and ideology in America.

More to the point, however, would be the response that students in elementary and secondary schools are no longer required to adequately study the "basics"--reading, writing, arithmetic, American history and geography, science, and civics. They must stop wasting time on "frills and fads" such as art, music, and social studies.

A high percentage of individuals in the sample will undoubtedly insist that "discipline" is far too lax at present. Schools and their personnel need to become tougher in this regard. They should also return to the practice of instilling solid old-fashioned American traits in youngsters, such as respect for authority, belief in God and country, desire to work hard and to compete strenuously for a higher rung on the ladder of socioeconomic success.

Some selected persons who have read approvingly the 1983 *A Nation at Risk* report[1] put forth by former President Ronald Reagan's National Commission on Excellence in Education will, no doubt, speak excitedly about returning to "excellence" in the schooling of our children so as to enable America once again to compete favorably in the world market with economically aggressive countries such as Japan, and to restore a semblance of unity and cultural integrity to our increasingly fragmented and directionless society.

Still others will enthuse on the need for school programs designed to arrest the growth of drug abuse and alcoholism among young Americans and the distressing increase in sexually-transmitted diseases, especially AIDS. Like the above respondents, many Americans are outspokenly conservative to reactionary in their thinking about education, regardless of their views about other social, economic, or political matters. And in the past fifteen years, educational policymakers have been listening to them seriously enough to attempt major retrogressive school reforms in each of the fifty states.

Among the more ideologically left-leaning respondents in such a sample will be a few radicals who believe that the basic traits of American schools are their authoritarian character and their "hidden curriculum" designed to insidiously reproduce an unfair system of social class distinctions by indoctrinating youngsters to stoically accept their ascribed place in the capitalist scheme of things. Some of these radicals would prefer to see schools become more "humane" and honest places in which children study in depth contemporary social problems and are taught how to think critically in the hope that as adults they can either overthrow that structure or at least quietly undermine it.

Less extremely alienated liberals, while not anxious to destroy the existing system of American life, nonetheless maintain that it needs considerable reformation in areas such as race relations, economic opportunity, the treatment of women, quality of the physical environment, and health care. In the minds of the most modern liberals, schools have a potentially significant role to play in gradualistic, albeit focussed social reform. Accordingly, they should be desegregated forcibly not only along racial and ethnic lines, but also to allow and encourage girls to study the same academic subjects as boys and be treated equally in athletics. Furthermore, classrooms should become more democratic environments in which caring and thoughtful teachers and free-spirited learners actively and rationally explore through social studies the character of contemporary life and its problems. Only in that way will they be prepared for the sportsmanship-like give-and-take of democratic civic interaction and progressive improvement of their communities later on after they have graduated.

In a random sample of Americans today, a small but rapidly growing percentage of respondents may even have become completely disillusioned with the public schools, and desire to abolish them altogether or, more commonly, force them to compete on a more nearly equal footing with inexpensive private schools, non-school "learning networks," and private home tutoring by parents. (About fifteen percent of American parents possessing varying ideological outlooks now send their children to private schools or educate them at home.) Interestingly, however, more proponents of private learning arrangements want essentially the same kinds of things that public school loyalists seek--that is, a diversity of educational goals and the means to achieve them. The major difference between proponents of an increased role for the private sector in educational affairs and the public sector majority appears to lie in their interpretation of the term "public." To those who espouse private arrangements, "public education" increasingly connotes moral and financial support by government for a free market of minimally or maximally regulated, yet competing learning arrangements.

In this view, educational free enterprise via universal parent choice of schools and teachers should replace the prevailing "monopoly" or formal learning by one agency; i.e., the compulsory, tax-supported, and bureaucratically-dominated and operated "state" elementary and secondary schooling system that has become standard over the last one hundred and fifty years. What should transpire educationally and otherwise in such preferred private agencies and for what ends can arguably be as reactionary or revolutionary--or anywhere in between--as what different individuals and interest groups supportive of the traditional concept of public schooling have long contended should go on in pursuit of their preferred ends.

The point is that whether Americans are "public school" advocates, as the majority will be, or retreatists to the growing "private" educational arena, most share one belief in common: formal education in the United States urgently needs to be overhauled so as to more effectively serve certain cherished ends. Those preferred ends, as well as the means envisioned to achieve them, differ widely depending on one's placement in the socioeconomic status structure and upon where one fits on an ideologic continuum ranging from the reactionary far-right to the equally rigid revolutionary left.

Despite their differences, however, these ends are almost invariably of a highly **utilitarian** character. Implicit in each and every conception of the direction our schools ought to take is the notion, the belief, indeed the conviction that formal education in America has tangible "commodity value" for its consumers; i.e., students and, more broadly, American society at large.

Whether labeled "public" or "private," schooling is considered by the great majority of our people to be a **public utility** comparable to the telephone company or the electric company or, perhaps, the county hospital. It is supposed to be "useful" to individuals and the community at large, however utilitarian functionality is defined.

I am suggesting that elementary and secondary formal education in this society is typically expected to accomplish something palpable and measurable for its clients, although there is wide disagreement about what that something ought to be. Most Americans, including the lay public, professional educators, and educational intellectuals, are to a greater or lesser extent concerned that schooling at the pre-collegiate level is currently failing to perform its utilitarian functions adequately. Something is wrong with our system of schools that needs "fixing." And most want schools fixed in such a way that their particular conception of the system's utilitarian purposes can be efficaciously achieved. Some want SAT scores raised; others insist that schools increase patriotic values among the young; still others seek more harmonious relations between blacks and whites. Most frequently cited as a desired function of schools between 1960 and 1980 was greater socioeconomic opportunity for the underprivileged to compete on an equal basis with the privileged for solid footing on a higher rung of the American Dream. Today it is restoration of United States leadership in the world economy. Whatever their special ideological biases and interests, the great majority of Americans of every income, educational, and occupational level believe in their hearts that if it is to continue warranting the expenditure of considerable amounts of time, effort, and money on its operation as a major institutional enterprise, schooling ought to prove its worth in "practical" terms; i.e., as a productive utility.

This ubiquitous belief in the commodity value of schooling implies that the institution is presumed **capable** of accomplishing the diverse purposes that the American people have assigned it; that it **can**, indeed, do what they believe it ought to do, that it **is** efficacious as an instrument for improving the welfare of individuals and the social order as a whole. Americans do not merely give lip service to the ethereal notion that schooling **should** have practical utility for living in some mystical otherworldly sense, but that it **actually does** in the here and now. (However, if pressed, most could not explain why they believe that it does.) Without such a **faith** in its capacity to accomplish the useful ends Americans demand of it and given no other plausible rationale for valuing schooling highly, the American people would simply give up on the schools. They would cease to support them legally, fiscally, or emotionally in the intense way to which they have become accustomed.

In the past several years a small number of educational historians and sociologists have argued that many Americans are, indeed, beginning to reconsider their unbounded faith in the power of schooling to effectually accomplish what they would like it to--hence, the growing trend to private educational services. I think their judgment is premature, and contend that most Americans have **not** stopped thinking of institutionalized schooling as a viable public utility. I maintain that most do, in fact, continue to place great hope and faith in one or another version of the school's capability to perform quite practical functions as a utilitarian social institution, much as they do "public" and "private" hospitals and other human service institutions.

A thoughtful examination of major concerns (e.g., classroom discipline) cited in recent Gallop Polls of educational attitudes will readily confirm this assertion. The very fact that so many Americans do complain vehemently nowadays that something is drastically wrong with the schools, requiring major repair work, is evidence of their almost desperate need to believe not only in the school's power to **educate**, but in its meliorative social and cultural efficacy, as well. Let us secure better teachers, overhaul the curriculum, bus blacks and whites across town for desegregation purposes, persuade parents to assist their children more with assigned homework, censor "unAmerican" textbooks, and so forth. In believing that the mounting problems said to be afflicting schools can be corrected in these and other ways, the American people demonstrate the persistence of their enormous faith in the schooling institution's essential ability to "deliver on its promises" to the society by converting knowledge formally taught and learned into individual and collective capabilities of living more comfortable lives and creating a better world.

In sum, Americans continue to want a great deal from their schools of a narrowly pragmatic character. They expect their schools to "work" in tangibly demonstrable ways to improve the quality of life, to meet their heavy "meta-educational" normative demands because they assume that it is **possible** for schools to do so. So great is their faith in the utilitarian capabilities of public schooling that Americans are increasingly willing to threaten to withdraw their children from the "public" schools and enroll them instead in competitive private sector schools.

A Heresy

It is nearly tantamount to a major heresy to question the basic premise outlined above; that the American school is a highly practical and efficacious instrument of individual and social benefit, a primary public utility. Most scholars, intellectuals, professional educators, and members of the general public alike do, indeed, take that premise for granted; accordingly, contemporary educational debates concentrate almost exclusively upon the issues of whose ends deserve implementation and by what means.

But, that assumption is open to challenge. The widely accepted **faith** claim that schools possess considerable instrumental efficacy, particularly to reform or reconstruct society, may be wrongheaded. Their utilitarian power may have been greatly overrated both by the public and the professionals. Such skepticism is not meant to imply that schools cannot do **anything** useful for people, only that Americans may have become excessive in their expectations of them, particularly in isolating them ecologically from their broader community base and, thereby, almost guaranteeing their failure to accomplish even their more limited possibilities.

Such a state of affairs cries out for correction. If the popular mythology about the school's utilitarian benefits is allowed to sustain itself uncritically, the probable consequences are likely to be increasingly social and cultural entropy which might otherwise yet be reversed with only minimal damage to the superstructure of American society. We are already witnessing entropy from failure to abandon myths in other institutional sectors, notably the economy.

The United States is well on the road to becoming what is variously termed a postindustrial, postmodern, or superindustrial society. We no longer are a preeminent industrial nation, as undeniably we once were. Granted that our factories continue to produce carryover products from the past, such as shoes and a few tools, alongside competitive goods from foreign factories, but heavy smokestack industries such as steel and steel-fabricated products have been in precipitous decline since World War I. Writing in *The Atlantic Monthly* recently, Charles Morris illustrated the purity of this decline as follows:

> ... Just a few statistics convey the speed and extent of the humiliation. In 1975 America's machine-tool manufacturers dominated the world markets; in 1985 machine-tool exports were virtually non-existent and German and Japanese machine-tools were standard throughout American industry. In just a few years America's share of world semiconductor fabrication dropped from 60 percent to 40 percent. For all practical purposes, American companies simply exited the consumer electronics industry. No home radios, phonographs, black-and-white televisions, or cassette players are made in the United States any longer; American companies' share of the color-television market is minuscule. No American company makes VCRs or CD players. Industry after industry told the same story. "We were oxyacetylened," one Rust Band executive says--"it was like being taken out with a blowtorch."[2]

Detroit-made automobiles have been especially affected by competition from other countries, particularly Japan. Many experts, including some American automobile designers and engineers themselves, agree that Japan--and certain other foreign nations--now manufactures cars superior to most built by Detroit, excepting some made in Japanese-owned and managed factories located in the United States and those imported from Japan but sold in this country under American trademarks (e.g., Chrysler's "Dodge Colt" which is manufactured in Japan by Mitsubishi). This notwithstanding recent efforts by Detroit to substantially upgrade new domestic automobiles. Without going into elaborate detail in a book on education, suffice it to say that a strong case can be made to support the judgment that, despite vigorous efforts to regain its former standing in the world marketplace, Detroit--and, by extension, the American industrial sector in general--probably will never redesign its operations sufficiently to make cars of comparable quality and par monetary value with those produced in Japan or by Japanese manufactures in the United States. The whole notion of "reindustrialization" is merely wishful thinking that wards off the day of reckoning for a while longer.

But, if the reality of our times is that the United States is rapidly becoming a **post**industrial society, logic would tell both managers and workers, as well as political leaders, to concentrate on the kinds of economic activities that such advanced societies do best: producing human services such as health and welfare, information and mass communication, education, public transportation, family planning, recreation and leisure, home maintenance, neighborhood beautification, and so forth. Rather than trying to return to what we once were but no longer are, we ought, logically, to be content to have Japan, Korea, and other interested and capable countries manufacture high quality products such as automobiles that are sturdy, pleasant to drive, fuel-efficient, and (other things being equal) relatively inexpensive to purchase and operate, while the United States moves "ahead" of technologically advanced industrial nations such as Japan as a world leader in providing people with high quality **services** of every type and level of complexity.[3]

Obviously, a balance of trade between the countries involved would need to be worked out in regard to the most effective functioning of this rational view of our future national development, one based upon what each respective country would be able to offer the other that the other needs. This poses a challenge that Americans admittedly have not had to face before in their relatively short history, but one far less insurmountable than expecting Detroit and other former manufacturing centers to come up with a miracle that will make it truly competitive with Asia and even Europe in heavy industry productivity.

In spite of the misery and havoc it wreaked on individuals and institutions as it proceeded, few would deny that the industrial age was a time of dynamic growth and vitality while it lasted; now it is over. It is time to move on as a culture. As Paul Hawken has generously stated the point in his book *The New Economy*:

> ....The industrial age was not a failure but an unmitigated success. If we refuse to change and try to extend the industrial age beyond its useful life, we will change success into failure by not recognizing our maturation.[4]

The analogy between schooling and manufacturing is far from perfect; but, it is useful, nonetheless. Precisely as Americans should abandon their self-destructive patterns of thinking about the United States as an industrial society and turn instead to a postindustrial model of economic reality, so should they rid themselves of their outmoded expectations of the functions of schooling if schools are no longer (if they ever were) **capable** of producing the narrowly utilitarian ends that the American people have hoped they could. It is dangerously self-delusory to pretend otherwise. Rather than expecting the impossible of their educational institutions, the people of this society ought to be investing in the realistically attainable, given the institution's unique character. This entails that they learn to be objective about what schools are capable of doing and not doing, and that they support them adequately in their wholehearted efforts to accomplish what they are able to do best--**educate**--while turning to other more effective avenues for pragmatic solutions to the concrete problems that have hitherto been displaced onto the beleaguered schools.

A Brief Prospectus

Suggestions for modifying our unhealthy expectations of the schooling enterprise in light of changing sociocultural reality will be provided later in this book. Nonetheless, the greater portion of the material to be presented will attempt to describe those exaggerated expectations more elaborately, and to analyze their causes. If there is one overriding idea at the heart of the book, it is the idea that there is in America today a monumental faith in the culturally "redemptive" power of schooling, which I term the **Educational Messiah Complex**. The reasons for this deeply rooted faith in the school's power to do good works will be discussed in the following pages. The issue of why Americans uniquely are so attracted to the notion of individual and cultural salvation via the efforts of schools and teachers will be addressed. I will also outline the major contemporary ideological expressions of messianic faith in schooling, those passionately held systems of belief articulated by certain educational intellectuals and charismatic leaders of groups interested in what the schools do. The general manner in which educational messianism is spread, or diffused in our culture will also be examined. Given the empirical possibilities and limitations of elementary and secondary schools; i.e., what they can and cannot do for their clients and the public at large, I will show how the prevailing hegemony of educational messianism affects teachers and pupils in our schools negatively and how the American people as a whole are the ultimate victims of a cultural mythology which allows them to escape from their most serious existential responsibilities by displacing them onto the false messiah of schooling. In the final chapter of the book, after portraying several undesirable--but not improbable--scenarios of the future of educational messianism, I will offer a conception of a viable socioeducational order greatly to be preferred; and propose a quite practical, publicly acceptable, and democratic strategy for getting back on track as a "nation at risk."

The material to be treated herein is intended to contribute in some small way toward provoking educators, scholars, social scientists, public policy leaders, as well as the concerned and thoughtful laity to reassess their expectations for schools and their professional personnel in light of what is both educationally defensible and attainable.[5] In turn, my own faith in the American people makes me optimistic that as a result of seeing the appropriate role of the school for what it clearly is, they will, accordingly, recognize the necessity for taking some first halting steps toward restoring a sense of vital and compassionate cultural community to their lives; and therewith become socially self-reliant in their vigorous pursuit of strong democracy.[6]

Chapter 2

The Educational Messiah Complex

The Grand Metaphor

Those who stay abreast with expository literature on modern life and its problems are accustomed to the literary usage of the "grand metaphor." The grand metaphor performs a valuable function for both the writer and his or her audience. It enables the writer to distill a wide a variety of particular ideas into one overriding framework which unifies and synthesizes those particulars. Thus, it facilitates intellectual coherence for the author who is attempting to articulate complex ideas on paper. More importantly, perhaps, it facilitates understanding by the reader who must struggle with the author's attempt to communicate those difficult ideas meaningfully.

Once the metaphor is grasped in its essence, the overall thesis of an original work is much more readily comprehended than would be possible otherwise, and the details provided easier to follow because they are clearly keyed to some central conceptual schema. Instead of appearing as disparate and fragmented bits and pieces of isolated information, they fit together purposefully and bring the work alive.

An illustration of the usage of the grand metaphor which underscores the points I have been making is a recent book by Martin Gross, entitled *The Psychological Society: A Critical Analysis of Psychiatry, Psychotherapy, and the Psychological Revolution.*[1] As the title suggests, this is a social critique of the United States today. The author contends that we have become a society more or less obsessed with the "pseudo-science" of psychology and psychiatry. Americans place unwarranted faith in the cure-all possibilities of psychotherapy and the promises of its practitioners; so much faith that they can hardly take a step on their own any longer before talking to a therapist, obtaining advice from some "expert" in the newspaper or on radio, or reading a popularized how-to book by a self-acclaimed authority on the human condition.

In Gross' psychological society we--especially if middle-class--must question our every motive and analyze our every *oedipal* guilt. We must ask ourselves not only why we feel the need to smoke or drink, but also whether our marriage partners of twenty-five years are any longer "compatible," whether we are "abusing" our children by spanking them, and, if teachers, how to discriminate between "hyperactive" pupils in our classrooms and students with "normal" discipline problems. (Note: "discipline" itself is considered an outmoded word in the psychological society; teachers are urged by experts to ask "what needs disruptive children are acting out and how they should respond to such needs affectively and motivationally.")

The metaphor of a "psychological society" is useful to Gross and his readers; so, for this volume, is that of an "educational messiah complex." It suggests something very basic and significant about modern Americans and their schools. It is helpful in organizing a great diversity of data and concepts into a coherent model of the possibilities and limitations of organized education in the context of what the American people **wish** those possibilities were. In the pages to follow, I will be discussing a propensity of Americans to view schools in a certain way--as agencies of "messianic redemption." I will be employing a "figure of speech" to develop the general idea that the American people as a whole tend to expect far more of the nation's schooling system than the latter can conceivably deliver; their exorbitant expectations laid upon a single social institution constitute an impossible burden for the schools.

The Messiah Concept in General

The Educational Messiah Complex is a true complex in two interlinking senses of that term: first, in the anthropological sense, referring to a culture-wide cluster of values and beliefs about the meaning and importance of schooling that is accepted by most people in American society--in the same way as is, say, the notion of monogamy; and, second, in the psychoanalytical sense, signifying some neurosis or more debilitating mental health problem (e.g., the so-called "inferiority complex"). It is my contention that the "messiah complex" that Americans have about the institution of schooling, although sufficiently widespread and deep-seated to be considered a genuine cultural complex in the first, or anthropological sense, is also dysfunctional for our society and its members in the second, or clinical sense. The manner in which the Educational Messiah Complex viewed as a cultural universal, in the anthropological sense, is linked causally with its clinical or dysfunctional correlates is quite important, and will be treated in some detail as the discussion proceeds. In the present chapter my remarks will be limited to an explanatory overview of what this organizing metaphor means in the former sense.

When I speak of the Educational Messiah Complex, hereafter to be signified by the initials EMC, I mean an extensive and passionately possessive **faith** on the parts of most Americans, including scholars and intellectuals, in the efficacy of one particular social institution, the pre-collegiate public schooling system, to improve the conditions of people individually and collectively, or even to save them from some perceived catastrophe (e.g., an AIDS epidemic).

In its least pronounced, and possibly most common form, given the American penchant for "rugged individualism," it is articulated in such perennially satisfying words as "Anyone in America can make it to the top if they want to and work hard in school, **the** royal road to success in American life." In its more extreme version, the metaphor can be expressed in language such as "If we will only educate youngsters in the 'proper' way, salvation, or redemption for the American people is inevitable." Rarely, if ever, is such language actually employed to express feelings about the redemptive power of schooling. Instead, intellectuals and public opinion leaders discourse emotionally about "nations at risk," "graveyards of the American dream," or "schooling as the critical factor in equalizing opportunity for all Americans regardless of race, creed, or color." Nonetheless, what true believers of every ideological stripe disclose about themselves in common when they articulate their views as above is a deep-lying **faith** in the **capacity** of **one** social institution, formal education, to change society redemptively, to act as a powerful force for individual and cultural salvation.

Thus, the metaphor signifies a virtually obsessional belief and attendant trust in the capacity of schooling to, somehow, make life more bearable and satisfying in the near future, because healing qualities have been attributed the institution by those who have pinned their hopes on it. And, it bears noting that such faith is on the increase in modern America, particularly with regard to the institution's presumed role in directly improving the collective conditions of our national life. Indeed, whether focussed upon individual or collective salvation, educational messianism in America is quintessentially a matter of **social** rather than merely individual concern. That is to say, our culture's stress upon individual achievement and success via the schooling process has always been harnessed to one or another conception of the welfare of the community and the larger society. What is best for **my** child educationally must, in the American view of schooling efficacy, also be good for the children of my neighbors and, ultimately, for the advancement of the nation as a whole. In short, the EMC metaphor signifies a peculiarly American outlook on the phenomenon of **social change**. As an explanation of that outlook, then, this book is an attempt to better understand the process of social change generally.

It is appropriate at this point to examine the word "messiah" in some small detail. The term has traditionally been associated with some individual person who typically emerges in times of exceptional social unrest and turbulence to play a central leadership role in calming the anxieties of his or her suffering disciples and followers who are most frustrated and distraught by current events (e.g., Mother Ann Lee in England; Ann Hathaway in the American colonies). The "messiah" arises out of relative obscurity at such troubled times in real or imagined response to the perceived need of the oppressed and disenfranchised, who seek someone "Godlike"--a hero figure--to help them rekindle their flickering hope, and, thereby, relieve their sense of emptiness and alienation from each other and their communities.

Throughout history, certain periods--including the present--have been fraught with greater societal instability and concomitant alienation than other more steady, quiescent, and psychologically secure and culturally integrated periods. Always under conditions of exceptional instability and anomie, some among the most helpless and alienated have tended to "seek and find their answers in an individual whose needs are as their own. They call him messiah."[2] Of course, it bears noting that others, whether equally miserable or not, may learn to cope differently by accepting their lot in life resignedly, seeking some prevailing form of psychological help in overcoming their personal problems, or developing their own non-messianic causes and directions; e.g., through social protest movements, ambitious careers, artistic endeavor, criminal activity, spectator sports, and other pacifying enthusiasms.

Traditionally, the person laying claim to, or attributed by others the title of messiah (literally "anointed one") has been a religious luminary. The obvious example is Jesus of Nazareth; perhaps among contemporary American civil rights proponents might be included the charismatic Reverend Martin Luther King, Jr., martyred as a result of an assassin's bullet. The Jewish people, who were chiefly responsible for the formulation and development of the messiah (in Hebrew, "Messiah") concept in ancient prophetic Israel and who transmitted it to the modern West via Christianity, even today continue to believe in the imminent coming of the Messiah and final redemption of His people that He will bring about upon His coming in the future millennium. More precisely, some of the more religiously orthodox among contemporary Jews do.

However, the narrowly religious conception has been maintained only peripherally since the Enlightenment. Since the Age of Reason the messiah concept has been extended greatly beyond its original meaning as found in prophetic Judaism and in Christianity. Far from remaining the exclusive domain of religion, the concept has become secularized, as Jack Gratus observes:

> Messiahs are no longer the exclusive concern of religion... Their religious convictions are considered of less importance than their social or political views or the effects their movements had on their society.[3]

Not only has the concept been secularized, but we are no longer confined to thinking of messiahs as individual human beings; now, the messianic metaphor can be applied as well to systems of ideas (ideologies such as radical feminism, which professes that only women are capable of saving humankind by ending wars, etc.), social classes and ethnic groups (for example, the familiar "oppressed and militant proletariat" upon which Marxists pin their hopes for the restoration of Eden throughout the world), the nation-state (America as the "redeemer nation" for the downtrodden of the earth), or major social institutions (for example, science, free enterprise capitalism, modern psychotherapy, universal education, etc.)

Thus, the messiah concept has been both secularized and socialized in modern millenarian thought and action. The EMC is actually only one--albeit vitally significant and interesting--variant of this secularization and socialization of the ancient millenarian quest for individual and collective salvation.[4] Like the cultural complex surrounding the growth of the extraordinary faith that members of the "psychological society" place in "therapy" as a *weltanschuang* of self-improvement, the EMC has taken root and rise to ascendancy as a panacea for all manner of social problems in the fertile soil of this still spiritually hopeful society "at a time when sociopolitical ideologies are unfashionable."[5]

In fact, it is physically dangerous for most contemporary Americans who are frustrated with their lives and their dreary perceptions of the future to become embroiled **directly** in extremist ideological and political movements, in spite of the conventional textbook rhetoric about freedom of speech and the Constitutional right to dissent in this country. This is especially true of movements on the radical left, as the post World War II McCarthy era demonstrated. And, the "fashionableness" of the more recent countercultural Vietnam protest period was short-lived. Right-wing extremist movements, including fascistic ones, have typically been less severely dealt with in the United States than left-wing movements, but have been contained to date by the same normative and legal controls that have made it ill-advised to be an outspoken Communist in the United States. How much longer such a steady state will prevail is a strongly debated question in some intellectual circles; some scholars are especially fearful of a full-fledged outbreak of fascism here in the not-too-distant future if the "crisis of capitalism" which, they believe, frustrates and alienates large numbers of socioeconomically disenfranchised Americans, is not resolved, and quickly.[6]

However that might be, it is still more difficult for Americans than for citizens of most other democratic societies to become directly involved in potentially inflammatory social movements, either of a revolutionary or reactionary character. Even comparatively mild "in-system" reformist efforts are frequently suspect, as contemporary environmentalists and other liberal activists have been discovering.

Furthermore, it is considered primitively naive and even mentally unbalanced for persons living in the late twentieth century to place intense hope for salvation in a single charismatic individual, particularly one associated with organized religion; after all, we do live in an age of scientific secularism, despite sporadic attacks on the "dehumanizing" implications of science and correlative periods of religious revivalism when sizable numbers of the alienated are spiritually reborn. This is not to imply that many Americans would not prefer their national leaders to possess "messianic" qualities--witness the extraordinary devotion to Ronald Reagan by his constituents under conditions which would cause defection from any other President (e.g., Irangate) and an unusual degree of grudging admiration for his leadership qualities even by Reagan's opponents. Still, Americans tend to balance their appreciation of the efforts of individual leaders by a recognition that those leaders themselves are influenced and controlled by systemic forces which no single person, however talented, can overpower.

Conversely, however, it is both "safe," "sophisticated," as well as normatively "responsible" for concerned members of a troubled modern society which denigrates and seeks to restrain potentially volatile and brutal ideological conflict to look to the formal education component of the overall system for a way out of their most immediate and pressing quandaries. The schools are a "respectable" means of channeling individual and civil discontent and of pursuing personal happiness and social reform goals. For many Americans schools symbolize the institutionalization of the "American Creed" as no church or even political party possibly can in the modern world. Indeed, as David Tyack and Elizabeth Hansot--historian and political scientist respectively--have pointed out: "The public school system is probably the closest Americans have come to creating an established church."[7]

Schools are seen as the incarnation of what we want to say we are--or at least ought to strive to be at our best--i.e., progressive, scientifically rational, open-minded and tolerant of our differences as a people, and conscientiously civic-minded. Our schools are commonly viewed as the last bastion of calm, deliberate growth and change for our own children and for the cultural collective via reasoned and fair-minded discussion and deliberation. In a crazy world, the schooling system of America is a safe harbor, a refuge of sanity; depending, of course, upon whose version of saneness is being espoused. As one eminent educational scholar and ideologue, social reconstructionist Theodore Brameld, once put it: "Only the power of education is capable of controlling the other powers that man has gained and will use for his annihilation or his transformation."[8] And that is precisely what the American people have decided to use it for, although, as we shall see, most have not subscribed to the democratic socialist ends advocated by Brameld.

They are instead relying upon the schooling system with a vengeance to secure for themselves and the rest of us their various conceptions of the good life. Schooling is the new "messiah" in the United States. Always considered by Americans an important aid to individual and societal advancement, since the 1950s schooling has become the **key** to our continued progress as a culture and the restoration of our preeminent position among the leading nations of the world.

So, in sum, the EMC metaphor represents well the modern American tendency to place large amounts of genuinely inspired faith in some singularly powerful agency which will, presumably, guarantee beneficial results on our behalf, especially in the relatively near future, and quite directly. We have, in effect, endowed the not reluctant school with unique capabilities and attendant responsibilities for leading us triumphantly into our varied and sundry versions of the New Jerusalem. We have invested immense faith and trust in formal education, and we expect that "anointed" institution to prove worthy of our investment.

The EMC's Uniqueness to America

The EMC is a peculiarly American phenomenon. Nowhere else in the world is formal education quite so widely regarded as a major public utility for promoting societal interests directly, efficiently, and in the relatively short term. Yes, it is true that practically all modern and modernizing nations today depend considerably more than they once did upon elementary and secondary schooling as **one** among many essential ingredients in the human capital development mix. Who can deny that, within carefully plotted limits, wise investment in schools **may**, hopefully, pay handsome dividends in the future of progressive societies in terms of highly literate and trainable manpower, of capacity for intelligent and responsible civic involvement, and of increased ability of the masses of individual people to understand and control their personal destinies, and to enjoy their lives more than did their ancestors.

But, nowhere else than in America do governments, scholars, and everyday citizens appear to take such assumptions quite so literally or depend so heavily upon the public schooling system for bringing about large-scale and difficult social reforms almost single-handedly. Other modern nations do, indeed, place **guarded** optimism in the utilitarian power of their formal education systems and then go on to work out their most severe social problems via the informal and formal **sociopolitical** process. This guarded optimism is evident, for example, to any student of the social sciences familiar with the current British literature on the relationship between formal education and society. The level of discourse by British scholars in this regard is, on the whole, infinitely more tentative and cautious in making pronouncements about what the schools presumably can and cannot do than the typically hortatory polemics by American intellectuals as well as lay writers on the subject. The same is true for the French, the Italians, the Germans, the Swedes, and the Israelis, to name but a few counties.

Other non-totalitarian nations live more "directly" than we who place such rare faith in indirect institutions of learning (and totalitarian ones, such as the U.S.S.R., lived "directly" prior to the revolutions which institutionalized their current regimes, with their non-messianic educational conservatism). As a result, schools elsewhere in both the "free world" and the communist and fascist nations are under less severe pressure to perform with missionary-like zealotry; they are far more relaxed and spontaneous places in which to live and learn than schools in the educationally pragmatic United States. Nonetheless, as the most reliable studies clearly indicate, their students generally out-perform our own on almost every **educational** index imaginable, from academics to vocational studies.[9] Some of these countries have comparably diverse and challenging demographic factors to take into account in the overall schooling equation; so the currently fashionable liberal rationalization about "underachievement" by our American students being due to the large numbers of ethnic minorities here is misleading.

In short, far greater respect is elsewhere displayed for the purely educational functions of schooling in contrast with the United States which stresses almost exclusively what Richard Pratte calls their "non-educational," or "social benefit" value.[10] Does this mean that most people in these other nations are less contented with their lives than we are because they expect and receive less of practical utility from the public schooling process? As the following section should make evident, the answer is an unqualified no.

The Israeli Educational Context

By cursorily examining Israeli conceptions of schooling efficacy, we can begin to understand just how genuinely messianic are those held by most members of American society. Such an examination will help demonstrate the contrast in faith between the United States and the land from whence the messianic idea primarily originated and flowered over 2,000 years ago. One might suspect that since the United States has exerted a more profound influence upon modern Israel than any other country has since its founding in 1948; and, since this little nation, which shares our relatively progressive outlook on life generally, is comparably pluralistic culturally and ethnically, as well as idealistic and secularly modern, one might further suspect that it would also share our powerfully utilitarian expectations for the role of formal education. That is not the case, however.

One should, of course, keep in mind that unlike the United States, Israel is essentially a **garrison state**, a country under interminable siege from hostile surrounding nations; that reality alone may have a telling impact upon its people's demands of their schooling system as contrasted with those made of our own. Just how much faith, then, do the "people of the book," so long directly associated with messianic movements, place in their own schools today as they struggle literally to stay afloat militarily, economically, and socially? To what extent do modern Israelis value formal education for its utility in resolving pressing problems, particularly those of a collective character?

To find out, I went to Israel in 1983. I spent a sabbatical semester there conducting qualitative research on attitudes toward education, in part as a participant-observer and also as an interviewer. Ironically, my first intimation of how the Israelis view education arose from a preliminary private correspondence with a widely respected professor of education at Bar Ilan University in Tel Aviv, an institution with a primarily religious focus as contrasted with the other leading universities in Israel. According to her, the major "redemptive" power of schooling resides in its potential to bring a person closer to his or her God. Education is an essentially **spiritual** endeavor. The Israeli philosopher, educator, and theologian Martin Buber perhaps best exemplifies this spiritualist notion of education in his almost mystical writings concerning the holy relationship between Teacher and Student, an I-Thou relationship.[11] The ideal educational transaction is a dialogue in quest of Truth rather than of some predetermined and necessarily mundane end (although the two are not necessarily mutually exclusive).

This negation of the American conception of the redemptive power of schooling in secular, or mundane affairs--as distinguished from affairs of the spirit--was reinforced over and over during my stay in Israel. Although in my reading and conversations with many individuals in all walks of life I did find a variety of views concerning the nature and purpose of formal education, nowhere did I encounter anyone who expressed a strong belief in the school's utilitarian value comparable to that commonly held in the United States.

Many modern Israelis, including most politicians, industrialists, labor unionists, and professional educators appeared to value the role of **higher** education in **training** the intellectually superior student for science-based careers believed vital to the defence and upgrading of a postindustrial nation under siege; e.g., engineering, mathematics, nuclear physics, agronomy, etc. Indeed, there is much concern being expressed currently in the Israeli press that too many students accepted by the university system want to study humanities and the social sciences while far too few are interested in becoming engineers or computer specialists.

In any case, both career training and humanistic scholarship at the level of advanced formal education--despite their blatant differences--have in common goals vastly different from the American notion of utilizing public **elementary** and **secondary** schools for the explicit purposes of advancing materially and resolving major social problems in the short term.

The state of Israel operates a compulsory system of tax-supported public secular, as well as public religious schools, from which parents may choose to send their children from ages five to sixteen (roughly comparable to the "voucher" system that American educators are currently debating, but limited to the public sector). Most parents select the public secular schools for their children. In addition, there are private tuition-charging schools of various kinds available from pre-school through grade twelve. Owing principally to the diversity of schools available to meet the demands of a heterogeneous society, there is no highly standardized curriculum as we know it in the United States, even within the public sector. However, students attending publicly supported schools, whether secular or religious, are required to pursue certain core subjects, such as the *Bible*, history, mathematics, etc.

In general, students at both elementary and secondary public schools that I visited seemed enormously free and happy in comparison with American students. There was a "permissiveness" in most classrooms observed that Americans would typically find intolerable except, perhaps, in some "country club" schools for the upper-middle classes. Yet, in one slum school in Tel-Aviv where I spent a day, the economically and "culturally" disadvantaged students of "Oriental" background (recent immigrants from Africa and other Eastern countries) were busily learning to read, write, compute, draw, and solve problems, all in crowded classrooms (thirty-five to forty children) with a high noise level managed by affable, easygoing teachers who were clearly enjoying themselves as much as the children were. The students had no inhibitions about demonstrating their newly learned knowledge and skills to me, my sabra guide, or their German-born and non-English speaking principal.

The same relaxed geniality pervaded a middle-class "*Ashkenazi*" (European origin) high school in Jerusalem. Teachers and students alike were either lounging around informally outside of class, some preparing to leave for a week of pre-military training in the Negev, or comfortably interacting in their respective roles inside of class. Teachers and school director were called by their first names by the students at this large urban high school. As an aside, an armed Israeli soldier stood in front of the entranceway. Initially, I assumed that he was guarding the building, since there had been several bomb threats in Jerusalem recently. It turned out that he was an eighteen-year-old member of the paratroopers proudly returning to his high school to visit one of his favorite teachers and show her how well he was doing since completing high school.

At a *kibbutz* school near Jerusalem that I visited during my stay, my guide, a leader of the commune, smoked a cigarette in the classroom where preschool children were engaging in learning activities and in the shower room where three youngsters were being bathed by their "*metapalet*" (nurse). He told me that it was perfectly acceptable for me to smoke my pipe, but my cultural conditioning in the "Victorian" United States inhibited me from smoking in the presence of young children in a school setting. Nonetheless, this example of relaxed attitudes toward interpersonal behavior in a structured learning environment had a most telling effect upon me, reinforcing my perception of the open and flexible approach that Israelis in general have toward the educational experience compared with the powerfully role-restricted orientation of Americans.

Finally, it became apparent to me in travelling around the country and several of its major cities that school-aged children and adolescents, on the average, spend more time than American school children in non-school socializing with their peers; for instance, engaging in the many organized sports available, walking interminably around downtown, eating kosher pizzas (pizzas without meat) and non-kosher *falafel* at outdoor stands, attending movies and rock concerts, and so on. One gains the impression that most do even less homework than American youngsters. But, it bears noting that only about twelve percent of all high school graduates are accepted by the eight universities in the country; apparently, the remaining majority do not yet feel sufficient urgency about a prestigious career to sacrifice their youthful energies on the extra-school study demanded to pass the rigorous entrance requirements. The suicide rate among adolescents and young adults is negligible. Upon leaving school and completing military service, there is suitable work for everyone who wants a job; and there is life beyond the job in this vibrant society, particularly in the extended family and more generally in the pervasive feeling that something exciting is going on--that a new nation is being constructed, one which requires the willing participation of each and every citizen, type and level of schooling background notwithstanding.

My point, then, in briefly describing these formal and informal observations and experiences, is to demonstrate not a low regard for schooling on the parts of the Israelis--quite the contrary. Rather, I wish to emphasize the lack of frenetic urgency and anxiety that almost all of the Israelis I met displayed about schooling, teaching, and learning. The overall impression I received from my reading, my varied interviews, and my observations was one of far greater acceptance of the non-utilitarian role of schooling in Israel in comparison to the average American's deep faith in schooling as a significant--therefore, to be carefully monitored--instrument of individual and social development and change. In contrast to the Israelis, we in the United States seem clearly "afraid" to moderate and let our elementary and secondary schools, and, increasingly, our colleges and universities, proceed in terms of the spontaneous rhythms which are indigenous to schools and classrooms wherever they are to be found throughout the world.

Americans constantly attempt to impose a necessarily distorted urgency and artificial rhythm on their schools and classrooms in the seemingly irrational fear that, otherwise, they will fail to "reach" every last student. Such an imposition, supposedly, will enable our schools to create unaided a highly competent, loyal, and well-integrated citizenry and to bring about desired social reforms of either a progressive or retrogressive nature. We take our lower schools, especially, far "more seriously" as important tools for accomplishing specifiable "meta-educational" objectives than do the Israelis; for, as I maintain, we have invested them with "messianic" attributes.

In short, Americans virtually expect miracles from their public schools; the Israelis look for their miracles elsewhere, expecting only modest demonstrable results of the schooling process, and those primarily educational in character. A small percentage of the student body will ultimately attain advanced degrees and other certifiable advantages from that process. For the vast majority of youngsters, attending elementary and secondary schools is no more nor less than a regularized institutional activity of the culture--part of the inevitability of trying to grow up with their peers in the modern world, some of whom will become their lifelong comrades and friends after they have left school, entered the military, and gone to work. It is ironic that the Israelis, far more than the Americans, appear to take seriously John Dewey's ideas about education being an integral part of life in and of itself; yet the American people who nurtured Dewey artificially separate schooling from the rest of life in their zealous efforts to utilize the institution as an instrument for the improvement of life.

The frenzied anxiety about "every child a winner," etc., that we in the postindustrial United States display is not an obsession in postindustrial Israel. Naturally, some children will be "winners" and some "losers," but the terminology itself is inappropriate and demonstrates an impoverishment of values. According to the prevailing *zeitgeist*, most will eventually turn out to be what most people everywhere may realistically expect to become--imperfectly socialized and encultured or acculturated to the ways of Israeli society with the help of an unpretentious schooling process guided by unharried, highly "competent" professional teachers who, in contrast to American teachers, normally enjoy their work. Many are genuine *artists* of the classroom.

As adults, these products of the Israeli schooling system will go about their daily lives in a social order under constant seige without the gnawing compulsiveness and restlessness that most contemporary Americans are increasingly experiencing in their comparatively safe and non-demanding society. They will make big and small mistakes along the road of life, yet few will blame the formal educational system, as Americans are wont to do, for producing a nation of largely ordinary, imperfect mortals who make mistakes in life. The ideology of educational messianism does not enjoy cultural hegemony in Israel as it does in the United States.

And yet this seemingly haphazardly reared people is capable of becoming superlatively disciplined at a moment's notice. The highly regarded (even by its opponents) Israeli Defense Force (IDF) most spectacularly symbolizes and epitomizes this capability of coming to order and "getting the job done" when deemed necessary. (I saw an example of this while visiting a *kibbutz* in the Galilee when a nationwide drill alert took all male and female soldiers to Lebanon overnight.[12]) And well it should, since Israel is, after all, precariously situated geographically and demographically; therefore, it must maintain a dependable and respectable military stance at all times.

A few more illustrations of this capability for discipline and preparedness: People stood literally for hours in the bank patiently waiting their turn to cash their weekly paychecks; they did the same in the few always crowded supermarkets. They argued fiercely and often articulately about politics and religion, without coming to physical or emotional blows; only recent immigrants from the U.S.A. and the U.S.S.R. seem to display the kind of raging fanaticism for which the police may occasionally be called in. There is enormous tolerance for difference of opinion in this tiny democracy.

The imperfect Israeli **community**, including but not singling out its schools, holds itself "accountable" for its members' welfare and the resolution of Israel's unparalleled social problems. Because it is an intrusive entity in the largely Islamic Middle East, formed and developed primarily by the efforts of persecuted castoffs of other societies, Israel knows more than most nations that it cannot afford the luxury of over-relying upon a single social institution, be it the school, psychotherapy, or any other. It is acutely aware that never again can its undeniably "bookish" people rely upon the book alone for earthly salvation--spiritual redemption, perhaps; but not societal.

Redemption in this world is for the self-reliant, interacting members of the holistic and goal-oriented community, according to the Israelis. As I was informed more than once during my stay, "We cannot afford to lose another war. Therefore, we must work together, not allow others to act on our behalf."

American Schools in Contrast to Israel's

In contrast with the Israelis and most other modern nations, the American people ask their schools to solve their major problems of individual opportunity and social cohesiveness **for them**. They expect schools to **lead** the rest of society in reducing the crime rate, lowering the incidence of venereal diseases, and resolving racial/ ethnic antipathies. American schools are expected to almost single-handedly strengthen patriotic values while simultaneously equalizing the opportunities of members of minority groups who have been unjustly treated in the larger society.

Schools as institutions are considered to possess the social power necessary to accomplish such broader-than-educational objectives in the United States. Moreover, practically alone, they are being urged to solve the drug and alcohol problems besetting our stress-ridden social order and to produce more efficient assembly line workers for increasingly obsolete industries. The American school is presently being directed to raise the general level of morality in this normatively fragmented society either through inculcating official platforms of "universal" ethical principles, as some districts have recently ordered, or through Constitutionally sanctioned prayers, as the 40th President urged. For the last twenty years or so, schools and teachers have even been expected to make the American family flourish once again via family life curriculums and by extolling the nuclear family while denigrating newly emerging family forms based on serial marriage, etc.

In short, the American school is being urged to lead society in either restoring the lost past that alarmed sentimentalists yearn for or to bring us reinvigorated into the new and brighter future that visionary prophets create in their mind's eye. In contrast with most other countries throughout the modern world, which view schooling as only one of a number of important interactive elements of community and societal development, the United States expects its schooling system to **take the place of community**, to stand in its stead as its principal agency of individual and social redemption. The EMC represents to the American people the symbolic incarnation of the restoration of their increasingly disconnected sense of genuine cultural community. More than church, family, free enterprise, or even political democracy, the school has been handed and has compliantly accepted the demanding role of prime mover of corrective reform and progress into the uncertain future.

However, there is no convincing **evidence** that the school can successfully perform the community replacement functions that it has been asked to. The most sophisticated research indicates that "the effects of education are conditioned by wider contexts. That is, more is not necessarily better."[13] The contemporary example of racial desegregation by itself makes it apparent that the school has only very limited power to bring about social change on its own. The *Brown vs. Board of Education* decision of the United States Supreme Court in 1954 and the subsequent heavily research-based civil rights legislation which followed upon that decision promised that American schools would not only bring blacks and whites closer together in this society, but would also guarantee equal opportunities via the educational process for blacks who attended desegregated schools with whites. But they did neither. When, after long and frequently violent battles between parents of both races, schools **were** officially desegregated in cities across the nation, many white parents simply withdrew their children from school and moved to different districts in the general vicinity which had not been required to desegregate. Such white flight, in turn, frightened school officials in desegregated districts sufficiently to rescind original desegregation programs where possible or to drastically modify them so as to seem less offensive to nervous white parents (primarily by "magnet schools" which not infrequently discourage blacks). Furthermore, by the 1980s in many cities minority children had themselves voluntarily left their "desegregated" schools and returned to segregated inner city schools. They gave as their reason that they had been mistreated and discriminated against both by adults and white students at their "desegregated" schools, or that the bus ride to and from school was excessively long, resulting in both reduced extracurricular and family activities and contributing to undue fatigue and lack of time for homework.[14]

Thus, thirty five years after *Brown*, school desegregation is, for all intents and purposes, moribund. Such a state of affairs would not surprise the renowned social psychologist Thomas Pettigrew, who has spent his entire academic career studying race relations. Pettigrew has long been an advocate of school desegregation and busing to help end pernicious patterns of racial separation and inequity in this society. Note, the key work is **help**. Pettigrew would **also** redraw school district maps so as to incorporate the entire county, thereby more effectively preventing white flight. More importantly, he would also desegregated **residential** patterns meaningfully. In short, Pettigrew is not an educational messianist, although he does believe that formal education is **one** of several institutions in the community that may contribute to the improvement of race relations and equal opportunity for all children. Desegregated schools may assist in an overall reform movement to change society, but the entire community must be committed to such reform. All of a community's social institutions must contribute their unique strengths to successfully bring about substantial change in the ways human beings think about and interact with each other. Granted their importance in such a reform agenda, desegregated schools alone cannot be expected to carry the ball for the entire society. Pettigrew realized this, but many of his equally renowned colleagues at Harvard do not, as yet. Like the average man or woman in the street, they still operate on the false premise that the hearts and minds of men and women must always precede institutional change and that a single institution is the panacea for dangerous fragmentation of the social structure writ large.[15]

Chapter 3

Some Well-Embedded Historical Roots of the Complex

Education and the American Dream of Eden

Educational messianism has been a feature of American life from the earliest colonial days, albeit not as a full-blown cultural complex. Indeed, belief in the redemptive power of formal education goes back a long way to the Judeo-Christian and Hellenistic sources of our Western civilizational complex in general. For instance, educational theorist Robert Mason, speaking of the historical precedents for recent thought about educationally led social utopias, asserts that the notion that a just society may be established and sustained by an educational program devoted to that end has appeared many times in the history of thought. It is present in Plato's *Republic* and in Comenius' *Great Didactic*. The works of Herbert Spencer and other late nineteenth and early twentieth century writers such as Edward Bellamy involve the idea of a deliberately planned society... It was argued that the essence of intelligence is planning-foresight. An unplanned society would therefore appear to be a society dedicated to chance rather than controlled by intelligence."[1]

Notwithstanding this broader, more universal messianic tradition, throughout our own history Americans have been inordinately predisposed to viewing the school as an agency of individual and societal betterment, at least in part due to the overriding and ever-present influence of what is sometimes called the "American dream of Eden." Richard Whalen finds the roots of this dream

> in the traditional assumption that this nation is unique and enjoys a special dispensation from Providence... Our dream ideology tells us that we are purposely set apart... All this is true because we are pure in heart and endowed with a boundless moral force and energy. America is therefore the universal model and the preordained instrument of God's will in this world.[2]

And, Henri Desroche claims that this dream ideology has "shaped the American consciousness into the collective consciousness of a 'redeeming society,' dedicated to a millenarian role in the destinies of the world."[3]

Formal education has long been considered to have a prominent role to play in shaping that consciousness. Some of the uses to which American schools have been put throughout our history for more than strictly "educative" purposes (i.e., propagation of basic literacy, transmission of old and new cultural information, improvement of thinking and learning skills, broadening of aesthetic appreciation, facilitation of creative expression, etc.) include: restoring popular morality, preventing potentially disruptive radical movements from gaining headway, unifying a nation of immigrants, equalizing opportunity for the lower classes, reforming a changing and modernizing society progressively, and massively overhauling a "sick" society.

A full history of educational messianism would treat in elaborate detail these as well as additional concerns for which schools have been called upon to perform extra-educational services (e.g., the reduction of unemployment, preparation for the unanticipated vocational opportunity, promotion of harmonious relations between "incompatible races," and more). However, the intent of this chapter is merely to draw attention to the fact that, while the EMC is a recent development which must be analyzed in contemporary terms, it did not arise in a vacuum. Its antecedents reside in cultural history.

Faith in formal education's culturally redemptive power was widespread in America from the very beginning as the mundane embodiment of transplanted Protestant faith in education for religious salvation. For example, as educational historian Henry Perkinson has informed us, the first compulsory education laws passed in Puritan Massachusetts in 1642 and 1647 were intended largely to ensure that colonial children would not "degenerate into savagery, not an unlikely fate in this strange, wild, and dangerous land."[4] Thus, according to Perkinson, the earliest settlers believed in the regenerative, or "civilizing" influence of schooling "far more than they did in Europe."[5]

Early faith in the efficacy of schools and teachers to restore lost European civilization while ensuring spiritual redemption was secularized almost completely by the time of the American Revolution; and, thereby, extended down to the present day in the form of a national concern for character development and moral education. The teacher--especially the elementary school teacher--is still expected to be a paragon of middle-class virtue in an otherwise impure society. Most Americans become very incensed at even minor deviations from that assigned role; witness the upright citizen's hostility toward unionized teachers who go on strike, thereby displaying supposed lack of appropriate respect for duly constituted authority and, worse, immorality for "abandoning" the children in their custody while they rudely demand increased salaries.

Another illustration of our deeply rooted reliance upon schools for purposes of ensuring social security--again, like the "civilizing" function, conservative and bourgeois in nature--has been our enduring wish to use them to prevent or reduce "radical" tendencies among "unruly elements" in our society. In his path-breaking study of the social ideas of leading American educators, historian Merle Curti asserts that

> from the colonial period, when educational spokesmen urged planters and merchants to support their work on the ground that it would prevent internal dissention and upheavals, to the depression of 1929, when business was urged not to cut school appropriations on the ground that provision for broad educational opportunities was the best insurance against radicalism, there has been a constant tendency for educators to insist that schools are the most certain means for preventing violent overturns in the social order.[6]

More recently, urgent concern for preventing the spread of social radicalism has been manifested not mainly by professional educators, but by individual and organized superpatriots (Mary Anne Raywid has called them "axegrinders"[7]) worried that schools and universities run by educators have been "soft on communism." Senator Joseph McCarthy, who led the notorious purge in the early

1950s of alleged communists and communist sympathizers in the federal government, the film industry, and the leading universities, best epitomized the deeply ingrained belief of ardent American xenophobes that schools have significant potential both for subverting the citizenry, if left wholly in the control of "progressive" professional educators' and, conversely, of being capable of guarding against dangerous radicalism if closely monitored by "loyal" members of the local, state, and national lay community. Professionals cannot be trusted; they required loyalty oaths.

That is the type of thinking remaining as a legacy from the days of McCarthyism. Few on either the right or the left ever question whether it much **matters** that educators can or cannot be "trusted." It is an article of faith in this society that school knowledge is potential social power. Therefore, those who control the output of knowledge in schools must be watched to make certain that they do not use their positions of authority over the young to undermine extant values, norms, and institutions.

The theme of promoting nationalism as a major function of schooling and teaching is not new, of course. The American Revolution led to the institutionalization of education for citizenship in a republic to be undergirded, according to R. Freeman Butts,[8] by three basic and unique goals: liberty, equality, and the public good. Whether this trilogy of political and civic values is interpreted conservatively or liberally, for generations it has guided mainstream American thinking about what the school should and can instruct and inspire schoolchildren to commit themselves to furthering as a first priority of responsible membership in this society. For two hundred years this has symbolized the continuing American struggle for national unification and a unique identity among the nations.[9]

In a society of immigrants increasingly considered as sociological strangers from non-anglo and non-nordic countries, the public schools have been expected, almost singlehandedly, to "Americanize the foreigners" coming here to live. Principally through training in spoken and written English, the schools are to acculturate and socialize large new population groups to our cherished core values and habits, so that they eventually "melt" into the national cultural "pot" by virtue of hard work, respectable demeanor, and participation in the democratic process via the ballot box.

It is interesting to note that during the 1980s, after having been out of fashion for ten to fifteen years during which the idea of cultural pluralism was in vogue, the term "melting pot" once again regained popularity among journalists, politicians, and educators. The "new civism," which Butts advocates as the primary responsibility of modern schooling, largely repudiates the centrifugal outlook of the recent cultural pluralism. It exemplifies the longstanding--if temporarily interrupted--faith of many fervent nationalists in the power of formal educational institutions to revive or keep alive the political ideology of the Founding Fathers and the cultural unifiers who followed them in the nineteenth century. In this new civism, the public schools are to play a central role in renewing our tarnished American sense of the just national community, particularly through study of American law and analysis of moral dilemmas, such as those advocated by former Harvard psychologist Lawrence Kohlberg.[10]

Perhaps the single most important social benefit project assigned the American schools throughout our history has been the equalization of opportunity to rise from rags to riches. In the words of historian Butts: "For 200 years the creed of equality and the creed of public education have gone together, each bound to the other with extraordinary fidelity."[11] In 1779, Thomas Jefferson proposed a system of education for the colony of Virginia whereby after three years of tax-supported schooling for all free children, poor youngsters would be selected from what he termed the "rubbish" on the basis of academic ability to go on to a private Latin grammar school with full board and tuition paid. The top student of limited means in the graduating class would then be given a three-year scholarship to the College of William and Mary. Although Jefferson's Enlightenment ideas about equalizing social opportunities for the intellectually meritorious were quite modest by contemporary standards, nonetheless they helped inspire the nineteenth century architects of the American public school system to incorporate the notion as a significant component of their more ambitious educational plans.

In turn, the latter established a precedent for contemporary educational liberals to follow in their own efforts to achieve the American dream of a (semi) classless Eden. Today, educational liberals and mainstream conservatives alike are expected to pay enthusiastic or reluctant homage to this idèal, because it has been institutionalized by the United States Supreme Court in its landmark desegregation decision of 1954 and by major federal and state legislation since that decision.

In his twelfth annual superintendent's report to the Massachusetts Board of Education (1848), Horace Mann, the acknowledged "father of the American public school," optimistically unveiled his grandiose conception of the redemptive role of schooling in promoting a semi-classless society in the New Eden:

> According to the European theory, men are divided into classes--some to toil and earn, others to seize and enjoy. According to the Massachusetts theory, all are to have an **equal chance** for earning and equal security in the enjoyment of what they earn. The latter tends to equality of condition; the former to the grossest of inequalities.
>
> Education...beyond all other devices of human origin, is the great equalizer of the conditions of men--the balance-wheel of the social machinery...it gives each man the independence and the means by which he can resist the selfishness of other men...[12] (Emphasis added)

The words "equal chance" in the above quotation mark Mann and most of his compatriots in the Public School Movement (PSM) off from the radical edge of the true believers in equalization of condition via education. The **semi**-classless society extolled by these reformers was the guiding image that finally became normative in educational thought as the twentieth century was born and grew up. Most adherents to the idea of educational equality in recent years have accepted that limitation; namely, that via strong programs devised by experts and implemented by excellent teachers schools can be expected to, if not literally equalize the **condition** of all Americans, certainly give each and every child of this society an equal **chance** to compete for the trophies symbolizing societal success--money, position, fame, power, etc.

From the time of the PSM reformers until now, this deterministic faith in the capacity of the institution of schooling to eradicate handicapping conditions for competing in the game of life, especially ascribed poverty, has persisted. Rich and poor alike, "normal" and handicapped, male and female, and so on are to leave high school or now even college with virtually identical intellectual and socioemotional skills for getting started successfully in the adult world. According to this ideology of educational efficacy, the young black man or woman, for instance, possessing a bachelors degree in, say, accounting from a state college should be in a position to start out in his or her career in a corporation at a desk alongside a young white male with a B. A. from Harvard. After the first few weeks or months on the job, however, the more meritorious one is expected to begin advancing more rapidly than the other. From the equal opportunity perspective, that person should not necessarily be the white Harvard-educated male. How far we have traveled in our seemingly boundless faith in the possibilities of schooling since Jefferson's era.

Once the basic structure of American formal education had been built (by about 1880) as a result of the untiring labor of idealists such as Mann and Henry Barnard, it almost immediately started coming under attack as being obsolete and controlled by conservative administrators and policy makers. Let me explain.

Historians argue among themselves about whether the public school reformers were actually liberals and humanitarians, as they have been touted as being until recently, or conservatives intent on preserving the status quo through the aegis of a new instrument of social control. Neo-revisionist educational historians claim that schoolmen such as Mann were more interested in preserving the status quo than in changing it--that, in effect, they talked one way to the general public and another way to wealthy businessmen and industrialists in order to obtain moral and financial support for the new public schooling system they were attempting to build. Be that as it may, the fact remains that the PSM's great contribution, uncontested by both conventional and revisionist historians, was the institutionalizing in American by 1880 of one of the world's first secular, public, free, and universal organizational systems of elementary and secondary schooling. Today, over one hundred years later, that system remains for all major intents and purposes intact; indeed, as Michael B. Katz has made abundantly clear in his well-known radical critique of the system, it has hardened and become bureaucratically cumbersome over the years.[13]

Nonetheless, it did then and continues to mean all things to all people. All except the most extremely alienated are willing to accept the basic parameters of the American way of "doing schooling," even if reluctantly. They are willing to work within the system built by Mann and his associates. But, they have **different** hopes for what that system should produce. Some want the system to produce more superpatriots; others would like to see it produce critical thinking nonconformists; the variety of expectations for what the school should produce is quite astonishing.

My point is that the nineteenth century school reformers succeeded in achieving one prepotent objective--constructing a relatively long lasting **organizational superstructure** for American basic education. They did not succeed in determining what the lasting social **functions** of that framework would be, because their hopes in that regard were chimerical to begin with. What those functions ought to be were then, as now, heatedly debated by people who otherwise agreed on the essential parameters of the organizational structure. It happened that the liberal and radical ideologues among the organizational reformers were defeated by the conservative and reactionary ones. The institution of schooling sought to serve highly traditional functions for the most part at around the turn of the century: selecting and sorting people for their adult roles, building and maintaining American nationalism and citizenship, transmitting traditional European and American culture (to both natives and foreign-born youngsters), socializing children for the workplace and the family, propagating Judeo-Christian moral values (character education), training children to be literate (the three Rs), and so on. Practically everyone who worked in the schooling system--administrators, supervisors, teachers--took these essentially conservative values for granted as being appropriate and feasible, as did most scholars and parents of schoolchildren.

But, a few did not. These few grew in number until they became a movement which could not be ignored. And, finally, by the 1940s, they virtually controlled the public schools and the colleges which trained teachers and other skilled school workers.[14] They came to be known loosely as "progressives" in contradistinction to the "traditionalists" whom they hoped to overthrow. The essence of their challenge to traditionalist educational ideology is perhaps best understood through the prolific writing of their philosophical leader John Dewey who, in the judgement even of many of his detractors, was a man of profound genius.

Dewey's Special Influence on Educational Messianism

As is so often the case with critics of the schools, Dewey himself grew up and received a traditional formal education in Vermont and at Johns Hopkins University. It appears to have served him well personally all of his long life; for, as a scholar, teacher, and writer, few have exemplified the classical intellectual tradition more brilliantly or faithfully. But, Dewey's **ideas** about education were anything but traditional; they were unthinkably "revolutionary" for his time--and, I might add, still are, understood correctly.

Dewey believed that American schools had enormous social power to do good, but only if they were overhauled and completely modernized. Given that stipulation, he suggested in 1897 that the teacher is "the prophet of the true God and the sharer in the true kingdom of God."[15] It is difficult to find a comparably pure affirmation of faith in the redemptive power of schooling. Indeed, taken out of context with the rest of his written thought, the statement targets him as an educational true believer of the first order. And, it is interesting to note, this statement was made by one derogatorily labelled an atheist and secular humanist to this day by religious fundamentalists.

According to Dewey and his progressive disciples, the traditional school had outlived its usefulness, because America was at the time changing rapidly from an agrarian culture and becoming an urban/industrial civilization requiring new kinds of intellectual capabilities. He conceded that limited conventional training in the three Rs had, perhaps, been modestly useful to many ordinary people living in the simple rural society of the "feudal" past, although most of their "real" education had come from their families, their workplaces, their churches; i.e., their primary community. For the upper-classes, a traditional classical education had been appropriately decorative and, admittedly, even useful to those destined to rule or to engage in scholarly endeavor; e.g., the clergy.

In acknowledging the limited utility of traditional schooling in days gone by, Dewey was trying to convey his conviction that then as in his own time, education was life and vice versa rather than being a separate, isolated process apart from life--the proverbial ivory tower conception, which he deplored. In the past, most of what had been **genuinely** educative had not needed to be acquired in schools, but rather in the transactional give-and-take of daily living in the primary, or organic community. However, since schooling did not then occupy so central a place in American institutional life generally as it was now beginning to occupy, it did not much matter that a great deal of what transpired in places called schools had been relatively meaningless or even modestly detrimental to the average rural or small town youngster then growing up. Their out-of-school educational experiences in the life of the times more than compensated for the minor inconveniences of provincial schoolhouses manned by roughhewn young men or women for a few years of their early upbringing.

But, now--in the first decades of the twentieth century-- schooling had come to matter significantly, not only for the elite, but for the great majority of youngsters, because the "organic" community no longer could adequately prepare most people for life, as it once did. Modern children would be increasingly growing up and coming of age, not in unified *gemeinshaft* communities, but rather in anomic urban industrial settings where, unavoidably, the existential problems of daily living and planning for the future would be vastly different from/and tremendously more complex than in the simple pastoral settings of America's early days. Most of the problems they would face could not even be accurately anticipated, given the enormous change occurring and the great differentiation of life circumstances in an increasingly culturally diverse population living in large metropolitan complexes devoted to manufacturing and retail trade.

So, if a semblance of democracy--both political and social--was to be retained in the future, and if modern youngsters were to grow up capable of effectively striving for the vaunted pursuit of happiness, American society and its schooling institution would be required to change drastically, Dewey believed. And, this prototypical liberal reformer of his time, influenced more by Darwin than by Hegel and Marx,[16] decided to focus his scholarly attention on the latter as the single most promising institution to help bring about evolutionary change and renewal in the former. I hesitate to label him an educational messianist, despite his enormous faith in the reformative capacity of formal education and despite occasional lapses into simplistic interest group reformism, because the **overall** tenor of his thinking about education and society throughout a long career was cautious and moderate.

This was in contrast with many of his overzealous followers in the progressive movement who imputed a **narrowly deterministic** potency to the schooling process--they were, of course, obvious true believers in the miraculous power of schooling. Dewey was normally far more circumspect in his views than were his disciples. As I have expressed it elsewhere in trying to sum up the essence of his socioeducational thought:

> Anticipating the future, John Dewey directed his efforts at such a reasonable goal [restoring integral community to America] many years ago, focusing upon the **unique role** of education in the **transactional** give and take of the community building process....[17]

In Dewey's educational "instrumentalism," or temperate "transactionalism," the essential contributory function of schooling in a changing, industrializing America was to help people learn to live harmoniously with each other, yet remain authentically true to their individual beliefs and values. Such a function was quintessentially democratic in character. The basic job of the school was to stimulate youngsters to think effectively about the unpredictable personal and interpersonal problems they would encounter along the course of life in a changing social order. They had to learn a method of problem solving which enabled them to analyze, criticize, and select from among alternative courses of action the most pragmatically valuable ones.

Dewey believed that the scientific method is applicable to all areas of **intelligent** living. Learning is a process of developing intelligent ("scientific") thinking skills to cope with real human problems. Learning entails confronting and clarifying existential impediments to perceived goals, hypothesizing insightful solutions to such dilemmas, deliberately evaluating alternative hypotheses in terms of their probably pragmatic consequences, and finally acting experimentally upon the apparently most reasonable course(s) of action determined. Although desirable results could never be guaranteed through such a scientific process of thinking, they were far more likely to ensue than via exclusively rationalistic strategies for coping with modern life.

As Dewey pointed out, some rare individuals have always thought "scientifically"--they have been the success stories of history. No longer, however, can we afford to trust in sheer luck. Everyone today must know how to think scientifically, merely to survive, much less rise to the top without trampling others into the ground in the process. In contemporary American society, therefore, the public schools must become community **centers** for teaching **all** children to live intelligently, to approach life critically as scientifically humanistic thinkers and doers. The schools should be transformed into micro-centers of democratic living and learning. They should provide continuous opportunities for children to meet and solve dynamic, timely problems real or simulated through social self-directed participation among their student-citizens. Ideally, the program of the school should be dependent upon no pre-established subject matter, as has always been the case in traditional schools, but rather upon increasingly complicated challenges subsumed within relatively long term projects demanding individual and team investigation by student researchers guided by research director teachers.

With the help of intellectual disciples such as educational philosopher William H. Kilpatrick at Columbia, who translated them into widely comprehensible form, and curriculum theorist Hollis Caswell of Peabody and Columbia, who advocated a modern problems-centered curriculum for improving life in an emerging urban industrial age,[18] Dewey's nonconformist ideas about education were quickly diffused among early twentieth century schoolpeople eager to jump on the progressivist bandwagon--not all, but the interlocking directorate of the liberal educational establishment and their lieutenants, those who increasingly controlled the curriculum and the teachers around the country; i.e., school administrators, supervisors, teachers of teachers, leaders of teacher organizations, etc.

Such people tend to be extremely busy, both by necessity and by temperament. Perhaps with the exception of some theoretically inclined teachers of teachers, they are the "doers" of the formal educational enterprise, the "executives." Dewey, on the other hand, was himself principally a theorist, a thinker rather than a doer. Therefore, his novel ideas, so elaborately worked out in his voluminous writings, were frequently distorted as they were diffused by the new liberals taking over the educational establishment. Dewey's philosophical and social psychological instrumentalism/transactionalism (which extolled genuine intellectual education more even than had the ideas of the best traditional educational thinkers preceding him) became **popularized** (and vulgarized) everywhere in the United States among schoolpeople, in the guise of "progressive education."

In conservative historian Diane Ravitch's words:

> While educators differed in their conception of its necessary features, 'modern' education generally emphasized: active learning (experience and projects) rather than passive learning (reading); cooperative planning of classroom activities by teachers and pupils; cooperation among pupils on group projects instead of competition for grades; the recognition of individual differences in students' abilities and interests; justifying the curriculum by its utility to the student or by the way it met identifiable needs and interests of students; the goal of "effective living" rather than acquisition of knowledge; the value of relating the life of the

> school to the life of the community around it; the merging of traditional subjects into core curricula on functional problems related to family life, community problems, or student interests; the use of books, facts, or traditional learning only when needed as part of students' activities and experience. In the pedagogical literature, the new education was consistently described as democracy in action, because it substituted teacher-pupil cooperation for teacher authoritarianism, stressed socialization to the group instead of individualism, and championed an educational program that was for all children in the here-and-now rather than the minority that was college-bound.[19]

This type of "life adjustment" pedagogy, essentially the softened, vulgarized popularization of Dewey's tough and disciplined theory of education as the intellectual reconstruction of experience, began to dominate American thought and practice about schooling by the 1930s, and remained in vogue until its decline shortly after World War II. At that time, it began coming under increasingly strong attack by traditionalists who variously saw it as anti-intellectual, overly permissive, a communist plot, too demanding of the average teacher, etc. By the late 1950s, Life Adjustment education was finished, replaced by a conservatively messianic emphasis on mathematics and science--the "basics" or "essentials"--intended by traditionalists to lead America to victory in space over the U.S.S.R. As we shall see, progressive education had a resurgence in the 1960s, along with a number of other liberal and radical social ideologies possessing elements of messianic faith in the school's culturally redemptive power.

Whatever their philosophical and/or ideological differences, most instrumentalists and progressivists did possess in common a considerable faith in the American public schools' capacity to lead society in reforming itself along increasingly modern lines. That they were taken seriously enough by educational conservatives following World War II as to warrant a relentless campaign by the latter to undo the work of Dewey and his followers may be testimony more to the messianic faith in schooling held by traditionalists than to any excesses and waywardness on the parts of liberals. The ongoing traditionalist attack on progressive education since the late 1940s has been undergirded by a rather evident fear that educational liberalism, left unchecked, will be the undoing of the vaunted "American way." Accordingly, the "common sense" course of action for those who wish to prevent this from happening and to restore the old way before it is too late is to throw the rascal progressive/liberals out of the schools and teachers' colleges--along with their "soft pedagogy"--and to put the "hard basics" back in.

Such fear has been greatly exacerbated by the fact that twentieth century educational progressivism/liberalism has spawned an embarrassing stepchild known as social reconstructionism. As if it were not bad enough to be attacked by the educational right for allegedly being intellectually flabby, since the Great Depression of the 1930s progressive education has been accused of harboring blatantly Marxist tendencies, a taboo unusually strong in the United States. As recently as 1983, one of my students in a graduate course in contemporary educational ideology accused Dewey himself--an extremely complex personality--of having been a Godless communist whose entire life had been devoted to undermining the "Judeo-Christian spirit which had originally made America the greatest country on earth."

Indeed, a small minority of those who had allegiance to the tenets of progressive education did possess radical leanings. Until the Depression, that minority had remained quiescent in the background of the progressive education movement. However, the enormous letdown of that unhappy period of bread lines and pervasive fear for the future brought to the foreground this disenchantment with what they considered the excessively gradualistic, individual-centered, and upper middle-class elitist tone of mainstream progressive education. The "new frontier" social reconstructionists, as they were then called, led by George Counts of Columbia, urged that the American school and its teachers should "dare" to lead in the creation of an entirely new and more viable social order.[20] Such a non-violently reconstructed social order should be predicated upon social democratic values borrowed from European radical thought and adapted to the unique conditions of American life:

> ....It was not to be capitalist, for capitalism was based on selfishness, which was morally reprehensible, and was, besides, a demonstrated failure. The future order should be planned, coordinated, socialized, humane, and collectivist; it should be built on the democratic and revolutionary traditions

of America's past....[21]

Teachers were to be the leaders of the reconstructive movement in America, not factory workers and peasants, as in Europe. Their job was to act as missionaries on behalf of a holy causes; albeit sophisticated missionaries who subtly inculcate new core values and specific strategies for peacefully achieving them in collaboration with like-minded others in the society, especially their students.

In the view of the new frontier reconstructionists, then, the school represented the last hope of a befuddled and corrupted America for redemption from its greedy, materialistic sinfulness. Only the public school and its missionary teachers could salvage this increasingly decadent society from the error of its ways, and **lead** it to a higher plane of civilized community life.

Is a more extreme form of educational messianism faith conceivable--that schools possess the **capacity** to actually lead American society to Eden by teaching children to depreciate its "central" institution, capitalism, while seeking to achieve a radically new and desirable image of a collectivist future? Seemingly not. Yet, some fifty years later, it is fashionable to assume that schools can, somehow, lead America **backward** to a sentimentalized vision of a revitalized "world leadership role in the international marketplace," as Ronald Reagan's 1983 President's National Commission on Educational Excellence does.[22]

At any rate, World War II brought to an end, temporarily at least, the crisis of capitalism known as the Great Depression. It also doomed for the time being any prospects that radical progressives might have had of the public schools leading in the comprehensive reconstruction of American society.

Solidification of Messianic Faith Following World War II

Historian Diane Ravitch recently addressed the question of what she terms the "faddism" of American education over most of the past half century. She asked why there has been so much of this faddism. Her answer supports what I have been saying about education in this society from the time of our earliest colonial roots:

> ....Our educational faddism stems from the **deeply ingrained conviction** among many Americans that the best way to reform society is to reform the

> schools. Awareness of a social problem typically leads to the creation of a new school program: To curb the rate of traffic fatalities, a driver-education curriculum is devised; a rise in the divorce rate is followed by new courses on family life; demands for racial integration are met with school busing. Since the needs of society change depending on the social, political, and economic climate, the educational pendulum is pushed first in one direction, then in another.[23]

Since those words were written, a new "fad" has attracted reform-minded Americans--sex education intended to end premarital promiscuity as a **direct result** of the "AIDS epidemic," advocated by the right as well as the left as a specific means to halt that epidemic.

Americans had sought to employ their schools for narrowly pragmatic/utilitarian purposes--even for messianic ends--from the time of the first colonists, who relied upon them to prevent their isolated children from "degenerating into savages" instead of embracing the new by raising their children to interact caringly in the new land's own terms. This tradition of reliance upon the institution of schooling for leadership in preventing or resolving large and small social problems and creating a more humane society continued until the eve of World War II, when the new frontier visionaries made their move to politicize public education for the purposes of building a socialist utopia out of what they believed were the ashes of decadent capitalism.

Throughout all that long history, the schools had never fully lived up to the burdensome expectations placed upon them; but Americans continued to hope that they would. They never lost faith in the redemptive power of elementary and secondary schooling. After all, they could see that there had, indeed, been more or less sustained social progress over the past 350 years. The schools "obviously" must have been central to that progress, so they wanted to believe, because in the American dream of Eden, knowledge **is** power. As Curti concluded in his historical analysis of the social ideas of leading American educators, almost all agreed that "if only our social problems were **understood**, faults in the existing structure would ***ipso facto*** be remedied by a new generation of upright and intelligent citizens."[24] (Emphases added.)

"Common sense" led most Americans to agree with the educators that such knowledge-born power must be transmitted to members of the community via the agency of schooling tightly supervised by lay members of the community. And, if the community is no longer viable? Then, as Dewey and certainly the progressivists who listened enthusiastically to his and his colleagues' lectures and read their books believed, the school becomes the **incarnation** of community. That is what seems to have happened increasingly over the years in the American case, although World War II temporarily interrupted the pattern by **forcing** the American people to come together in a unified fashion to protect themselves and their allies from perceived threats of Nazi invasion.

After the war ended, however, that social self-reliance faded quickly as the returning soldiers and their families settled down in the newly burgeoning suburbs that went up almost overnight across the land; and, the schools of America were almost immediately **reinvested** with community redemptive power--so much so that what had previously been a consistent and growing tendency toward dependence upon this institution for social problem solving became a full-blown cultural complex in a few short years. By about the mid-1960s, the process of building that complex had been completed; and that period marks the beginning, roughly, of the contemporary situation regarding Americans and their obsession with schooling as a symbol of **displacement** of their anxieties about themselves and their future.

Chapter 4

The Birthyears of the Educational Messiah Complex

The Transformation of Responsibility

The point was made in the previous chapter that Americans have always been unique among the nations of the world in attributing significant ameliorative power to formal education. But it was not until recently, beginning in the early 1960s, that interest in and reliance upon the institution of elementary and secondary public schooling for purposes of collective salvation and cultural redemption became so sufficiently widespread and intense as to constitute a ruling cultural complex, herein termed the Educational Messiah Complex.

Prior to the 1960s, most educators and lay people relegated the role of schooling to a subordinate position in the hierarchy of major influences upon the development of the American character and the direction our society would take as it moved into the future. They gave lip-service to the by then well-established axiom that schooling was an important public utility. But most saw the schools as possessing a mysterious kind of behind-the-scenes potentiality to impel behavior indirectly. Few considered them capable of exerting a highly direct and immediate force for altering circumstances in any way comparable to political or economic or even familial or religious power. It is true that throughout the 1950s an unprecedented number of articles and books critical--often vitriolically so--of the so-called "life adjustment" education then in vogue in some suburban school systems had been published and widely disseminated, thus seeming to belie the relative indifference and placidity of the times. These conservative and reactionary attacks on modernist educational values ranged from strident polemics by muckraking opportunists eager to make a name for themselves by scapegoating John Dewey to sober analyses by thoughtful scholars who seemed genuinely concerned about the undeniable excesses of progressive education.[1]

Moreover, the liberal educational establishment was extraordinarily defensive about the programs and teaching strategies they supported that were coming under concerted attack by the "essentialists," as most of the conservative critics of public education were then called. But this noisy debate of the 1950s between critics and proponents of the "new education" really did not significantly affect the average teacher across America. The latter was seemingly content to conduct business as usual in his or her rectangular classroom by implementing a mostly nineteenth century curriculum in highly traditional ways.

Nor did the average man or woman in the street appear to care very much that a heated debate about proper schooling was, in fact, going on at some rarified level. They were too busy worrying about making mortgage payments on their split-level homes in the mushrooming suburbs across America; and making certain that their children obtained suitable grades on their report cards in order to meet college entrance requirements. They displayed little interest in such "peripheral" matters as whether "intrinsic" or "extrinsic" motivation should undergird classroom learning theory, or whether the primary social function of schools ought to be the promotion of social democracy in a welfare state or rugged individualism is a laissez faire plutocracy. Actually, what most Americans had in mind when they thought of a school was the image of a hurdle to be overcome on the royal road to personal success in the workplace (especially for boys) leading to a middle- or upper-middle-class lifestyle.

It was drilled into the heads of innumerable youngsters growing up in the 1950s that in order to get ahead in the modern world, one must graduate from college with a bachelor's degree. No longer was a high school diploma sufficient. Therefore, one must first do well in elementary school and then in junior and senior high school. These youngsters' parents were concerned individually with their son's or daughter's using the schooling system to their personal advantage.

An incautious interpretation of the above truism might suggest that such limited concern is evidence of a tremendous faith not in the schooling system's broader social power (the vaunted equal opportunity motif), but rather in the **family's efficacy** in convincing its offspring of the potential benefits resultant from a calculatingly pragmatic approach to life in America generally. But a closer scrutiny of those concerns would show that most parents then as now did not take major credit for their offsprings' decision to manipulate the formal educational system's growing gate-keeping monopoly to their advantage. In the 1950s their faith in **America**, the country whose streets were paved with gold, was still strong enough to preclude such "immodesty" while yet permitting them to see the school fairly realistically as one of many tools that great America made available to the shrewd for gathering in the gold.

The Shift Toward the EMC

At any rate, the 1960s changed all that. Almost overnight, schooling began to be perceived by practically everyone--not only a comparatively few vocal enthusiasts and critics--as a national resource of immense significance; indeed, as the necessary **and** sufficient condition for creating any worthwhile future, both for the individual person as well as the societal collective. Abruptly, the school ceased to be seen as a secondary institution; it entered the foreground of American life. America as a comprehensive society made up of many contributing institutions led by the so-called "military-industrial complex" came to be seen as America the "schooling society." Going to school and college became our national way of life.

No longer was the school considered merely a useful, but ancillary tool in the arsenal of the pragmatic go-getter for making it in America; now, the responsibility for "making it"--and much more--shifted from the individual client of schooling services, the student, to the **supplier** of those services, the school's teachers, administrators, curriculum development specialists, testing and guidance experts, psychologists and social workers, and, of course, university-based trainers of these various institutional functionaries, the educational professoriate--the teachers of teachers.

Going to school in the 1940s and 1950s, one was expected to assume virtually all responsibility for one's successes as well as failures as a student, regardless of the quality of the instructional staff. In those decades students at all levels, from elementary school through the university, were expected to take major responsibility for their own education. In the 1960s, things began to change; students were to share responsibility with their teachers for the formers' education. Since the mid-1970s and as we move into the 1990s, the teacher is expected to assume virtually total responsibility for the learning of his or her students, as well as (if a college professor) continue to carry out the longstanding academic tradition of advancing and diffusing knowledge.

The above illustrates what I mean when I speak of a major shift of responsibility from the individual client of schooling services to the supplier of those services. Most students today place their wholehearted **faith** in the efficacy of the school to secure their education **for** them. They expect the implantation of knowledge from outside by experts.

In its most extreme form, such an expectation is systemized in the learning theory popularized by B. F. Skinner, known as behaviorism. Through highly strategic maneuvering based on what Skinner thinks are scientific principles, the teacher--or computer--is to efficiently manipulate learning, viewed as the modification of a passive or reactive organism's environmentally produced behavior. Such a shift is epiphenomenal in the history of the world. And, it is a result of basic change over an extremely short time period in our entire society's view of the role and associated social power of schooling at every level. As such, the EMC is strictly a contemporary phenomenon, although the propensity to messianism was always there under the surface of things in the American context, one wrought through and through with the mystical dream of Eden.

What has happened since the early 1960s to bring about this shift in responsibility from client to provider of educational services? What were the essential social events that produced the new outlook, the new and greatly expanded universal faith in schooling efficacy, herein being discussed under the metaphoric rubric of EMC?

The takeoff point for change occurred in the late 1950s when the Soviet Union launched the first manned space flight, thereby provoking the U.S.A. to become nervous about its ability to compete technologically with the Russians. For the first time in American history, education became an official tool of warfare:

> The Congress hereby finds and declares that the

> security of the Nation requires the fullest development of the mental resources and technical skills of its young men and women...The national interest requires...that the federal government give assistance to education for programs which are important to our defense.

Thus began the preamble to Title I of the National Defense Education Act (NDEA) of 1958 (PL 85-864), an emergency act by the United States Congress passed in response to a fear of losing the ongoing Cold War with the U.S.S.R.

Immediately, pleasantly surprised college and public school people seized the unprecedented opportunity to upgrade their services by writing grants to develop federally funded programs for the training of teachers and the construction of language development centers, the improvement of teaching in areas deemed relevant to national security such as the sciences and engineering, the expansion of guidance, counseling, and testing programs, and much more. Change was in the air. I felt it as a third year teacher in 1961 when the "New Math" was first experimented with in the Cleveland Public Schools. It was exciting to be part of the national reinvigoration of education, with its promise of an unfamiliar central role for schools and teachers in the rebirth of American greatness--even if one did not agree with the militaristic rationale for the new nationalism. At least it was a start, a breaking up of deeply ingrained tendencies to what then seemed like dysfunctional stability.

The spirit prevailed and expanded as the 1960s wore on. After Lyndon B. Johnson replaced the charismatic liberal John F. Kennedy in the White House, the Civil Rights Act of 1964 was passed by Congress. This complex document covered a wide range of activities abolishing discrimination against blacks, Jews, and women under the law in voting, in hotels, restaurants, and theatres, in parks and municipal auditoriums, in any federally assisted program, in employment, and, of course, in schools. It sought to positively implement the Supreme Court's decision of ten years earlier that public schools must no longer be segregated. As one historian has written:

> ....The passage of the Civil Rights Act marked a turning point in the evolution of the Civil Rights movement as well as in the larger issue of the role of race and group consciousness in American life....[2]

Then, almost immediately following upon the heels of the Civil Rights Act, came the landmark Elementary and Secondary Education Act (ESEA) of 1965. To many, that act represented the formal culmination of the American dream of equality of educational opportunity first articulated over 150 years earlier by Thomas Jefferson and other founding fathers and promulgated by Horace Mann and the other nineteenth century leaders of the public school movement.

According to political scientist James Sundquist, the impetus given by the (conservative) NDEA of 1958 and the (liberal) ESEA of 1965--not to mention the (liberal) Civil Rights Act of 1964--multiplied federal expenditures for formal education by all levels of government "more than ten-fold in a decade--from $375 million in 1958 to an estimated $4.2 billion. [It is now over $30 billion.] The federal share of all expenditures for education has risen during the decade from less than 3 percent to about 10 percent."[3] (However, since the early 1980s, that percentage as well as real dollar expenditures for education have declined.)

The ESEA initially contained five titles to which several amendments have since been added. Title I, the heart of the bill, provided for grant money through states to local districts for the purposes of upgrading programs and facilities specifically for poor children (e.g., Project Headstart). Other titles authorized funds for various educational services: school libraries and textbooks; counseling, remedial instruction, and vocational guidance; creative arts; educational reform; support of increased pure and applied educational research; and the strengthening of state departments of education. Later amendments have included funds for programs for handicapped children, for bilingual education programs, and for career and consumer education. It is hardly exaggerating to suggest that the ESEA was the single piece of high point federal legislation that concretely changed the course of American school history--probably for all time--and exponentially accelerated the development of a true educational messiah complex in the United States.

But, this legislation and the circumstances leading up to it are still only the beginning of our story. The quiescence and relative indifference toward educational controversy of ordinary people observed in the late 1950s and early 1960s was abating rapidly by the time of ESEA in 1965. Americans everywhere were beginning to be confronted daily by television with the mind-boggling sight of students at Berkeley and other major universities defiantly rebelling against the ivory tower system which was nourishing them and the government which was entering more and more into a shooting war in

Vietnam. Hippies, yippies, and the new left counterculture were beginning to stir up the fury of some staunch defenders of the status quo and the allegiance of other, more like-minded members of the "baby boom" generation now coming of age.

Books were being written by many angry young and middle-aged rebels during this period extolling the virtues of the imminent "cultural revolution" led by young people, and waxing enthusiastically about the inevitability of the "greening of America."[4] Willingly or reluctantly, most professional educators were being caught up in the new spirit of what Arthur Wise later called "legislated learning;"[5] that is, a system of schooling increasingly influenced and even directed by judges, politicians, and bureaucrats at the federal and state levels (grant writing had by now become a high art form).

At the same time, a vocal minority of disaffected idealists were speaking and writing about radically reforming the American school. It was portrayed as a virtual prison for all children, but especially those living in the "culture of poverty," and a repressive arm of a bankrupt capitalist economic system. The "ecstatic movement" of the young and not so young was spawning a variety of literary exposes condemning what were considered the vile purposes and practices of conventional schools. Venting their spleen in the opposite direction of the most vitriolic of the 1950s "essentialists," these new left muckrakers demanded the alteration of schools into more humane places where children could happily enjoy their young lives, free places where minority children could study their own historical roots instead of only the dominant "WASP" group's history and culture (preferably in their own native language), and non-sexist places where girls could compete in all sports with boys and learn physics and chemistry if they preferred (while boys should study homemaking and cooking in preparation for the unisex world which radical feminist groups began to actively promote in the early 1970s).

In the later 1960s and early 1970s Marxist-oriented members of the counterculture attending college, employed on college faculties, and seeking teaching credentials began urging that the public schools seek to reconstruct American society (reminiscent of George Counts in the 1930s and Theodore Brameld in the 1950s). This objective was to be achieved by subversion if necessary or by unveiling the "hidden curriculum of capitalist hegemony" or by fostering the unification of proletariat workers in the schools--teachers and students--on behalf of a "critical" expose of the unjust American system.

At the same time, Ivan Illich, a radical priest living in Mexico, bettered educational anarchist Paul Goodman by taking the ultimate step of advocating the "disestablishment" of schooling altogether, the "deschooling" of society as a central means of ending what he considered the extant order of oppression throughout the world wrought by the crisis of social class inequity in capitalist as well as state socialist societies. Illich was urging the deschooling of society precisely because he himself believed the institution had gained such totalitarian power as to, in his words, "threaten all political systems that rely on schools."[6] Illich, the wrathful prophet, was calling for the killing of the (secular) messiah turned devil.

Getting rid of schools altogether did not, however, appeal to many of the liberals and radicals who had been stirred up by events of the 1960s and early 1970s to seek the greening of America. They had too much messianic faith in the institution to join Illich, Everett Reimer, and the other utopian anarchists of the period. Instead, some of the more severely disaffected among the anti-establishment baby boomers and their elder comrades decided to establish private alternatives to the public schools, known as "free schools." (It may be recalled that the term "free" refers to their program and climate, which sought to offer maximum student choice, not to their financing, which required tuition payments by parents.) These marginal men and women sought to enlist alienated youngsters and their parents in grassroots efforts to create their own idea of what learning should entail. They wanted to escape from the rigid and oppressive bureaucratic paraphernalia that they believed made public schools untenable for most students. They wanted to abolish grades, adult-imposed curricula, teacher-centered instruction, and administrator-dominated organization. They wanted children attending to determine freely--largely along the lines of A. S. Neill's Summerhill experiment in England[7]--what they preferred to study and the means by which they would learn. In that way, the seeds of a more humanistic social order, one founded upon a Rousseauian and Freudian conception of educational dependency, would, hopefully, sprout.

During the early 1970s, when the free schools movement was vaguely catching on, some professional public school leaders who were experiencing serious discipline and dropout problems as a result of all the furor in the society conceived of the idea that if they established their own "free schools" within the public sector, they might substantially diminish their difficulties. At the same time, such a venture might help retain the public schools' increasingly tenuous competitive edge over the private schooling sector which was beginning to be a force to be reckoned with once again. Small as it was at its peak, the free school movement frightened public school people who envisioned it as the signal for a more general, hence, potentially dangerous flight from the tax-supported educational sector into the private educational sector. Alarmed by this potential loss of institutional dominance, they tried to repulse the free school movement by coopting it. They established a "public school alternative movement" replete with its own literature and gurus.[8] They built "schools within schools," "schools without walls," and a number of other alternatives for students who did not quite fit in with conventional programs and personnel.

Turning of the Tide Toward Conservatism

But their efforts were fruitless; perhaps too little and too late. For already the tide of liberalism/radicalism in education was beginning to turn. Bear in mind that the public school alternatives movement of the 1970s was largely an effort to compete with the newly worrisome private educational sector. While most of the free schools went out of business after a year or two as a result more of poor planning and administration than of anything intrinsic to their goals, some of the more successful and long-lasting private school ventures that were initiated during the late 1960s and early 1970s in reaction to perceived public school inadequacies were anything but liberal, much less radical in their outlooks. They were secular or religious schools, frequently with strong right wing neo-fundamentalist leanings. If religious in character, they attracted individuals of all major spiritual persuasions--Protestant, Catholic, Jewish, even Islamic.

The incipient public school alternatives movement quickly abandoned its liberal character and, chameleon-like, turned colors in order to fit in readily with a growing backlash against the "excesses" of the anti-establishment, "overly egalitarian," "overly permissive" period of the 1960s and early 1970s. Far more parents were taking their children out of the public schools and enrolling them in private schools to escape having their children "forcibly bused" across town to mingle with blacks or Hispanics in recently desegregated public schools than were leaving to enroll them in countercultural free schools. So, reading the omens clearly, the public school alternatives movement rapidly became dominated by the back-to-basics, or "renaissance" school mentality, rather than retaining its mission of providing a variety of humanistic program options as had initially been promised.

By the mid-1970s, the massive socioeducational change movement which had been ushering in a new era of educational messianism directed at reforming or reconstructing American society along liberal/left lines had, for all intents and purposes, run its course. Even the mildly reformist and eminently respectable futuristics movement (spearheaded by Alvin Toffler's immensely successful *Future Shock*,[9] envisioning a postindustrial world of computerization, abundant leisure, and material plenty within the capitalistic economic model and guided by a schooling system that prepared students for the "history of the future") was on the wane. The socioeducational pendulum was beginning to swing back toward the conservative/reactionary right. The liberal/radical left, including millions of once hopeful parents, students, and teachers had developed what some called "battle fatigue." Its members were tired.

On the other hand, the conservative right was emerging from the shadows once again, aggressively hostile at what they considered a decade and a half of the ruination of the real America by culpable politicians and schoolpeople and radicalized students who had turned their backs on their parents and their national heritage. They saw their chance, and seized it. They looked around, and then fixated on certain symbols of the seeming decline of America, which they blamed substantially on an increasingly decadent schooling system.

For instance, they gazed obsessively at steadily declining SAT scores, and blamed the decline on what they assumed was the unforgivable erosion of standards of academic excellence fostered by uncaring teachers and opportunistic administrators who cared more about ADA (average daily attendance) and free lunch programs that about a demanding academic curriculum with built-in teacher accountability. They read about unprecedentedly rapid rises in the divorce and crime rates, and blamed them to a considerable extent on overly permissive and morally neutral schools that failed to indoctrinate the young with appropriate values and character traits. They watched Japan take over the world automobile and electronics markets while American workers allegedly produced shoddy products, cursed their foremen, and took excessive days off from work to get drunk or indulge in the ingestion of illegal drugs. The schools were to blame for subverting the American character, and unforgivably sanctifying the "socialistic" welfare state and its abuses at the expense of the traditional work ethic.

Meanwhile, as noted earlier, the liberal/left baby boomers had grown weary; especially once the Vietnam war was finally brought to an undignified conclusion, accompanied by the realization that most of their countercultural heroes had, in their terminology, "sold out" or had "failure of nerve." For example, one time student movement leader, Jerry Rubin, who had brazenly called for the elimination of everyone over thirty during the high-pitched 1960s, now had abandoned his cause to become a New York stockbroker. So, most of the former dissidents on the left decided that they might as well follow his example by rejoining their once-despised martini-drinking parents in their "bourgeois" groping for the American dream of material affluence.

The former yippies of San Francisco, led by Rubin in the 1960s, were heard of once again at the Democratic convention held in that city twenty years later. This time around they were being courted by then-Colorado Senator Gary Hart, a seemingly esoteric conservative liberal seeking the Presidential nomination for the first time. In 1984 they were called "yuppies" (young urban upwardly mobile professionals); and the Democrats' great fear was that these former cultural rebels now clad in three-piece suits would vote for the Republican ticket led by Ronald Reagan. Many, in fact, did. Certainly, it is interesting to observe that many of the new corporate/computer set now had their own children who were being groomed (as their parents once had been) for the ivy league universities by being sent to very expensive elite private schools from as early as age two.

So, the pendulum has swung backwards twenty-five years after the drive was first launched to build a Great Society in earnest via the messianic efficacy of a mostly liberal/left-oriented schooling system. The American nation has reversed itself. Its people have determined that its educational redeemer shall have conservative/right-wing inclinations and objectives. Its schools are presently expected to secure the ancient American dream of Eden not through equalizing opportunity so much as by insuring that in the next war--be it with Central America or whomever--the nation's youth shall not run away to Sweden or Canada, as considerable numbers did in the 1960s. They shall have been trained by a refocused schooling system to be "patriotic" enough to fight to the death for their country, right or wrong, as their forebears purportedly did. And, they shall learn to respect hard work again, and to be respectful of their elders and their superiors in the workplace. Women (and homosexuals) shall regain their "virtue" and not be sexually promiscuous in the future. The society shall reindustrialize by virtue of a well-trained corps of disciplined and proud factory workers and high technology professionals; and, thus, no longer be "at risk" in the world market because of an inferior academic foundation. America's dangerous flirtation with "progressive education," convenient symbol of all the wrong-headed liberal/left tendencies that had been building up since John Dewey first began being taken seriously over eighty years ago, and that exploded into a myriad of dissonant and crazy fragments during the Great Society period, is over. The country is back educationally to what the new right calls "sanity" in its schools and its teaching personnel.

But, if we have "returned to the 1950s," it is with a difference. Today's educational conservatism is not quiescent and passive as it was then; it is passionately and hortatorily redemptive. Not just a few obscure theorists are seriously interested in what the schools are about today, as they were in the 1950s; practically everyone is, regardless of social class or occupation. The error of those who have been claiming recently that Americans have lost faith in the power of the school to lead society in its reformation (and their number is not inconsiderable) is directly related to the fact that most of them are disenchanted liberals and radicals, not the neo-conservatives who have regained actual control of the schools. The former group is "out of office" for the moment, and capable only of equating educational efficacy with liberal or radical versions of reform, so narrowly centered are they upon themselves and their allies in the ecstatic movement for left wing social change. Insofar as their particular values have failed to be inculcated for the time being by their preferred instrument of sociocultural problem solving, the school, they obviously have reason to feel frustrated. But they should not err, as they have, by assuming that everyone else in America has given up on the school as a redeemer institution; or even that the pendulum will not swing back their own way sometime in the foreseeable future, and, thereby, quicken the pulse of their hope once again.

The fact is that, largely as a result of the very same cultural forces that in the 1960s and 1970s gave rise to serious prospects for the victory of American liberalism via the aegis of school-diffused knowledge, American conservatives today are unprecedentedly dependent upon the schooling process to secure their unique version of the Eden dream. It is **American** faith in education--magnified by events of the past two decades--not exclusively liberal/left faith--that was deeply affected by the concatenation of change forces depicted in this chapter. The Cold War, the Great Society, the Student Movement, the Arab Oil Embargo, Vietnam, the Collapse of Detroit, the Civil Rights Movement, the Women's Movement, the Depression of the 1970s, the Revival of Fundamentalist Religion, and many more big and little sociocultural factors have interacted to produce unanticipated repercussions in the form of invigorated and reinvigorated mental and emotional states, both radical and restorationist, in the American people since the early 1960s.

The battlefield upon which these diverse forces have contended has been so viciously crisscrossed and torn up that not a single participant in the fray has escaped being affected deeply by the changes wrought over the past twenty-five years. Practically everyone has come to believe that the schooling process is somehow vastly more significant as a utilitarian agency for good or evil than was thought to be the case a mere thirty-five years ago. Virtually all Americans, whether left or right on the ideological spectrum, have been convinced that formal schooling has a messianic role to play in the rebuilding of this society. The left imagines that the institution's redemptive role is to foster one or another version of social democracy, while the right wants the schools to bring back the economic, political, and social norms of the eighteenth or nineteenth century, dressed up in the cosmopolitan style of the computerized late twentieth century.

It is thus incorrect to imagine that the EMC was a mere flash in the pan phenomenon, as the recent highly superficial liberal/left critique of American belief nervously claims. On the contrary, the EMC, which the liberal/left nurtured early--only after having been born by the conservative/right fears of Soviet dominance in space--is alive and well. The liberal/left has been **contained** by the conservative/right, for the time being. Faith in the messianic power of elementary and secondary schools and their professional personnel to redeem America from the social pathologies produced during the tumultuous 1960s and 1970s, and to restore the founding fathers' conception of what the republic ought to be, is at an all-time high, and gives every promise of remaining high for a number of years to come.

Viewed from the classroom teacher's perspective, one can be fairly certain that the great majority of students of the future will not believe that it is their duty to be nearly as self-reliant in obtaining an education as pre-1960s students were brought up to believe. The shift from student initiative in the formal educational process to teacher responsibility for ensuring that learning occurs in the classroom, if necessary by entertaining strategies, is too far advanced for any quick and easy return. Today's mostly conservative students will continue to expect to be guided and nurtured by their mentors as much as, if not more than, the liberal and radical students of fifteen years ago did--and far more than students expected to be guided and nurtured prior to the 1960s--at least as long as the EMC prevails as a major cultural universal in this society. That universal fosters ever-increasing dependency upon teachers at all levels (even including the university) and decreasing intellectual demands of the individual self in a society that appears to be ineluctably determined to sacrifice its social self on the altar of educational messianism.

Chapter 5

Contemporary Ideological Manifestations of Educational Messianism in the United States

Introduction

"Hope is a rope," in the words of Henri Desroche.[1] Like a resting hot air balloon, messianic expectations for schooling are always attached to a mooring of concrete images of what the schools should be doing for Americans, what the practical results of going to school ought to be; i.e., to an ideology.

An ideology is a socially embedded and emotionally provocative system of values clearly aimed at determined kinds of behavior and action. Ideologies are held with greater or lesser passion--even fanaticism--by "true believers," including charismatic leaders and their followers, or disciples. The ideological point of view cannot be questioned with impunity, as can a philosophical viewpoint. Faith by the community of disciples in their leading ideologues' beliefs, objectives, and means of attaining the latter is demanded. The unfaithful are the enemy. Many people have been slaughtered, banished, or ostracized throughout the centuries for appearing to lack "appropriate" belief and faith in the dominating religious and political ideologies of the day; e.g., Jews by Christians, South African blacks by proponents of apartheid, Native Americans by frontier colonialists, Armenians by Turks, communists by Nazis, non-communists by communists, etc.

The thread of messianism runs through a bewildering array of dissonant ideologies of educational purpose and efficacy competing for adherents in this demographically heterogenous land. These ideologies range from the highly reactionary, seeking to turn back the hands of social and cultural time in America via the educational process, to the radically liberationist, hoping that schoolteachers and their students will unite in the common cause of proletarian revolution to overthrow the prevailing socioeconomic system and institute a collectivist utopia. In between are a number of more or less conservative and more or less liberal "mainstream" conceptions of the school's social mission and strategies for accomplishing that mission.

The currently fashionable President's National Commission on Educational Excellence report, cited in previous chapters, represents a mainstream conservative ideological point of view which seeks to have our schools restore a "nation at risk" to a preeminent place in the global economy after years of foundering and decline.[2] The recently powerful agitation for bilingual education, largely by Hispanic interest groups, illustrates, for the most part, a moderately liberal ideological belief about educational efficacy; mainstream elements of the latter movement have been seeking to equalize opportunity for social mobility among recent immigrants via special language training in the schools.

Not all contemporary American educational ideologies plead for the school to redeem us as a people; indeed, one of them ("Educational Anarchism") calls for the "deschooling" of society so as to reclaim a meaningful educational experience for the people. But most have a messianic component to them. This suggests that in regard to formal education, most Americans simply cannot resist being overcome by emotion-laden faith and hope that, somehow, schools will do more for their children and those of their neighbors than make them learned. Our schools are invested with the obligation to **improve** society as well as help individual children acquire knowledge for its own sake.

In this chapter, I will present the major educational ideologies holding sway in contemporary America. I will be employing a classification system which includes nine basic ideologies, three of which are conservative, four liberal, and two radical. It should be readily comprehensible and useful to readers.[3] The purpose of presenting the nine ideologies is to aid the reader in understanding how primitive **faith** in the capacity of schools to improve human life is invariably leashed to some organizing framework of values and beliefs which serves as a readily accessible guide to action on the part of the faithful in efforts to utilize schools for particular purposes.

Nine Contemporary Educational Ideologies

A. Conservative/Reactionary Ideologies

The following three ideologies all seek, each in its respective way, to perpetuate the socioeducational status quo or to restore a past believed to have been unfortunately lost. Adherents to conservative and reactionary ideologies of educational purpose and practice range from everyday citizens who want little more from the school than to ensure that their children succeed in a highly modernized America through disenchanted marginals who feel left out of the mainstream as a result of geographical immobility, vocational obsolescence, inflexible religious convictions, or social legislation and policies favorable to "new populations" (e.g., Southeast Asians, women, etc.) at the perceived expense of those who "built this country" and now feel shunted aside. A third group consists of intellectual conservatives or reactionaries, individuals who read books supportive of their carefully articulated rationalizations for preserving the status quo or for turning further to the right--books written by such distinguished spokespersons for the philosophy of conservatism as Russel Kirk, Frank Meyer, William F. Buckley, James Kilpatrick, George Nash, and Milton Friedman, among others.

1. Education as Human Engineering

This is a mainstream conservative conception of formal education as an instrument for efficiently adjusting American youngsters to the status quo, particularly to the capitalist economic framework which prevails in the United States. It is the dominant American educational ideology at present, and probably always was. Perhaps the chief reason for its comparative "obscurity"--i.e., the limited focussed attention paid it both by intellectuals and the general public--is that it has been taken so much for granted by so many for so long. Americans as a whole are a rather conservative people when it comes to schooling, even when they are more progressive politically, sexually, or in other ways. It is a relatively "safe" ideology, meaning nearly all things to all people. Therefore, it is also the ideology adhered to by most professional educators (contrary to the frequently heard claim by conservatives that our schools are manned by left/liberal teachers and administrators unduly influenced by the ideas of John Dewey).

The central idea of Human Engineering ideology is that, by application of scientific principles--notably psychological--educational experts in a variety of professional specialties are able to "engineer" the kinds of learning demanded to fit or adjust successfully to contemporary American society; especially to its increasingly technocratic occupational system. Adjustment to the entrenched institutional and normative core cultural principles by advanced educational engineering is the key here. There is no strong zeal on the parts of Human Engineering ideologues to return to nineteenth century values (as there frequently is among Revivalist Fundamentalists) or, conversely, to move forward to the challenges of the twenty-first century.

We **presently** live in an incipient post-industrial society rooted in classical liberal values, and youngsters must be taught in school to fit into that society without undue friction. They must learn to live "functionally" in an "information society" dominated by a corporate capitalist economy, replete with computers and massive urbanization. The new "essentials" required for such smooth adjustment are to be determined by university-trained adults who are presumed to know better than children what such socialization and enculturation entail; and, adult professionals--preferably with graduate degrees--are to implement these "essentials" of learning scientifically.

This new "scientific realism" depends upon a catalogue of familiar educational **technologies** intended to ensure that the **products** of the engineering process (students) will learn what adults think they ought to in order to operate smoothly once they leave school to enter the competitive game of life. Some of the technologies most widely discussed in recent years include: the testing and measurement movement--including minimum performance testing through the grades and in order to graduate from high school; career education; Skinnerian-style behavior modification in the classroom; the teacher accountability movement--including written behavioral lesson plan objectives and lists of "competencies" for each student to achieve; performance contracting with business and industry (to make the learning process more "efficient"); programmed instruction and teaching machines for skills training; the "new civism" referred to in previous chapters (which a critic terms an attempt to "conserve and preserve the values heritage of the society, but cast it in contemporary terms"[4]; and related "social skills training" for surviving in the new corporate workplace, family, and on the urban freeway; and, last but far from least, "technological literacy"--in the form especially of advanced training in mathematics, science, and computer literacy in order for the United States to become more competitive economically with Japan, Germany, Korea, and other nations that are currently making us look bad. As Secretary of Education, William Bennett, put it in a 1985 speech to the American Legion, "Our national security is no less at risk from a poor school than from a poor army or navy."[5]

And, while the goals of this ideology are normally not so farfetched as those of other more extremely right or left wing educational ideologies (Bennett's assertion quoted above admittedly is an exception), that is, adjusting children to the contemporary status quo, the **messianic** component of the ideology resides in the **unproven** belief--held by great numbers of lay and professional people alike--that schools and schoolpeople can take an extraordinary human welfare enterprise, education, and operate it on the model of a modern business or industry. The new essentialist "cult of efficiency,"[6] Human Engineering, does, however, possess enormous faith in the capacity of schools and teachers to manufacture highly adjusted and socially well-integrated building blocks of "human capital" for the modern post-industrial socioeconomic system. Detractors would prefer the word "robots."

2. Education as Revival of the Fundamentals

Perhaps the most graphic way to describe the currently fashionable educational ideology of Revivalistic Fundamentalism is to quote from the writings of some of its leading proponents, particularly in regard to what they are **against** (almost everything that contemporary schools allegedly stand for, consistently--and incorrectly--blamed on "progressive education"). To give the reader some idea of how extreme the negative emotional content of this ideology can be, consider these comments made by then California Superintendent of Public Instruction Max Rafferty in 1970:

> Its ["progressive education"] a way of thinking and of teaching with which American democracy cannot coexist. Within it lie the seeds of the rumbles and the riots, the frantic search for "kicks," the news-

> stand filth and the cinematic garbage that mark the last descent into the cloying, clinging sickness of ultimate decay by every civilization that has ever permitted this infection to overcome its resistance.[7]

Or local school board member Henry S. Meyers in 1977:

> Of the myriad problems our public schools face today, none is more serious than the lack of competition. In fact, most of the other problems would simply fade away if we were somehow able to put competition back into our schools as well as into our lives.
>
> And right here is the crux of the problem. Nearly every major accomplishment in the history of the world has been brought about by honest, free enterprise competition. Conversely, as soon as competition is eliminated, deterioration and inefficiency are inevitable.[8]
>
> ....Our backs are up against the wall. We fully realize that we are engaged in a life-or-death struggle. If we should lose, there will be no second chance.
>
> **The nation you save may be your own.**[9] (Emphases added.)

Or President Ronald Reagan in 1983:

> We must move **forward** again by **returning** to the sound principles that never failed us when we lived up to them. Can we not begin by welcoming God back in our schools and by setting an example for children by striving to abide by His Ten Commandments and the Golden Rule?[10] (Emphases added.)

Each of the statements quoted above, in its respective way, is a strong plea for messianic redemption via the schools--salvation of the nation by **restoring** the revered past when social and cultural life was so much more simple, stable, and morally pure than it has become in the twentieth century, particularly since the hated 1960s.

Revivalistic Fundamentalism is a contemporary backlash not only against the reviled "radical sixties," but all of the forces of educational modernism that have been building up in this country since its adherents' major scapegoat, Dewey, first began complaining about the failures of traditionalism at the turn of the century. Educational Fundamentalists made a concerted effort to overthrow modernism during the Cold War days of the late 1950s; but were quickly overwhelmed by partisans of the Great Society movement and its offshoots in the 1960s and early 1970s. Now, Fundamentalist neo-conservatism is back in the ideological fray.

Journalist Ben Brodinsky describes the new right faithful best in these words:

> During the past two decades...while educators' eyes were on themselves and on the rush of developments in education and in society, large groups of parents and taxpayers were becoming increasingly disillusioned with their schools. They began to look at educators and their doings with mounting distaste.
>
> The alienated, the disappointed, and the irate gathered together under the banner of an aberrant conservative movement--a movement that includes concerned mothers and fathers but is led by zealots and extremists. Some manifestations of the movement are rational. But its rabid core, now known as the New Right, has loosed dogs of war against the public schools, using the accumulated ire of some segments of the population as a justification to wage warfare against the schools for what they have done and are doing, as well as for what they are **not** doing that the zealots wish them to do.[11]

Just what is it that these plainspoken secular as well as religious neo-fundamentalists wish the schools to do in order to restore to America their version of the lost Eden dream?

Partly, it depends on which particular "aberrant" interest group they belong to; i.e., among others, especially: the "evangelicals" (Jerry Falwell and the Moral Majority, for instance); the "pro-lifers" (e.g., American Life Lobby); the "anti-pornographers" (e.g., National Federation for Democracy); the "anti-homosexuals" (for example, Anita Bryant's Save Our Children); the "educators" (e.g., Norma and Mel Gabler of Educational Research Analysts in Texas); the "Congressional component" (e.g., Senators Jesse Helms of North Carolina, John Paul Laxalt of Nevada, and Jake Garn of Utah, and Congressman Bob Dornan of California, as well as others); or the "Washington connection" (e.g., Bob Baldwin of Citizens for Educational Freedom, Bill Billings of National Christian Action Coalition, and Phyllis Schlaffly, former head of Stop-ERA, etc.).[12]

But taken together, educational neo-fundamentalism can be

said to want the following: renewed emphasis on the three Rs--especially reading (taught exclusively by phonetic methods) and including American history and government (not "social studies"); fewer electives in secondary school (in this regard they differ more extremely even from the conservative supporters of Human Engineering in wanting to get rid of such "extraneous" subjects as driver training, career education, consumer education, and "big-time interscholastic athletic competition and all that goes with it"[13]); ultra, or "love it or leave it" patriotism, including, in Florida, for instance, courses explicitly denigrating "communism"; indoctrinative moral training (e.g., anti-homosexuality, and respect for such things as authority figures, rugged individualism, proper dress and neatness and cleanliness, hard work, etc.); censorship of "indecent" and "unChristian" text and school library books (e.g., *The Diary of Anne Frank*) and other materials (the Gablers in Austin send out a regular listing of "forbidden books"); public school prayer (so far the new right has only succeeded in securing the legal right of religious "clubs" to utilize building space for after school meetings; relatedly, "creationist science" (still being heatedly debated in state legislatures and the courts; more homework, and in all subjects; stricter discipline and restored authority by teachers to administer corporal punishment when deemed necessary; better preparation for living in a competitively materialistic society by returning to strict letter or number grading and elimination of automatic passing (including minimum competency testing throughout the school years and in order to obtain a high school diploma); far more parent involvement and influence in school affairs, and if parents are dissatisfied with public schools, the availability of tuition-tax credits or vouchers to enable them to enroll their children inexpensively in private schools of their choice (supported as well by certain liberals for different reasons entirely, as shall be brought out in the final chapter of this book); concomitantly, a return to principal control of schools by local boards of education and elimination or drastic curtailment of federal financing and influence upon public schools; and, finally, termination of what fundamentalists consider the pernicious influence of "soft" and "overly permissive" "progressive educational" pedagogy--especially as represented by the designated leaders of the "liberal" educational establishment, professors of education in teacher training institutions.

To return to the first two writers quoted in this section, both ardent supporters of Revivalistic Fundamentalism, let us summarize the ideology's idea of schooling in their own words, first those of Meyers:

> A Fundamental school is simply a school where basics of education are stressed with little or no experimentation; where discipline reigns and patriotism flourishes.[14]

And then Rafferty:

> Three things have all schools, and no more than three: pupils, teachers, and books...[If Americans were to return to the basics], then in about one generation **we could eliminate all our reform schools, most of our prisons, and a good many of our asylums.**[15] (Emphases added.)

Such abundant faith in the healing power of fundamental education in schools is distracting to the mind accustomed to more elaborate prescriptions for ameliorating complex sociocultural problems such as crime and insanity than those formulated by Rafferty. Nonetheless, his influence on the American people has been considerable; and the educational new right, or back-to-basics movement is currently enjoying unprecedented influence in this society.

3. Knowledge-for-the-Sake-of-Knowledge

Not quite so for the third of our nine contemporary educational ideologies. Still, Knowledge for the Sake of Knowledge lends intellectual respect and credibility to educational conservatism in general, and--therefore--serves to sustain American faith in the school's culturally redemptive power at a time in history when superficial socioeducational constructions of reality could otherwise be in danger of being toppled by more sophisticated analyses of organized human behavior. The recent *Paideia Proposal*[16] by philosopher Mortimer Adler and his colleagues has been a godsend to educational conservatives and reactionaries searching for an intellectually respectable rationale for their *a priori* faith in the power of ancient and medieval knowledge to improve human affairs in the modern world.

It is an updated version of what, in the 1940s and 1950s, was considered by liberal and radical detractors to be a reactionary theory of education, with highly elitist overtones; then known variously as perennialism, neo-Thomism, neo-scholasticism, classical realism, or classical humanism. Adler, an Aristotelian classical humanist himself, makes a sincere effort to rectify that earlier negative impression in *Paideia*. He attempts to show how a common "liberal education" can and must be offered every American youngster from about age four on regardless of socioeconomic and cultural circumstances or ability. The messianism implicit in what some scholars--e.g., Richard Pratte[17]--think of as an ideology largely disinterested in societal benefits, is apparent in the following words of Adler:

> Our country faces many insistently urgent problems, on the solution of which its prosperity and even its survival depend--the threat of nuclear war, the shrinking of essential resources and supplies of energy, the pollution or spoilation of the environment, the spiraling of inflation accompanied by the spread of unemployment.
>
> To solve these problems, we need resourceful and innovative **leadership**. For that to arise and be effective, we must have an educated people. **Trained intelligence, in followers as well as leaders, holds the key to the solution of the problems we face.**[18] (Emphases added.)

As the above quotation makes clear, what Adler and most other proponents of Knowledge for the Sake of Knowledge, past and present, are after is actually **not** knowledge for its own sake in the final analysis. It is knowledge for the sake of social problem-solving by an intellectual elite, much as that advocated in Plato's *Republic*. In modern American, however, that elite is to be democratically selected and supported by its inferiors who possess sufficient school-trained common-sense to realize that it is in everyone's interests to allow their intellectual betters to lead and for them to follow.

The argument of modern perennialism--whether secular as in Adler's case or ecclesiastical, as in the Catholic Church's official education policy--is that: (a) We live in a civilization in grave crisis, and knowledge is required to end that crisis; (b) All significant knowledge has been available to us since the birth of Western Civilization, particularly since the time of the ancient Greeks, although refined during the Middle Ages--such significant knowledge is **timeless** and, organized in curricular form, is commonly called the liberal arts; (c) While a liberal education should be at the heart of what a university offers, particularly through intense study and discussion of the great classics of Western thought, training for the rigors of such study must begin in the primary grades with the "basics" and proceed through secondary school years where the rudiments of formal logic and rhetoric are to be taught; (d) A genuinely liberal education means a common general education for all that should be viewed separately from mere vocational training (career education is **not** the function of the school, as many other conservatives believe)--schools should operate upon the assumption that "we remain at least vaguely aware that we are the inheritors of civilization and that our task is to preserve it, to enrich it, and to pass it on through study of the past and cultivation of our own power of thought and responsible action"[19]; (e) The end product of a good liberal education will be a well-rounded generalist possessing highly disciplined intellectual capabilities--some individuals more so than others owing to innate differences in talent and scholarly disposition; (f) The crisis of our age can be overcome only by the best, most highly disciplined of the school's products, the intellectual elite formed by a broad and deep liberal education from grade school through the university applying their superior minds to the resolution of the problems contributing to the crisis (Plato's philosopher-kings)--this elite to be enthusiastically selected by their followers who recognize that equal opportunity to a common general education does not guarantee equal intellectual achievement.

According to this approach, after an extended liberal education, only the most intellectually meritorious of the material that the school has to work with should be expected to make the life and death decisions required for ending the crisis of our age. As Plato believed, participatory democracy destroyed Socrates' Athens, and it will destroy our America unless we stop adulating mass man at the expense of superman; we are to return, instead, to a meritocratic, or truly republican form of highly limited democracy based on success in school and university.

Thus, we may conclude that in the ideology of Knowledge for the Sake of Knowledge, the messianic element is at least as great as in the first two conservative ideologies discussed; however, the results of educationally messianic endeavor are to fructify more indirectly and over a longer term. That is to say, schooling is expected to **directly** produce liberally educated people--the best of whom, in Aristotle's view, find that the greatest personal happiness resides in the most human of all activities, leisurely contemplation for its own sake. However, more **indirectly**, as both Plato and his favorite student believed, the most intellectually able and learned men have an obligation, at times, to their fellow human beings, to the *polis*, to the society within which they become fully human. That obligation entails that their superior knowledge be employed in the service of the general public, as a form of "noblesse oblige." And, since we in the United States currently live in the throes of great national and world crisis, now is the moment for the second, or indirect function of a liberal education to come to the fore. Leisurely contemplation for the sake of personal happiness is presently an unaffordable luxury because of the tenuousness of modern life. Perhaps later on. First, the havoc we have wrought upon our country and the planet must be eliminated by relying upon the institution of schooling to produce a newly public-spirited citizenry of capable leaders and equally capable followers--a happy collaboration of the "gold" and the "iron."

Whether or not one agrees with the perennialists, it must be conceded that theirs is an amazingly hardy and influential position and a brilliant rationalization for anointing the school with quasi-divine powers of redemption. After all, in a nuclear age not many Americans are prepared, as they once were, to publicly disagree that the liberally educated "wise" man or woman--the most "rational" citizen--should be entrusted with key decision-making privileges. To challenge such a seemingly obvious notion seems almost to smack of churlish resentment, so great has become the hegemony of intellectual, as distinguished from political, liberalism in post-industrial America.

B. Liberal/Reform Ideologies:

The liberal/reform educational ideologies have in common a belief that society can and should be continuously modified in a forward direction, but within norms and values currently considered acceptable to the general populace rather than preserved or turned backward; and, that such **progressive** social change should be guided significantly by the formal education process. Liberal/reform ideologies all hold in high regard the overriding goodness of the American dream as its specific elements become codified through time and experience--in unbroken continuity from past, through present, into emergent future. The responsibility is not to adhere rigidly to the obsolete elements in this Eden ideal, as reactionaries and conservatives are accused by liberals of doing, nor to abandon the ideal *en toto* as revolutionaries unwisely prefer; but rather to preserve its civilizing aspects while constantly striving to improve upon it where it is weakest and in clear need of reform. Within this context, the "progressive" school is expected to foster the needed intelligence, persistance, creativity, and concern for others--not for elitist purposes, but in the interests of social and political democracy.

4. Education as Ethnic Revitalization and Cultural Pluralism

The 1960s spawned many ideological movements in American education, including social reform movements based explicitly on the long suppressed belief that minorities had a right **not** to be assimilated into the mainstream, not to become homogenized, but to remain identifiably unique within the broader sociocultural conglomerate if that were their choice. To most dominant group Americans--and a good many minority group members--such an idea was amazing and dismaying, since they had grown up on the opposite notion. The controversial doctrine of cultural pluralism, nonetheless, was not an innovation of the 1960s in any strict sense. It had been amply discussed earlier in the century by Dewey, Issac Berkson, Horace Kallen, and many other liberal observers of and participants in the successive waves of Southeast European immigration that had occurred between about 1880 and 1925.

The establishmentarian concepts of Anglo conformity and the melting pot had come under attack by pluralists from abroad and within ever since people of British and Northern European origins had ceased to be the almost exclusive members of the American population. Even so, throughout the late 1800s and the first two-thirds of the 1900s, the public schools had operated on Anglo conformist and melting pot assumptions in their culturally protective efforts to "Americanize" the foreign strangers.

However, with the mid-twentieth century civil rights movement and the Great Society ideal, both of which reached their heights in the 1960s, huge numbers of blacks, Hispanics, Native Americans, Asian Americans, and other non-European minorities from both abroad and within our borders--the "new immigrants"--began to assert themselves by demanding the right to educational opportunities to become socioeconomically equal to other Americans while simultaneously remaining culturally different. And they had great faith in the schooling system as the chief means for achieving their goals of successful separatism.

Programs in ethnic studies for each of these groups were developed first in colleges and universities and then in secondary and elementary schools across the country. In time, the ethnic studies trend spread to include groups which had formerly submitted to melting pot values. Thus, depending on location, educational institutions offered Armenian studies, Polish studies, Jewish studies, Irish studies--even WASP studies for the "Protestant minority" was seriously suggested. Multicultural education programs that treated a variety of subcultural themes of concern not only to ethnic minorities, but to females, homosexuals, and other emergent ideological interests blossomed as an offshoot of the new ethnic pride. Liberationist ethnic and other minority revitalization via the aegis of formal education has become a contending ideological feature of the messianic urge in modern America.

One of the most vociferous ideological demands on behalf of subcultural revitalization has been for inclusion of bilingual education programs in public schools which have a substantial limited-English-speaking clientele. For instance, in California during the 1970s, the most intense of the earlier advocates of "maintenance" bilingual programs were often fanatical in their organized efforts to utilize school systems in the state for the purpose of replacing Anglo culture with Mexican cultural values and norms, and to develop an identifiable base for eventual political control of the region. Bilingual programs throughout elementary and secondary schools were to be the primary tool of the educational messiah for working the miracle of reclaiming for downtrodden Hispanics territory taken from Mexico in 1848 by the Anglos. But the vast majority of Hispanic bilingual ideologues were far less chauvinistically utopian in their objectives, seeking **equality** with Anglos rather than cultural and political domination over them.

Transitional bilingual programs relying upon the native tongue in early grades and gradually switching to English were deemed to be acceptable by the more moderate of the bilingual ideologues, especially after the rout of Democrat Jimmy Carter in the 1980 Presidential election by conservative Ronald Reagan. Although deeply concerned by the backlash of the American people against the cultural separatism which Reagan's overwhelming victory at the polls partially symbolized, many bilingual enthusiasts had, nonetheless, not yet conceded defeat for their ideology in the early 1980s, as the following statement by the former vice-president for academic affairs at my own institution demonstrates:

> Hispanic parents and the supporters of bilingual programs know that these programs work, and understand also the key role played by the federal

> government in the establishment of such programs. It should surprise no one that Hispanics tend to view any and all attempts to cut back or to discontinue bilingual education as anti-Hispanic action. Early actions by the current [Reagan] administration would seem to indicate a very serious lack of appreciation of that fact.[20]

Such ethnic revitalization developments as ethnic studies, multicultural education, bilingual education, and community control (largely an aborted movement by black inner-city parents to gain control of the public schools in their segregated neighborhoods in the 1960s and 1970s and to hire more black teachers and administrators for those schools instead of pushing for desegregation) really represent only the tip of the ideological iceberg sometimes known as "radical cultural pluralism." Some educational theorists and intellectuals in other disciplines as well as disenchanted spokespeople for the lay public are now claiming that the very notion of a common school experience for all American children--the essence of Horace Mann's 140-plus-year-old vision--is obsolete. At present, disillusioned people from all walks of life and all income groups are claiming that the public school has failed dismally in strengthening our nation, as it had long promised.

They say that the public schooling system across America has become an inefficiently bureaucratized, arrogantly unresponsive, financially wasteful, and inhumanely demoralizing institution that robs youngsters of their individual creativity, their chance to learn what they need to know in order to fit into the mainstream, as well as any ethnic or religious identity with which they may have come to school in the first grade; this whether they are poor, middle-income, or rich. We have no recourse, they assert, but to greatly expand the schooling options of all American parents and their children, if we are to preserve what they cherish; namely, the unifying cultural diversity of our pluralistic society.

One educational scholar who has written extensively on this position is Seymour Itzkoff. He argues as follows:

> Education is a process of creating and shaping human values of culture building. By giving citizens choice, a great measure of choice, we can begin to nurture those qualities of mind and soul that are intrinsic to the educational process. To choose, people also have to reject. By forcing student and

> school upon each other, we already limit choice.[21]

And the authors of a widely circulated 1980 treatise on educational options, attorneys John Coons and Stephen Sugarman of the University of California, Berkeley, argue that significant opportunities for choice in schooling would promote both social unity at the same time as valuable subcultural diversity was preserved and extended:

> Far from threatening an existing consensus, an end to official culture could strengthen the social bond...In actively encouraging families to express their cultural and ideological diversity, the nation would substitute mutual respect as the ground of a social accord that has been based too long in the acceptance by minorities of an elite model. The bestowal of choice implies **trust**, and trust can beget trust, even among those of strongly different persuasions...The message that society respects the values and tastes of the non-rich in the formal training of their children could be a stride toward a more stable civil order.[22] (Emphases added.)

So, here we have the ideological belief of the leaders of the nineteenth century PSM turned on its head: The development of a harmoniously **integrated** social order is, according to the pluralists, to be the outcome not of a system of common public schools, as Mann wanted; but instead, ironically, of a loose confederation of private (as well as public) schools supported financially by public monies in the form of tuition-tax credits and vouchers. For several years now, those two proposals have been defended not only by certain educational intellectuals such as Itzkoff and Coons and Sugarman, but also by private school interests in the U.S.A.--most noteworthy, the Catholic Church which supports the majority of private schools in this country.

Senator Daniel Moynihan of New York has written vociferously on the subject in his efforts to have laws enacted in Congress supportive of the private educational sector. He argues that America is in danger of losing much of its valued pluralism, and that tax-supported private schools, not only Catholic but Jewish and Protestant as well, are a major hope in stopping such a threat:

> I take pluralism to be a valuable characteristic of education, as of much else in this society. We are many peoples, and our social arrangements reflect this disinclination to submerge our inherited dis-

> tinctiveness in a homogeneous whole.
> Our private schools and colleges embody those values. They provide diversity to the society, choice to students and their parents, and a rich array of distinctive educational offerings that even the finest of public institutions may find difficult to supply, not least because they are **public** and must embody generalized values.
> Tax credit for school and college tuitions furnish an opportunity to support these values. And they do so without raising any question of constitutionality.[23]

Public opinion, led by both former President Reagan as well as by George Bush, is becoming increasingly favorable to educational alternatives supported by public funding. Religion appears to be a major stumbling block to passage of facilitative legislation. But, even in regard to this volatile issue the barriers are slowly crumbling. Warning that since the 1960s our public schools have been fostering the collapse of moral consensus in a once unified America, and that "the great danger confronting our schools is the slow, quiet spread of the moral nihilism of Nietzsche into every corner of our lives,"[24] some conservative educators and citizens are demanding that religious studies emphasizing traditional Judeo-Christian moral values be required in public schools. They argue that such studies will profoundly help avert the dangerous tendency toward national disintegration. The schools have supposedly been the prime movers of such disintegration because of their extreme value relativism and refusal to face the reality of what parents and students really want taught. As James Lee puts it:

> Any school which deliberately avoids giving learners what they and their parents claim they need to be truly educated as human beings is not authentically educational because it is **unreal**. Such a school is based on and permeated with unreality--the unreality that religion, like sex, does not exist or if it exists should be totally closeted with the private non-school domain.[25]

However, since it is unlikely that public school interests will, in fact, concede the logic of Lee's argument, the tuition-tax credit and voucher alternative may be the only way out for ideologues who favor including religious content in school. So, for instance, Alan C.

Carlson believes that "a joint program of tuition-tax credits and vouchers would open all elements of the population, not just the relatively wealthy, to the contemporary imperative of choice in education. In this respect, tax credits and vouchers become the vehicles for **true equality and democracy** in the late 20th century."[26]

The ideology of Ethnic Revitalization and Cultural Pluralism is clearly messianic in terms of its overall objectives; although, as will become clear later, the means employed to achieve them (tuition-tax credits and vouchers) may be utilized to achieve other, non-messianic educational objectives. A large and growing array of special interests ranging from linguistic particularists to religious regenerationists believe that attending the kinds of schools they approve of, public or private, will, somehow, alter significantly the fabric and moral character of our "endangered" nation. The point is that a single social institution, the school, is to be the agency of cultural redemption for most ethnic and value pluralists seeking their own special version of the Eden dream, just as it is for their opponents on the side of cultural uniformity and homogenization.

5. Education as Social Reengineering

Human Engineering, the first ideology discussed, seeks to adjust children to the status quo by means of efficient application of scientific methods to the learning process. It is a conservative educational ideology. Its liberal/reform cousin, Social Reengineering, similarly advocates reliance upon science and technology; the difference being that Reengineering aims its technocratic arsenal at the legal system, educational policy and management, and instructional methodology in the overall interest of ameliorating dysfunctional social conditions in America via schooling.

This reformist ideology came to prominence in the 1960s, largely under professional aegis influenced and heavily supported by the federal government, which has, until recently, encouraged innumerable public education programs under its welfare state banner.

Largely in the name of **equal educational opportunity**, liberals in the field of education have, for the past thirty-five years, been developing a wide variety of educational "innovations" highly dependent upon the application of "scientific" principles of curriculum development and pedagogical reform. Examples--some widely diffused, more gone from the scene--include: the New Science and New Social Studies (in general exile since the mid-1970s neoconservative backlash); compensatory education for the so-called "culturally disadvantaged" (still in some vogue in a variety of remaining federally and state-assisted programs for the poor, including, for instance Operation Headstart); court-ordered desegregation and busing (a major example of the employment of the legal system to order school reform, but now in substantial rout as a result of white flight coupled with big school district efforts to appease opponents of busing); affirmative action recruiting and hiring of minority and female personnel and advancement of students in higher education institutions (currently being closely controlled by both liberals and conservatives anxious not to offend opponents of its extreme end product, quotas); a comprehensive special education program for the physically and mentally handicapped--PL 94-142--which requires that schools guarantee equal educational opportunities for such students in the "least restrictive environment" (currently one of the few Social Reengineering efforts that has retained much of its integrity, because of built-in legal safeguards); mandated eradication of sexism in sports and other formerly male-dominated school activities (some gains for female students have been made as a result, but less significant than feminists had hoped for); the high school reform movement, a long struggle to overhaul secondary education in order to make it more relevant to the masses of modern adolescents, including reducing the leaving age to fourteen (most gains to date have been cosmetic, and the recent interest of a variety of conservative national commissions in high school reform promises to have marginally greater impact upon the institution than liberals have had); and the student rights movement, a legally based humanitarian movement to allow school pupils the same Constitutionally guaranteed civil rights as other citizens.

The Vietnam era precipitated the students rights movement with a Supreme Court decision (the *Tinker* decision of 1969) allowing students to wear black armbands as a symbolic form of free speech in protest to that war. (Over the years, the growing conservative trend in education and society and attendant fears of declining academic and disciplinary standards have eroded the movement's momentum, but very recent events may bode well for its gradual revival; e.g., Court decisions limiting search and seizure of students by school authorities, the uncovering of disturbing widespread child abuse by school personnel and other child custodial workers, etc.)

Social Reengineering, perhaps the central liberal ideology of the second half of the twentieth century, urges socioeducational reform by fiat of professional educational experts and specialists in the schools and universities under the protective legal and bureaucratic mantle of the state and federal governments, in particular the all-powerful federal courts. As suggested above, its major goal is the expansion of socioeconomic opportunity and the broadening of civil rights in American society. So massive had the legal-bureaucratic apparatus become under the broad framework of this educational ideology by the late 1970s that one writer, Arthur Wise, used the derisive words "legislated learning" as the title of a book highly critical of what he termed the "hyper-rationalization" of American schooling.[27] He was referring to the excessive employment of scientific technology to achieve liberal educational objectives efficiently and effectively.

Furthermore, since most of the vaunted results promised by a plethora of bureaucratic, legislative, judicial, and academic social reengineers have failed to materialize (for example, the welfare rolls have not receded as a result of improved educational opportunities for the poor, school desegregation efforts are in shambles, and racial tensions may be more explosive than prior to the 1950s), we are witnessing a powerful pendulum swing back to the basics in this country, led by Revivalistic Fundamentalists and the less polemical, but equally anti-progressive devotees of Human Engineering.

But, even in areas where Social Reengineering innovations seem to be adhering (e.g., special education reform), one relatively unnoticed factor mitigates against long-term success via the hyper-rationalistic mode of securing school related social benefits. Practically all such efforts place voluminous paperwork demands on underpaid and harried teachers who resent being unduly imposed upon by ambitious administrative bureaucrats and an apparently unsympathetic public. The unanticipated consequence of those demands has been a reduction rather than an increase in the efficiency of schooling.

Yet, despite gradual erosion of liberal faith in the American school's power to fulfill the promise of a more egalitarian society, there are modest signs that some of the faithful refuse to admit defeat. For example, as late as 1983, the United States Commission on Civil Rights was admonishing Americans to continue to believe that education is a "**key** element in efforts to **eradicate** racism and violence...Parents, educators, leaders of religious institutions, and other opinion-makers should work together to develop educational programs designed to produce cognitive and **emotional** change with respect to racism and anti-Semitism."[28] (Emphases added.)

Another noteworthy liberal/reform effort to use schools to reengineer society addresses itself to "peace education"--particularly through nuclear disarmament. Educators for Social Responsibility is a recently formed "national, non-profit organization...committed to helping teachers, school administrators, and parents respond positively, through education, to students' concerns about nuclear war, and to developing community action/education projects to end the arms race." One of its programs involves "consulting with parent groups and school systems about how new curricula can be introduced...[and] exploring how students can best be educated to become socially responsible, well-informed, active citizens, capable of critical thinking and moral reasoning."[29]

But that organizational effort is modest in comparison with a contemporary program sponsored by the National Education Association. Our nation's largest professional education organization, with a membership of nearly two million teachers, has developed for national distribution a nuclear disarmament curriculum for junior high school students. It is boldly entitled "Choices: A Unit on Conflict and Nuclear War." The idea is to educate children on the need to change American foreign policy. Needless to say, the effort (and a number of its more localized spinoffs) has already come under sharp attack not only from conservative citizen groups, but from its normally more left liberal rival American Federation of Teachers, as well, for being manipulative, misleading, and undemocratic. From the perspective of the present study, a more important concern about such a school-based effort to bring about international peace than the ethics of indoctrination--important as such a consideration is--questions the sheer **efficacy** of the best-intended efforts of mice and men to bring about major social change through the diffusion of knowledge in places called schools.

6. Education as Therapeutic Interaction

The 1960s and 1970s were also noteworthy for an incredible outpouring of literary polemics by teachers, former teachers, college students, journalists, education professors, psychologists, and self-appointed human potential experts aimed at making public schools less miserable places for children than their authors believed they were; and for some, more productive of therapeutically healthy community life in an increasingly alienating society. Some of these moral tracts became best-sellers and went into paperback, to be consumed by millions of teachers, students, and members of the lay public.

Some examples include: journalist Charles Silberman's *Crisis in the Classroom*, a plea for a more "open education" mirroring the much admired British primary school; Jonathan Kozol's *Death at an Early Age*, reminiscent of Upton Sinclair's earlier expose of the meat-packing industry in its shattering denunciation of the "windowless, rat-infested," crowded conditions of schools for Boston slum children; Neil Postman and Charles Weingartner's *Education as a Subversive Activity*, a tongue-in-cheek attempt to convince would-be teachers to "sabotage" the rule-laden educational establishment by refusing to teach "crap;" *The Way It Spozed to Be*, teacher James Herndon's personal tale of subjugation to depersonalized bureaucratic norms and role expectations and how he and his minority students together freed themselves and went on to become authentic inquirers.[30] These were but four of the many books with titles sufficiently striking to appeal to the ideological imagination of youthful and older educational liberals alike during the heyday of America's most recent "cultural revolution."

This genre of book sought to impress upon the reader the horrors of traditional schooling and the desperate need to humanize what some considered a "fascistically" authoritarian institution. Such a view of the typical school of the times ran exactly counter to those held by ideological conservatives themselves--to whom schools has long since been taken over by the left wing "demagoguery" of Dewey and progressive, or life-adjustment, education.

Although a number of those institutional critics have since moved on to other careers or literary interests, at one time they represented an educational ideology of passionate messianic fervor. Usually associated historically with the iconoclastic Swiss genius Jean Jacques Rousseau (who believed that all institutions were corrupting, and, therefore, advocated allowing youngsters to learn naturally from life rather than confining them in schoolrooms) as well as with Sigmund Freud (much of whose work stressed the evils of civilizational repression upon development of wholesome personality), this ideology today attaches great importance to the notions of such celebrated humanistic psychologists as Carl Rogers, Abraham Maslow, and Rollo May. These luminaries' commitment to individual authenticity have supported the Therapeutic Interactionists' conceptions of the overriding importance of the feelings, values, and creative needs of the student in educational arrangements, as have the assumptions of individual autonomy to be found in philosophical existentialism. Dewey's ideas on the transactional relationship between the teacher and the whole child are also credited on occasion, but, in general, the educational humanists feel that Dewey was too "logical," "linear," or "left-brained"--too "scientific" in his explanations--to be of major inspiration to them.

The affective, humanistic, romantic, or neo-progressive education movement, as this ideology is variously called (Morris Bigge dispatches the ideology with the rubric "psychedelic humanism" in his well-known comparison of learning theories[31]), seeks to open the public school classroom to children's real feelings--believed to have been outlawed in conventional schools--and to democratic interpersonal relations. It seeks to create "schools without failure," where each child is unique and, as such, may succeed in his or her own right. Youngsters are to move around unrestrained from one interest to another discovering for themselves the literary, scientific, and especially artistic secrets of the universe. Daryl Siedentop calls these last of the "basics" the "ludic arts," because of their "inherent playfulness." He complains that "we all still suffer from our historical tendency to view the world of work as the major end in life and the world of play as a peripheral, even potentially evil detractor."[32]

An excellent characterization of Therapeutic Interactionist ideology has been provided by Israeli educational theorist Zvi Lamm. He calls it "radical" education:

> Creativity as a mode of life, subjectivity as a test of the validity of knowledge, and self-awareness as its goal are the dimensions of knowledge in the radical conception of education...In the radical interpretation knowledge is not an instrument to train the young to take part in social life nor to place them in defined social roles...but an instrument which is designed mainly to further the process of their emergence as unique individuals, i.e., their individualism.
>
> Self-regulation means a choice in favor of primary motivation, in favor of activity motivated by curiosity and not by competition, the need to belong or a sense of duty.[33]

This last deemphasis on the need to belong is clearly in contrast with the thinking of conventional liberal philosophy and ideology, much less conservative outlooks. It is far more in keeping with mainstream, non-theistic existential thought, except for its greater emphasis upon the managerial role of the teacher:

> ....In the view of radical educators, the teacher...is called upon to organize the environment of his students in such a way that it will provide sufficient stimuli to engage them in interaction with it....[34]

This expectation that the teacher shall take concrete responsibility for structuring the environment for student interaction also separates the newer progressivism from Dewey's older, more fluidly transactional conception of the teacher-student relationship; and seems to be more in keeping with both the Montessori approach (structured freedom) as well as with the British primary school "in the more active role of the teacher, greater emphasis on planned environment, clarification of the limits of the child's freedom, and greater concern about the curriculum."[35]

From the above, it can be seen that Therapeutic Interactionism is **not** a modernized version of progressive education, nor is it a form of quasi-anarchism, as in the free school movement, which advocates almost total student freedom.

Therapeutic Interaction is a hybrid liberal/reform educational ideology born of the 1960s. It has drawn upon a number of different theoretical sources for its ideas, as I have suggested, but its key thrust is upon the relative freedom of the child. Yet this child is seen as--if not necessarily "belonging"--certainly as **interacting** in an environment comprised of fellow children (and an involved teacher) with whom one must as least coexist in order to find authentic personal identity. Public schooling is not abandoned as a potentially valuable agency for helping the child discover who he or she is, but schooling needs to be radically **humanized** if it is to succeed in freeing up the child for such self-discovery.

In this perspective, the role of schooling is to act as a therapeutic community in microcosm, allowing American youngsters to live and learn in newfound joy and spontaneity. In turn, these qualities will lend them the psychological strength lacking in most repressed Americans. Such psychological strength will enable them to carry on enthusiastically and creatively--self-reliantly--in the larger community and society beyond school later on and throughout their lives.

Producing creative self-reliance is a **messianic** role for the school. One institution is called upon to provide the life-giving psychological and interpersonal resources that an otherwise repressive social order cannot or will not provide. In this view, publicly supported and controlled schools and teachers are attributed extraordinary powers with which to "manufacture" the sensitivity and the sanity that eventually are to restore a sick society to health once again. Thus, the schools are to lead in redemptive social change on the basis of an abiding faith in teachers' possessing "spiritually" enriching qualities that are infectious and that ordinary people presumably lack. Therapeutic Interactionist educational ideology is a modernized and secularized version of messianism akin to the early Christian conception of the absolute healing power of love.

7. Education as Exploration of the Future

The final liberal/reform educational ideology that may have messianic overtones came to fruition in the early 1970s following publication of several well-publicized essays on futurism, including Alvin Toffler's widely-heralded book *Future Shock*.[36] In that consciousness-raising effort, Toffler advised all Americans to prepare themselves for the massive and unremitting social, cultural, and technological changes and dislocations that are an inevitable and unavoidable accompaniment of our society's movement into the post-industrial age: in the basic character of the family, the workplace, the physical environment, religious values, the mass media, leisure and recreation, the scale and scope of government, and a great deal more.

In order to prevent catastrophic personal and societal consequences resultant from such change-based "future shock," Toffler and others advise us to prepare for the future as we would prepare for a visit to a Third World nation, only much more thoroughly. Once again, the schools emerge as the seemingly logical agencies for helping young people prepare themselves to live in the vastly altered future that they will inherit. Students in elementary and secondary school, as well as college, must study the "history of the future," grounded in extrapolated projections of the probable inferred from interpretations of constantly emerging trend patterns.

The futures movement may at first glance seem "radical," but it is not, because most of its participants are less interested in creating a markedly original future than in helping people **adapt** to what they predict is posited on the basis of current trend patterns. For the most part, futurists are liberals in the true sense of the word. They accept progressive reforms rather than urge social revolution. The movement was in considerable vogue among well-educated upper-middle-class intellectuals and professionals during the 1970s, but has become relatively quiescent in the 1980s. Young people today are more immediately concerned with preparing simply to earn a living in a difficult job market, as contrasted with their concerns a decade and a half ago. Still, staunch futurists argue that precisely **because** social and economic conditions have become so tenuous since the 1970s, an ideology that centers on preparing people adequately for the year 2000 and beyond is eminently sensible; and the schools are, in their opinion, the most appropriate agency for the bulk of such preparation.

To help the reader gain an insight into the thinking of main-stream futurism, Ronald Barnes, an educational consultant, not long ago offered the following imaginative look back to the mid-1970s from the year 1996, and described some important educational changes that "have occurred" during that period:

> 1. There is much less emphasis in 1996 on learning facts in school than on assisting students in learning how to learn.
> 2. A renewal of interest in learning as student discovery rather than as data transference from teacher to student occurred in the 1980s.
> 3. Preparing people to become generalists rather than narrow specialists is finally becoming a major task of education.
> 4. Lifelong learning--discussed for years--is now an actuality. People of all ages, rather than from five to eighteen or so, now depend upon schools as well as many other agencies to help them learn year round.
> 5. No longer are the traditional acculturation, enculturation, and socialization functions of education paramount. Now (in 1996), the individual really is the focus of education rather than the economy or the polity.
> 6. The history curriculum is now future-centered as well as past-centered.
> 7. The reality of one learner is now understood as being acceptably different from that of another.
> 8. We have moved from a strictly cognitive to a cognitive/affective approach to learning.

9. The separation of learning into fragmented courses and disciplines has given way to an integration of knowledge approach.
10. Textbooks no longer are used in schools. Now, open- and closed-circuit television, community resource people, films, tapes, and other modern technologies are employed to facilitate learning in schools.
11. Learning is now actively engaged in by the student rather than passively. Experiential and creative efforts are now rewarded instead of conforming docility.[37]

What is "messianic" above is the belief that schools are even capable of being modified as suggested to **try** to help people adjust more harmoniously to a new culture. For instance, consider Barnes' eighth prognostication about schools adding a significantly "affective" component to their conventionally cognitive focus. That is precisely what the Therapeutic Interactionists want; but, given the historical record coupled with the current political backlash by conservatives against what they consider peripheral "frills," its achievement is dubious. Or, to use another illustration: Barnes posits in number two above that student discovery, a central feature of philosophical instrumentalism/progressivism as well as gestalt/cognitive-field learning theory, will make a comeback in the 1980s at the expense of direct data transference from teacher to student. Precisely the opposite has occurred in the 1980s, in no small part because proponents of returning to the basics have so extensively influenced educational policy that even those comparatively few teachers remaining who might prefer teaching by the discovery approach rarely have time any longer to employ genuinely student-centered educational strategies.

On balance, it would seem that the liberal ideology of mainstream educational futurism may be considered **non-messianic** if judged exclusively by outcomes expected of the schooling process; i.e., seeking merely to find better ways of utilizing schools for fitting people into an anticipated status quo. If judged by more inclusive criteria, however, we may conclude that while the goals of exploratory futurism are only mildly reformist (or perhaps even conservative), the **means** relied upon to achieve those safely liberal ends (e.g., "integration of knowledge" approach--Barnes' ninth prognostication) seem farfetched, if not genuinely messianic. After all, the rhetoric of mainstream Exploratory Futurism is frequently quite passionate; to wit: "Education will be in the vanguard of urgently needed efforts to reconfigure and expand the role of education as the continuing social engine of our democratic system."[38] Overall, the urgency of that statement and similar ones made by mainstream futurists leads one to conclude, cautiously, that the ideology is, in fact, representative of the kind of faith we have associated with the Educational Messiah Complex.

C. Radical/Reconceptualist Educational Ideologies:

The third general class of ideology to have made some significant impact upon contemporary American thought, if not practice, is aptly termed radical/reconceptualist in that whatever form it takes, its proponents are deeply dissatisfied with life in this society. They advocate nearly complete overhaul of the social order. Radical/Reconceptualists agree that educational reform, preferred by American liberals especially, is merely palliative in its consequences. The crisis in modern American life is, purportedly, so advanced that only total redesigning of our basic institutions is likely to reduce that crisis and humanize society in any meaningful way for the long term.

Indeed, according to this approach, efforts to reform schooling and society, however beneficial over the short term, are likely to actually worsen the alienating conditions of modern life by solidifying the obsolete foundational structures that have produced such demoralizing and unwholesome conditions in the first place. That is why a thoroughgoing reconceptualization of our individual and sociocultural priorities is imperative today.

8. Education as a Strategy of Revolution

Futurism as described a few paragraphs back is primarily an ideological movement of mainstream America. For the most part, its adherents are middle-class, liberal professionals in a variety of respectably conventional fields who seek to prepare for a post-industrial age that they envision, optimistically, as evolving quite naturally out of the present corporate capitalist *Weltanschauung*; barring some completely unpredictable catastrophe such as defeat in a third world war with the U.S.S.R.

Mainstream futurism is grounded in a teleological metaphysic. Thus, the role of formal education in the minds of most futurist educational ideologues is, in effect, to help the American people acknowledge and plan ahead for an unavoidable, or imminent reality; hardly a utopian project, albeit somewhat daring.

However, there is another way of looking at the future--one that rejects the post-industrial model. That model is believed to help self-serving liberal or conservative efforts to perpetuate a fundamentally unjust and alienating society, a society in which institutionalized racism, sexism, social class elitism, poverty, and related forms of correctable inequity and oppression are inevitable by-products of the overwhelming dominance of the capitalistic ethos reaching far beyond the economic sector into all realms of institutional life.

According to this other perspective, capitalism by its very nature seriously exploits human beings, especially in its highly advanced corporate forms. Accordingly, those privileged to possess substantial investment capital are enabled to live parasitically as a ruling oligarchy without having to work for their necessities and luxuries by purchasing cheaply the productive labor of the great majority of less fortunate people. Thus, the rest of us are forced to live marginally and frequently in desperation off the sweat of our bodies, hands, or minds while the privileged minority possessing investment capital to buy the instruments of production and the labor to operate those instruments secure obscene profits that should, instead, have gone to the productive laborers themselves and to their families.

American Marxists have been interested in education for over a century. Yet, today, when their numbers are perhaps higher than practically ever before (certainly they were a few years ago during the height of the post-1960s upheaval of countercultural activism), they still are not agreed on what the school's special role ought to be in bringing about the utopian future of a classless, non-exploitative, humane society based upon cooperative rather than brutally competitive principles.

There are four distinguishable positions in this regard that have implications for education:

1. Some American educational radicals think, as did Karl Marx himself, that the schools have an essentially secondary role to play in major social change. That does not mean that traditional Marxists necessarily disdain the school. Antonio Gramsci, a founding member of the Italian Communist Party in the early part of this century, represents the traditional position well; he felt that the school had a definite role in the dialectical process eventuating in the revolution of the proletariat. According to one of his contemporary interpreters:

> ....Gramsci saw the futility of instruction in socialism outside the appropriate industrial context; commitment to revolutionary social change must grow out of industrial experience. But to believe that schools are neutral to social objectives and to emphasize that political education can only fructify in the practical experience of adults, does not rob schooling of its importance. On this view school is an indispensable foundation for further education by ensuring the necessary mastery of language and other intellectual tools and assimilation of the cultural past with which present experience must engage dialectically as the spur to social action.
> Viewing the school thus...helps to resolve the paradox of Gramsci's commitment to a **conservative** view of curriculum and method...this was the standpoint of Marx himself....[39] (Emphasis added.)

Thus, the first, or traditional Marxist position is emphatically **not** messianic about schooling; but, nonetheless, maintains that in their very conservatism schools inevitably reproduce the contradictions of capitalism. In performing such a latent function, they help pave the way for genuinely revolutionary education later on in the workplace for adults who can--as a result of schooling wedded to life experience--then appreciate the differences between core cultural mythology and sordid reality. Adult education, then, outside the school, is a prime mover of fundamental social change in the conventional Marxian view; childhood education supplies some of the fuel for this engine of change.

2. A second radical position first became prominent during the Great Depression of the 1930s when "social frontier" leader George Counts asked: "Dare the schools change the social order?"[40] For the time being, the answer was negative. But, Counts' question was asked again in the 1950s, and later--somewhat modified--in the late 1970s. The position espoused by Counts and other radical intellectuals sharing his educational outlook has come to be known as social reconstructionism. The social reconstructionists, who are usually affiliated with education directly as teacher trainers and scholars, typically place a far more significant burden on schools as leading agencies of basic social change than do conventional Marxists.

Reconstructionists would like to see schools and teachers become the prime movers of change to the kind of communal world order desired by most Marxists. As late as 1977, the late Theodore Brameld, the then-elder statesperson for social reconstructionism, called for a comprehensive agenda of "social frontiers" that America's schools should promote. Included on that agenda were:

> -a democratically controlled and planned world order
> -the outlawing of all nuclear military force
> -the replacement of so-called "free enterprise" by social democratic public enterprise
> -imposed "limits to growth" and reduction of global pollution
> -free education throughout the globe from cradle to grave
> -absolute elimination of sexism and sexual Victorianism
> -free health services around the world
> -free communication services (TV, radio, telephone, cinema) throughout the world
> -all art to be made fully available to all human beings as a public service and all artists to be guaranteed complete freedom of expression
> -scientific research and application to be governed by a World Science Authority
> -outer space exploration and habitation to be encouraged under global authority
> -world peace instituted[41]

Brameld admitted that the above agenda is "utopian;" yet (like the eminent sociologist of knowledge, Karl Mannheim[42]) unashamedly concluded that the search for the impossible dream of a glorious future by means of education and schooling is achievable if we put out minds and hearts to the task. Brameld was an educational messianist who probably would not have been embarrassed to be called that, so immense was his longstanding faith in the revolutionary potential of schooling.

Other social reconstructionists have become less sanguine in recent years about how much schools alone can do to bring about a collectivist utopia. In the words of Vincent Crockenberg and Richard LaBreque:

> Formal schooling is just one of the institutional processes of our culture. With respect to promoting desirable human growth and development, it is

> probably one of the less significant, despite all the rhetoric to the contrary...We renounce the...view that schools could build a new social order. Schools can do some things in this regard, but we must not continue to look to them as the **redeeming** institutions of the culture.[43] (Emphasis added.)

Such a dramatically limited view of schooling efficacy seems more akin to traditional Marxism of the sort enunciated by Gramsci than of social reconstructionism as usually understood; and it has come under attack recently by radical educational ideologues who are struggling to keep alive their faith in the social power of the institution. So, an alternative to what is considered the cynicism of the newer "reproductive" conceptions of schooling, which largely replaced "naive" social reconstructionism after the 1960s, is emerging. It gives renewed hope to some educational radicals that schools may, after all, have a significant role to play in basic social change, as Counts and Brameld thought in the first place; albeit perhaps that role needs some refining in light of recent curriculum theorizing and social psychological research.

3. Depending on who is doing the writing and the language employed, a third alternative could be termed either "subversive" or "micro counter hegemonic." When a writer talks about radical teachers infusing daily classroom instruction with values such as "groupism," altruism, cooperation, and welfare concerns for others, in the interests of long term revolutionary social reconstruction, he or she is talking about what most people would term quiet subversion in the schools.[44] More subtly, it has been suggested by Henry Giroux, among others, that radical teachers implement

> dialectics in the curricular process. In doing this, the notion of the common-sense understandings and daily experience of students as they are drawn from their cultural existence and wish to interpret, mediate, or even mystify the hegemonic ideology are reappropriated for curricular use. Gone is the sense that there is something called "curriculum," free-floating and unattached to human existence. Arising is the notion that teachers and curriculum must "take seriously those cultural experiences and meanings that students bring to the day-to-day process of schooling itself." Such a curriculum would capture the dialectic characteristic of totality,... media-

> tion, appropriation, ...and transcendence ...Curriculum can be formed by using these categories for self-examination as selections from the larger culture.[45]

Ann and Harold Berlak seem to be suggesting a similarly "micro counter hegemonic" mode of using the schooling process for radical social change, but with a focus on the finely tuned dynamics of teacher-pupil interactions as supported by recent advances in social psychology rather than on broader curriculum theory. They believe that the manner in which a teacher (the "change agent") **communicates intimately** with children via language can strongly influence and modify the child's receptivity to larger sociocultural values and norms. In other words, a highly skilled teacher can "subvert" students--can change students without the students "realizing it." This means that teachers have far greater potential for altering the consciousness of children under their tutelage than has hitherto been recognized by educators and lay people.[46]

Whether termed subversion or micro counter hegemony (or, more recently, critical pedagogy[47]), the notion that individual **teachers** possess the potential power to change society radically obviously implies a faith in schooling efficacy of great significance. If teachers can be **trained** to interact as the Berlaks suggest, consider what the implications might be for those who prepare teachers in colleges of education.[48]

4. Finally, I should mention a variation on the conventional Marxian theme of focussing on the workplace as the primary source of inspiration and impetus for revolutionary action. I refer to the idea of extending the workplace to **include the schools**--the "proletariat" in this view being both teachers and students, while the bourgeois "capitalists" who help exploit both groups are school administrators, or "managers," and, of course, educational policy makers. While "subversion" may be one of the tactics employed by the union comprised of teachers and their students, it is not necessarily the principal consideration in their efforts to bring about change, efforts which may, in fact, be quite out in the open. Martin Carnoy and Henry Levin explain how schools viewed as workplaces can become instigators of radical change:

> The strategy, then, is to establish in the workplace ...an antagonistic pole of power of challenge to management decisions. This anti-management organization, once it achieves its power, will be able

> to anticipate management decisions and to influence them before they are made...
> The short-term objective of the encroachment strategy, then, would be to win increasing control over what goes on in the classroom and what constitutes the educational curriculum. However, it is crucial that this control be won by teachers at the expense of central management, not students, and that control be won by students **together** with teachers. This requires reducing the antagonism between teacher and students which is inherent to the production of knowledge in capitalist societies, and implies a strategy of not only raising consciousness of teachers as worker-managers to demand permanent power over all aspects of work...but also to raise teacher and student consciousness as coworkers to demand **joint** control over the learning process.[49]

Of the various conceptions of education as an intentional strategy of revolution previously discussed--"naive" social reconstructionism," "subversion," "micro counter hegemony," "overhauling the workplace"--the last seems to be most specific in terms of a definitive strategy for accomplishing desired revolutionary objectives via the schooling process. It also lends itself to the efforts of already existing or potentially interested **organized** educational interest groups, such as teacher unions. (Of course, the same qualifier obtains in regard to organizing out in the open to resist management decisions as does in the case of the subversion model: public resistance to indoctrination of values deemed to be inappropriate. It is one thing for adults to risk their own livelihoods and more in their workplaces, but it is an entirely different matter for parents of schoolchildren to allow their progeny to be subjected to the revolutionary rhetoric and mobilizing efforts of teachers.) In any case, all of the conceptions outlined, with the exception of traditional Marxism, are grounded in a greater or lesser degree of faith in the power of the schooling institution to improve American society by changing it radically to the left.

It may be instructive to close this discussion of revolutionary strategies--a most contemporaneously significant genre of messianic educational thought--by reproducing the ideas of one such thinker.[50] I am not interested in "categorizing" his thought; but rather in giving the reader some inkling of the **passionate** fervor with which the messianically inclined frequently struggle to convince others of the remarkable powers of the schooling process of which they themselves are so enamored. In a critical review of a recent "functionalist" (i.e., to the reviewer, ideologically conservative) treatment of American public schooling,[51] educational theorist James McClellan presents his own "conflict" conception as an alternative:

> Let me make an alternative proposal. We use the System to **educate** the oncoming cohorts so that they can perform the duties that history has put upon them: to eliminate the Capitalist class and with it "others," i.e., unemployment, especially among our youth...Look, not by merit but by an accident of history, we inherited an eighteenth century political structure which guarantees us the right to peaceful revolution by Constitutional amendment. We have reached the state in the evolution of our political economy that we must exercise that right or lose it altogether in the deepening class, race, status struggles that lie just ahead. The material conditions for such a revolution are exactly right. What is lacking is the intellectual liberation which alone meets the honorable title "education." There's no reason, even in strictly orthodox Marxist theory, why revolution by education **must** fail. The odds are long, but the stakes are very high....As we free our minds from the hegemonic domination of bourgeois culture we set upon the road to collective self-knowledge.[52]

9. Education as Anarchy

The final of the major educational ideologies to be outlined is, at least on the surface, non "messianic." Ironically, its proponents want little or nothing from the public school, precisely because they believe the schools have **already** proven excessively powerful--in their capacity to cause personal and societal damage. This seemingly non-messianic ideology deserves attention because it has generated a substantial amount of heated debate over the past twenty years, and will help to round out our survey of contemporary expressions of the American people's diverse expectations for the schools that most rely upon heavily for salvation.

The ideology is radical/reconceptualist in tone, but the ends sought by proponents, i.e., cultural anarchy, are rarely as explicit as those envisioned by Marx and the contemporary Revolutionary Strategists. This is not an absolute assertion, since some Educational Anarchists do long for an eventual classless society but differ from classical Marxists in believing that it must be preceded by nearly complete sociocultural disorganization.

At any rate, educationally focussed anarchists not only refuse to consider education as being synonymous with schooling, but would like to see the latter done away with altogether; they urge that society be "deschooled." They feel that the main function of public schools has been not to educate, but rather to keep the masses in line; i.e., under cultural control by the more privileged classes.

Because they have been eminently successful in performing that undemocratic function, Anarchists have a healthy respect for the "enemy," schooling:

> ....Don't think that it is just a mistake that the school system is bad. It is not a mistake; it is not accidental, nor incidental. Schools are the way they are deliberately. They are set up to indoctrinate, classify, and control youth. The school system is part of the pacification and containment program designed for the youth of the country. What schools do they do on purpose and as effectively as is currently possible.
>
> It does no good to improve the school system--the system **is** the problem. Compulsory systematization (forming human beings to fit into systems) is itself anti-human; it is violence....[53]

Even if schools were once useful institutions, this approach suggests, they have become obsolete. Schools all over the world are presently organized as self-perpetuating bureaucracies merely to reproduce, through their credentials and degrees, the established order of things which, whether capitalistic or socialistic, is seen as oppressive to most of the world's people.

Ivan Illich, a major articulator of the ideology of Educational Anarchy in recent years, speaks of the "erosion" of contemporary civilization and urges the "disestablishment" of institutionalized schooling:

> The crisis is epochal. We are witnessing the end of

> the age of schooling. School has lost the power which reigned supreme during the first half of this century, to blind its participants to the divergence between the egalitarian myth its rhetoric serves and the rationalization of a stratified society its certificates produce. The loss of legitimacy of the schooling process as a means of determining competence, as a measure of social value, and as an agency of equality threatens all political systems that rely on schools as the means of reproducing themselves.[54]

Using advanced computer technology humanely, Illich and his disciples would replace schools with what they call "learning webs," "peer-matching," and other novelties that place "natural" teachers from the "organic" community in the willing company of learners of every age desiring to acquire the skills and understandings possessed by the former. Since access to elitist educational sources (i.e., schools) would be negligible under such a plan, all people at every age would have a more truly equal opportunity to utilize the revitalized educational institution to their advantage.

As noted above, deschooling ideology is non-messianic by definition; although some Educational Anarchists at least harbor faith that genuine **education**--to them a natural part of living in the "real world"--may be culturally redemptive. They are probably correct in the latter assumption; however, that assumption is not at issue herein. Whether or not education viewed broadly possesses culturally salvationary efficacy, the central issue under consideration for the present concerns the validity of the ubiquitous belief that **schools** possess positively redemptive qualities. The deschoolers are among the rare Americans who believe otherwise. Quite the opposite, as we have seen: they maintain that schools have nefarious qualities, and, therefore, deserve to be abolished.

Another interesting form of retreat from traditional conceptions of appropriate educational control and authority was the free school movement of the late 1960s and early 1970s (see Chapter 4). The deschoolers, including Illich, have been highly critical of this quasi-anarchistic ideological movement. They consider it to have been a subterfuge intended merely to ease the growing pains of deviant children from the more privileged classes. This despite protestations by movement leaders that free schools are not like other schools--that they are intended to salvage **all** human beings from the same oppression that deschooling anarchists claim are caused by schools.

The deschoolers' view seems cynical. Regardless of what most free schools eventually became in practice--or how far they may have strayed from originally conceived goals--the overall ideological thrust of the movement **was**, in my experience-based judgment, sincere in its messianism. That is to say, the authentic purpose of the movement was the liberation of American children's spirits from presumably corrupting capitalist values and norms via "counter hegemonic" schools operated in the private sector. In short, granted exceptions to the rule, fundamental free school ideology in America has much in common with Marxist ideology--Education as a Strategy of Revolution; although it differs from the latter in placing its faith in the culturally redemptive possibilities of private rather than public schooling.

An Illustration

To briefly sum up: Of nine strongly divergent educational ideologies competing for institutional dominance in contemporary America, nearly all including Exploratory Futurism are premised on the faith claim that schools possess messianic attributes which ideologues believe should be capitalized upon to benefit the American people. Of the nine, only conventional, or orthodox Marxism and Deschooling ideology appear to doubt the culturally regenerative power of schooling (although, as indicated, Deschooling ideology affirms the **degenerative** power of the institution). It is noteworthy, first, that both of these ideologies are radical/reconceptualist in their quintessential social goal orientation; and, secondly, that both have been taken seriously in this society by only a very small percentage of the American people, predominantly disaffected radical intellectuals and affluent professionals marginal to the upper middle-class. Conversely, we find that the great majority of Americans--including most radicals interested in education--do possess some greater or lesser faith in the singularly beneficent cultural power of the schooling process.

Are the conventional Marxists and the Anarchists, then, more in possession of a sense of reality than the rest of the American public, where schooling is concerned? Conceivably. One should remember that, at the outset of this book, it was acknowledged that in American society, it is considered "heretical" to doubt the considerable utilitarian efficacy of public schools and their teachers. American Marxists and anarchists are obviously atypical in their educational values; nonetheless, they are ideologues. In the final chapter, I hope to demonstrate that one may be a heretic without also being an ideologue.

At this point, it will be helpful to provide a highly specific illustration of how Americans place their faith in the public school system to resolve their problems for them. The illustration deals with "destructive" religious cults. The ideological framework, or model, for organizing belief about the school's social efficacy is Revivalistic Fundamentalism. The plea for school-based salvation by an apparently intelligent lay person is sufficiently straightforward and uncomplicated as to be ideal for illustrating what a tremendous hold the schools actually do have upon the American imagination in its search for educational panaceas.

The March, 1983, issue of the *Phi Delta Kappan* educational journal, one that ordinarily cannot be accused of sensationalism, included an article entitled "The Urgent Need for Education about Cults." The author was Shirley Hale Willis of Powey, California, a member of the Citizens Freedom Foundation, described by her as "an organization whose purpose is to educate the public about destructive cults."[55]

Willis informs readers that she has lost a daughter to what she alleges is a "destructive religious cult." She systematically explains how, in her opinion and that of selected "authorities" on cults, her daughter and over three million other young Americans have become trapped in cults. In short, she constructs a persuasive case that cults are bad.

Accordingly, something should be done about them. What does Willis propose? Not that people learn to be more tolerant or at least understanding about their children's choices of religious affiliations, as leading authorities on cults advise.[56] Nor does she have much faith in comparatively "direct" interventions, such as deprogramming, legal pressure, psychotherapy, etc., since, in her words, "My husband and I have spent thousands of dollars in fruitless efforts to free our daughter's mind."[57]

Not surprisingly, Willis takes the American road to salvation. She proposes that high schools teach courses about cults in order to prevent the "cult problem" from expanding in the future. "**The cult problem must surely be easier to prevent through education than it is to cure by any means.**"[58] (Emphases added.)

Specifically, she has three suggestions for the public schools:

> 1. High schools should "provide social studies programs that compare the methods of Hitler and of other repressive regimes to those of destructive religious cults."[59]
> 2. "A course in which the Bible is studied not as religion but as literature and as history would dispel some of the naivete about the Bible that makes young people so vulnerable to the cult leaders' manipulations of this most important book."[60]
> 3. There should be "more emphasis in our schools on teaching students to gather and evaluate information from opposing sources before making any decisions of importance in their lives...In short, students who recognize the ways of con artists and are aware of the dangers of a closed mind will be less vulnerable."[61]

Willis concludes her article with the following forceful profession of faith in the power of schooling to restore the status quo ante preferred by her:

> The program I have suggested might well be the most important program in the high school curriculum, both for the individual student and for society.[62]

My major purpose in presenting this material has been to illustrate just how real and how pronounced is this type of faith in today's society, even among relatively world-wise individuals, as well as to let readers see for themselves how generalized faith in the efficacy of schooling tends more or less to parallel a comprehensive schema, or ideology of school function and effectiveness; in this case, Revivalistic Fundamentalism in a fairly sophisticated and seemingly non-hostile key.

Note how Willis uses the term "social studies"--one offensive to most Neo-Fundamentalists--instead of "history" and "government" for her purposes of indoctrinating students. Also, she is careful to emphasize teaching the *Bible*, **not** as religion but as literature and history; but at the same time has no qualms about what she proposes to tell students are the "correct" and the "manipulative" interpretations of the *Bible*.

Lastly, she tries to win the hearts of all genuinely liberal disciples of Dewey (instead of angrily attacking many of *Phi Delta Kappan*'s readership as is customary among Revivalistic Fundamentalists) by carefully appealing to their predilection for "gathering and evaluating information from opposing sources," etc. Nonetheless, what she wants and forthrightly demands from those professional educators who read *Phi Delta Kappan* is a **restoration** of the fundamentalist status quo ante. Underneath her careful use of language is a plaintive cry for the preferred ways of the past before the American family and its conventionalized religious patterning had become unglued, as it apparently has in her own family's tragic case.

There is nothing inherently wrong with yearning for the past, even if it is often sentimentalized beyond any semblance of what actually went on. Americans have the privilege of **wanting** anything they please--whether it be a return to a reified period of the distant past; an uncomplicated and psychologically non-traumatic fitting in (conforming) with contemporary socioeconomic demands; or a chimerically utopian paradise set in the distant future. That notwithstanding, it ought to be a matter of profound concern to thoughtful people that seemingly responsible individuals, such as Willis, can take for granted the efficacy of **schools** as the appropriate vehicles for achieving their varied and sundry dreams of better days. And, in the year 1983 Willis personifies par excellence this penchant for placing naive faith in schooling in her forthright call for teaching about the evils of cults in high schools, and expecting such teaching to result in prevention of, if not a cure for, the cult problem.

Can it be substantiated that comparing Adolf Hitler with American cult fashions during high school social studies will make a significant difference in how many young people actually join them? Can becoming less "naive" about the *Bible* preclude being "manipulated" to join cults after graduating from high school? Finally, will understanding and skills in gathering and evaluating information systematically acquired in school actually make a person bound and intent on joining a cult (or taking hard drugs, gambling away their lifetime earnings in Las Vegas, or entering into a life of crime, for that matter) less likely to do these kinds of things in the future? In other words, can knowledge gained in school guarantee desired emotional and behavioral outcomes--assuming that one's ideologically preferred knowledge is permitted to be taught in school as a result of successful political struggle over disparate values in the first place?

Cult authority Saul Levine does not think so. According to him, none of the above educational "treatments" is likely to make a substantial difference in the decision about whether to join or not join a "dangerous" cult. The reason: The decision to join is predicated **not upon rationality**--which is purportedly what Willis expects the school to foster--but, rather upon **avoiding the personal dilemmas of having to grow up.**[63] Joining a cult is an act of intentional defiance of reasonable behavior; it is an **emotional** act. The issue at stake here as in all conceptions of the school's individual and cultural meliorative power is whether social life--which always involves deep emotions far beyond the purview of the school--can, for the great majority of human beings throughout the world, be controlled primarily by reason. Most people are motivated by **passion** far more than by reason, whether for the good or for the bad.

This is particularly true in matters of critical significance, involving intense personal and social values; *viz* cults. It certainly should be kept in mind that many of Hitler's most heinous henchmen were brilliantly educated and highly rational Ph.D.s and M.D.s. Those school-bred qualities did not prevent them from committing their atrocious crimes against other human beings. As political scientist Leonard Fein has aptly phrased it: "....though this be the century in which man masters space, this is also and ineradically the century of Auschwitz. Whoever remains invincibly confident of man's ultimate capacity to destroy the beast in man is historically illiterate."[64]

Contrary to what Willis and other educational true believers may think, the power of reason, alone, to control the behavioral impulses and tendencies of even the most carefully educated individuals is profoundly limited, both in terms of what schools are allowed to teach in the first place (their political "inputs") as well as what their clients are likely to base their lives upon after graduation (their educational "outputs").

Chapter 6

The Appeal and Spread of Educational Messianism

Educational Messianism as a Displacement Syndrome

Ubiquitous faith in the capacity of the public school to serve major utilitarian functions for the American people is largely the result of widespread **displacement** of their perceived ability (including their willingness) to resolve social problems **directly** at a time of profound change and dislocation in the basic structure of our society.

Instead of concertedly, yet self-reliantly grappling with the society's growing problems of poverty, greed, intergroup hatred, violent crime, ennui, alienation, and breakdown of the family, Americans seem to cringe in anxiety and indifference from these and other change-related challenges. Unable to live up to their overblown expectations of utopia, they dissipate collective and individual energies on what social critic H. Mark Roelofs terms "politically frivolous enthusiasms and pointless actions."[1]

Americans talk more than they act. They talk a great deal about coping with the **symptomatic** stresses and strains of daily living in a "future-shocked" world that (despite comforting denials by wishful-thinking authority figures and professional futurists who equate technological advances such as computers with human welfare) is, in fact, still changing far too rapidly for most. Indeed, important talk-- even more than the nation's almost fetishistic obsession with spectator sports--appears to be a substitute for carefully crafted action in a society that is increasingly incapable of acting efficaciously either at home or abroad (e.g., witness our profound failure in Vietnam and our continuing effort to deny it by rationalization in both conversation and the cinema). As Richard Whalen candidly put it:

> We are in retreat. The serpent of tragedy appeared in America's earthly paradise in the mid-1960s...The United States lost not only its moral self-image, but also its actual position and reputation of leadership, of guardianship of free-world interests and money.[2]

Symptomatic of this penchant for trivial talk is the now-ubiquitous "talkshow" on radio (as well as television) in which the moderator confabulates about every subject imaginable: sports, travel, movie actors, and the like. Not long ago when escapism was less profitable, talkshows dealt primarily with significant political and ideological issues such as the pros and cons of building more nuclear plants, the rights of homosexuals, the effectiveness of the President and Congress. Now, however, audiences are treated to a seemingly endless parade of shows hosted by experts in clinical psychology and the practical dynamics of everyday middle-class life. They advise forlorn men and women about their love lives, sex, failing marriages, coping with loneliness, interviewing for a corporate job, etc. Serious programming dealing soberly with issues of critical significance to the nation and the world is an increasing rarity; and, when available, is attended to least by those ill-informed citizens who most need such programming.

In addition, there has recently been an enormous outpouring of popular books by self-acclaimed authorities of every stripe on how to deal more successfully with the stresses of modern life, including not a few written by Hollywood celebrities about how to lose weight and be popular, how to present an "executive image," how to be a single parent supermom without breaking down, how to grow old gracefully, and the like.

As noted above, not all of this talk is frivolous, but most of it is. We have become a nation of petty gossips ripe for exploitation by the mass media "pundits" who prey upon our collective fears and anxieties. The point is that Americans engage in trivial conversation excessively, because with all of its immense problems waiting to be resolutely attacked, entertaining conversation has become a bearable substitute for serious dialogue aimed at acting authentically, which is always risky. In Martin Pawley's view, we want to live in "the triumph of sensation divorced from action,"[3] which television and other mass media especially encourage quite obligingly.[4]

What has been happening to the American people to make them so impotent as a society? In my judgment, the essence of modern America's damaged capacity for social self-reliance stems from a rather basic yet all-important idea: namely, the loss of a pervasive sense of **community belongingness** both at the local and regional/national levels. Only the **myth** of community, kept alive periodically during holiday seasons such as Thanksgiving and Christmas, and at Presidential inaugurations, remains for most people born in the United States. Privatistic individualism, goaded by the increasingly distorted ethos of ruthlessly competitive materialism, runs rampant, and further erodes our strength and resolve as a people daily.

Recently, anthropologist Marvin Harris treated this topic in depth in a book called *America Now*.[5] Although focussing on concerns broader than education, he argues that the ultimate source of most contemporary complaints about shoddily manufactured goods and services, breakdown of the family structure, rampant crime and violence, uncontrolled pornography and sexual abuse, etc. is a profound loss of authentic organic community in American society since about the end of World War II. In its headlong rush into the depersonalized future, he maintains, Americans have forsaken their parents, their children, their neighbors, their friends, their lovers. Americans are strangers to each other as never before in history.[6] Today, most think nothing of leaving their primary group roots to secure a supposedly glamorous corporate job in some large city hundreds or even thousands of miles from their cultural origins. And, most public personalities carelessly encourage such extremely individualist/separatist behavior on the almost unarguable ground of "getting ahead."

The focus of Harris' book is the loss of home and local neighborhood--the ultimate *gemeinshaftliche* community--by both men as well as women as a result to their being forced to work in **depersonalized** complex formal organizations in an increasingly technocratic and anomic *gesellshaftliche* society. His argument about the effects of such depersonalization are superbly illustrated in the following extended quotation about quality of goods produced past and present:

> A man is not likely to fashion a spear for himself whose point will fall off in mid-flight; nor is a woman

> who weaves her own basket likely to make it out of rotted straw. Similarly, if one is sewing a parka for a husband who is about to go hunting for the family with the temperature at sixty below, all stitches will be perfect. And when the men who make boats are the uncles and fathers of those who sail them, they will be as seaworthy as the state of the art permits. In contrast, it is very hard for people to care about strangers or about products to be used by strangers. In our era of industrial mass production and mass marketing, quality is a constant problem because **the intimate sentimental and personal bonds which once made us responsible to each other and to our products have withered away and been replaced by money relationships.** Not only are the producers and consumers strangers but the women and men involved in various stages of production and distribution--management, the workers on the factory floor, the office help, the salespeople--are also strangers to each other.... The larger the company and the more complex its division of labor, the greater the sum of uncaring relationships and hence the greater the effect of Murphy's law. Growth adds layer on layer of executives, foremen, engineers, production workers, and sales specialists to the payroll. Since each new employee contributes a diminished share to the overall production process, alienation from the company and its product is likely to increase along with the neglect or even purposeful sabotage of quality standards.
>
> My basic contention is that after World War II, quality problems reached crisis proportions as a result of the unprecedented increase in the size and complexity of the U.S. manufacturing corporations and hence in the quantity of **alienated and uncaring** workers and managers....[7] (Emphases added.)

The principles articulated in the above illustration may be generalized to American society as a whole. America has in this generation gone from a relatively affiliative condition operating on a socio-psychological scale of interpersonal bonding to a severely dehumanized condition, or what Vance Packard has called "a nation of strangers."[8] Its people are increasingly confused, alienated, disconnected. They are afraid to face themselves existentially, much less the strangers with whom they are required to play superficially interactive roles almost constantly. Most feel quite helpless and insufficient in their isolation; that is why they seek "messiahs," whether in the form of an authoritarian political father figure such as Ronald Reagan or in the kindly image of a Dr. Harvey Rubin, popular psychotherapist of radio talkshow celebrity.

In their perceived helplessness, they **displace** their fears and anxieties about facing themselves and their seemingly externally-determined future upon confident-appearing others who arrive on the scene promising peace of mind without much personal sacrifice.[9] This book concentrates upon one such would-be redeemer of the reluctant American people--not a person, but a complex institutional idea. The promises proffered by the idea of schooling as a redemptive institution is that, somehow, secular **knowledge** will bring socio-spiritual salvation to America. Knowledge has significant cultural utility in the short term, it is thought, because it increases a person's or group's ability to cope with practical problems at every level of complexity. If we all obtain more knowledge, presumably, we will all become more effective in coping with life. The major difficulty with that common-sensical and attractive Enlightenment-born notion is that in seeking to secure knowledge from schools, we continually put off until tomorrow or next year or the next generation the actual grappling with the problems that beset us **now**. In attributing redemptive qualities to school knowledge, we are admitting that we do not care to tackle our immediate problems head on. They are too frightening.

With the help of authoritative political leaders who symbolize the self-confident wisdom we no longer possess but are afraid to acknowledge, the secular messiah, schooling, will, we imagine, protect us from harm until our children grow up possessing an "education." Then, **our children** will use their school-based knowledge to resolve America's problems. Unfortunately, by then, those problems will have become magnified to even more monumental proportions than at present, like the national debt. But, the **current** generation, already formed and on its single-track life course, will not need to worry about them. There is yet time. Let us improve the public schools in anticipation that our formally educated children will use their more advanced intellects to restore societal integrity. We can afford to bumble and stumble along in the meantime until they, with their greater knowledge-based intelligences, take charge and rebuild the nation and the world.

Even if it were true (a) that adequate time remained in which to employ delaying tactics until this generation's more highly educated children went to work in earnest on a massive national reclamation project--which is doubtful--and (b) that the disparate values reflected in wide-ranging ideological conceptions of schooling efficacy discussed in Chapter 5 could be harmonized in a **political** consensus which enabled the institution to mobilize for concerted educative effort acceptable to most citizens, there is no convincing evidence available that trained intelligence by itself is the most effective mode of solving the kinds of problems facing America. They are grounded principally in deep-seated core cultural **values** and passions rather than in primarily instrumental considerations involving relationships between agreed-upon ends and the logical means to attain those ends.

One of the most rational, or knowledge-based societies in the world today is Israel; yet, it cannot rely principally upon the trained intelligence of its people to resolve its valuational differences with its Arab neighbors. No amount of time spent in school will result in Arabs and Jews liking and trusting each other in the Middle East. The only viable possibility of resolving the underlying value conflicts facing the people there rests on the continuing threat of war, on mutual accommodation based on threat of physical annihilation via military combat. And, probably because of Arab numerical superiority and indefatigability, coupled with the ideological as well as pragmatic need for a Jewish state to appear to the larger world and to itself as morally superior, sooner or later, the Israeli Jews will, as they have done before, reluctantly be the ones to make the greater concession in this mutual accommodation; i.e., by giving up most of the West Bank.[10] Even such a drastic step is risky, so it would be foolish for the Israelis to beat their swords into plowshares after conceding what they call Judea and Sumeria to the Palestinians. Intelligence alone will not work under the circumstances. Intelligence is useful, but sustained military preparedness is essential on an indefinite, and probably on a permanent basis. One does not need to go to school for a long time to obtain that level of "practical intelligence." One only needs to hear a bomb go off next door to a crowded downtown department store in Jerusalem after being pushed out of the way of danger by an armed soldier--as I was--to understand contemporary as well as historical reality in the Middle East.

The American people have not as yet felt the immediate imperative of arming themselves to the teeth and having soldiers carrying submachine guns along the streets of their cities, as in Israel. They have not learned from radical experience at the outer edge to appreciate the relative insignificance of trained intelligence produced by schooling in directly resolving most currently pressing social problems. Americans still think they have time on their side, and that they can afford to use it to displace their responsibilities for directly attacking their increasingly complex societal problems onto highly specialized institutions of knowledge diffusion. They are mistaken. They must alter their overblown expectations for schooling, and regain a sense of proportion, of collective responsibility equal to--indeed, greater--than their exaggerated individualism.

The Social Psychology of a Displacement Syndrome

It is important to bear in mind that, from the very beginnings of the American experiment, the members of this society were predisposed to place an inordinate degree of faith in the immediately foreseeable sociocultural efficacy of schooling. Still, it was not until a decade and a half after World War II, when the times were ripe, that educational messianism became more than a mere cultural predisposition; i.e., was transformed into a major cultural **complex**, the EMC.

Before then, the American people, by and large, still retained a semblance of organic community life which permitted them to give lip service to the cultural utility of schooling while yet maintaining faith in their own individual and collective self-sufficiency in resolving the manifold problems of living in what they took for granted was the greatest nation on earth. They had faith in American social self-reliance, because they had faith in each other--a function of relatively successful living in human scale communities tied interdependently to other communities and connected integrally with a sense of broader societal purpose sustained by still-vivid memories of the unquestioned victory of good against evil in World War II and its aftermath of global redemption and unprecedented material affluence at home.

When all this collapsed, and America was devastated by successive shock waves of massive social change beginning in the 1950s and continuing until the present, the vast majority of the people of this society were stung into a near-paralytic state of confusion and helplessness from which they have not yet recovered. They no longer could turn to each other for encouragement because most had left home and were now living alone in "new towns" such as Los Angeles or Houston, San Francisco or Denver or Atlanta. Americans were, increasingly, becoming strangers to each other as the society became compartmentalized. Under the forces of secularization, even the meaning of God was being redefined for modern Americans, so that, despite the rise of televangelism, the majority could no longer receive authentic spiritual and moral sustenance and courage from traditional religion.

Thus, the times were ripe for American's historic predisposition toward educational messianism to be transformed by displacement into an active, full-blown cultural reliance upon the public school for secular, post-industrial-age salvation.

The actual mechanics of this displacement phenomenon eventuating in the EMC are highly complex. Basically, we are dealing with the social psychology of public opinion and mass movements, of how educational belief and ideology are developed and spread throughout a social system--or, in sociological language, the diffusion of ("valuational") innovation.

The general theory which perhaps best explains the overall process of displacement of American faith in the culturally redemptive power of schooling during the contemporary epoch is reference group theory; more particularly, symbolic interactionism. Originally developed in the late nineteenth century by G. H. Mead, John Dewey, and other seminal social psychologists and philosophers, its value as an analytic tool is only now becoming widely appreciated among students of human behavior.

The essence of symbolic interactionism is that human beings are supremely social animals who obtain virtually all of their values, beliefs, and attitudes from their interpersonal relations with other people, beginning at birth with their "mothering ones" and expanding as they grow older to include neighbors, friends, teachers, bosses, co-workers, spouses, political leaders, favorite authors, and so on. Such relations give human beings identity and purpose, thereby poising us for what we consider meaningful behavior throughout our lives.

These various reference figures are termed "significant others;" and the employment of spoken or written language is of crucial importance in this interactive process. We "refer" to our significant others for confirmation of our developing personalities and role-associated ego identities. Largely through language exchanges, we learn from others who we are and even how we are expected to behave--as through a "looking glass," to use Charles Horton Cooley's famous analogy.[11]

Our significant others give us clues about how we appear to other people, whether we seem physically attractive or homely, smart or dumb, moral or immoral, personable or dull; in short, whether we are, in their eyes, worthy or unworthy. If we are fortunate, we grow up with what psychologists call a healthy self-concept, and, accordingly, believe we are more or less "in control of our own fates" as a result; if unlucky, with a great deal of **anxiety** about our worth and a greater or lesser sense of "externalized locus of control." For psychotherapists, highly anxious, "other-directed" (neurotic or psychotic) people are their bread and butter.

In symbolic interactionist theory the job of psychotherapy is to substantially reduce debilitating anxiety in highly insecure people, while simultaneously increasing autonomy, or "internalized locus of control." This is accomplished by one or more of several methods of convincing the anxious individual to see himself or herself as more worthy in the eyes of significant others, usually the therapist or his surrogates, a collaborative group of fellow counselees comprising what might be called a "quasi-family."[12]

It bears noting that most people in contemporary American society grow up with moderately shaky identities; i.e., most have a higher general state of anxiety than their forebears in the more stable and less confusing past, albeit not so high as to require professional intervention. But, that is not our immediate focus herein. We are primarily interested in the organizing principle that people acquire a unique identity, or sense of selfhood and existential justification, via the looking-glass self process of relating interpersonally to significant others all throughout their lives, primarily through the utilization of linguistic symbols.

Secondly, and--ironically--perhaps even more important for our present purposes, is the symbolic interactionist notion of "generalized other." We may thing of a generalized other as the totality of looking-glass images of self in a specific domain of our personhood (e.g., attractiveness or artistic talent) and/or our role identities (e.g., executive, earth mother, or relevist) abstracted to a more or less **consistent** general image.

Acquisition of personality and role identity--including values, beliefs, attitudes, ideologies, etc.--occur both as a result of face-to-face interpersonal communication with significant others in successive **specific** situations, or "episodes;" as well as a result of far less directly personal interactions via the written word, the mass media, the formal lecture, and so forth. In Everett Rogers' now classic sociological study of the process by which innovations are diffused, highly specific principles can be stated concerning which type of communication--personal and direct or less directly personal--is most important at each stage of a five-stage process of widespread acceptance or rejection of a new idea or technology. For instance, Rogers postulates that **personal** influence is generally most important at stage three, evaluation of the novel idea, when people tend to rely on local "opinion leaders" and close and trusted acquaintances.[13] On the other hand, **less directly personal** sources are most commonly relied upon at stage one, initial awareness of a new idea, and particularly for "early adopters."[14]

In what follows, I shall not adhere rigidly to the paradigm developed by Rogers and other researchers interested in the study of interpersonal and intergroup influence on public opinion. Instead, I will focus upon some of the key actors in the drama of educationally-related diffusion of a **faith** in the messianic properties of schooling. They occupy a variety of more or less influential role **positions** in the social structure of American formal education.

As Julie Evetts puts this idea in her 1973 study of the social psychology of educational ideas: "Individuals in certain positions react in predictable ways such that it might be possible to group them and generalize about their responses to certain educational ideas."[15]

Evetts, who is British, believes that two of the centrally important positions in influencing educational values are those of "teachers of teachers" (university-based professors of Education) and, at the local level, parents of children in school. Evetts makes one more salient point that warrants keeping in mind as we proceed; that has to do with the explicitness with which different segments of the population view an educational ideology:

> ....Educational ideas seldom affect public opinion directly, only when they have been filtered and incorporated into an existing body of social and

> political ideology. The ideas themselves have to be transformed for mass consumption, and climates of opinion seem to result more from successful **advertizing** techniques than from reasoned arguments.[16] (Emphasis added.)

In what follows, then, I will be considering how the generalized American predisposition to "educational messianism" is exploited intentionally and unintentionally today in such a way as to displace social self-reliance based on organic community involvement onto a universal faith in the school's prepotent cultural efficacy.

It does not occur out of a cultural vacuum; rather, in Evetts' words, it requires "an existing body of social and political ideology."[17] Stated differently: The EMC displacement phenomenon is dependent upon a singularly American cultural predisposition to place our faith vaguely in the school as an important instrument of direct social power for improving the human condition; however, when organic community and its accompanying social self-reliance are at a low ebb and ineffectual individualism runs amuck, such predisposing and vague faith are exploitable by our significant and generalized others. People then are "ready" to avoid confronting their collective problems directly at any cost and, instead, are prepared to let the schools act for them on their behalf. All they need is a push.

The process, or mechanics, of such displacement requires that certain **explicit ideologies** of schooling efficacy be developed and disseminated, or "advertized" widely by influential others. That is, diffuse faith in schooling efficacy remains mere predisposition until it is attached to a **specific cause** dear to some one or another organized and influential interest. As demonstrated at length in Chapter 5, there are many such ideologically-related educational causes ranging from reactionary to revolutionary in tone and purpose confounding our society as we move toward the close of the twentieth century.

People's predisposing and generalized faith in the school's social power is energized and activated by such concrete causes and their ideological support structures. Working competitively for their multifarious motives, people organized in interest groups to influence other people and the political structure controlling school policy eventually come to raise their already high expectations of the schooling "messiah" to a new plateau; and justify it by the overriding notion that in a service/information-centered society, knowledge acquired in schools and colleges is of supreme importance. Educational messianism is thus transformed from a vague predisposition to a major actuating cultural complex, replete with self-protective rationalizations for the massive displacement which has taken place.

The Key Actors in the Diffusion of Educational Messianism

Who are the key actors in this modern "religious" drama focussed upon the "secular" public schools of America? There are many, and from all walks of life. They include most saliently the following:

Educational intellectuals
Certain politicians
Important judges
Leaders of special interest groups
Independent pollsters
Teachers of teachers
Editorial writers and talkshow hosts
Public school teachers
Parents of school children
Taxpayers and other concerned citizens

Each of the actors listed can be viewed from a symbolic interactionist perspective in terms of identifiable **social position**--solidly embedded or marginal--with a concomitant **role-function** to serve in the drama of building the EMC.

A. Educational Intellectuals:

First there are those whose essential role in the drama is to **create** belief--the true believers who develop the ideologies upon which messianic faith in the social efficacy of schooling is predicated. These are the intellectuals, frequently rootless and marginal men and women with a mission in life, who are convinced of formal education's salvationary promise as a result of their research and thought. They write tracts and essays of varying length and quality proclaiming some one or another normative assignment for schools; e.g., the integration of a disconnected society by means of mandated school desegregation and busing, or the reinvigoration of Jeffersonian democracy by strengthening the social studies curriculum via "The

New Civism,"[18] or, especially influential in the last few years, the restoration of America's former leadership position in the world economic market by going "back to the basics" with a vengeance in elementary and secondary school.[19] And so on.

Educational intellectuals include among their ranks teachers of teachers dissatisfied with the status quo into which they fit poorly; they are especially prominent in developing the ideological support structure for the EMC by virtue of their intense career-vested interests as scholars in convincing themselves and others of the supreme importance of public schools as utilitarian agencies of redemption. They also include, intermittently, national commissions of eminent university professors and other prominent public figures assigned to prepare documents for mass distribution which recommend sweeping policies for rectifying the national plight by radically reforming the nation's schools.

Also included among the intellectuals are lay and religious dignitaries who believe that the character of the American people and their spiritual sensibilities have become increasingly weakened and corrupted over the years. They believe that the American character can be strengthened by overhauling a decadent system of pre-collegiate schooling, typically in a conservative or reactionary direction. Their books and speeches are frequently filled with hortatory polemics and vitriolic accusations based on little or no evidence other than their "intuition" or their literalist interpretation of the *Bible*.

Such lay and religious writers (former Moral Majority leader Jerry Falwell is a good example of the latter), with their typically simplistic and dogmatic style (e.g., reading should be taught **only** by the phonics method), are usually far more influential in swaying mass public opinion to their ways of thinking than even the most vivacious and brilliant intellectual ideologues from the academy. One exception, perhaps, was Max Rafferty, once the elected Superintendent of Public Instruction for the state of California. Rafferty was one of the most effective reactionary educational true believers in the history of the republic. His often snarlingly savage attacks on the devil of "progressive education" had profound influence in swaying popular opinion about schooling in a conservative direction between 1950 and 1980.[20]

But, whether scholarly or evangelistic in their approach to educational problems and their literary style, educational intellectuals have the important, if frequently understated, **role** of creating new or reincarnating old ideologies which attribute salvationary powers to formal education. Their unique function in the construction and perpetuation of the educational messiah mystique is to provide ideological fodder for other less constantly and obsessively committed educators and the public to chew and digest. Their malcontentedness, channeled into erudite or populist polemics, keeps the ideological debate fueled during times of exceptional unrest when the nation is desperately seeking easy answers to difficult questions.

B. Major Opinion Leaders:

Sooner or later, the ideas of certain of the more influential educational intellectuals are picked up ("adopted") by public opinion leaders of various kinds. The latter are capable of diffusing widely those ideas, normally in modified form. Former President Ronald Reagan is a splendid example of a major political opinion leader who, while in office, employed developed ideological faith in the messianic efficacy of schooling to further his own and the Republic Party's cause. He and his appointee as Secretary of Education, Terrell H. Bell, formed the commission that wrote the conservative to reactionary *A Nation at Risk* report extolling Human Engineering schooling ideology, a report which has had enormous publicity since 1983 and has been a major influence on counter-progressive type educational reform.[21] Reagan personally has been unswerving in his oft-stated Neo-Fundamentalistic conviction that prayer in school will be good for America, that it will contribute to the moral regeneration of the nation.

Politicians of lesser stature than the President also perform the role of trying to diffuse widely their own and their constituents' conceptions of the school's redemptive mission, especially by seeking to have legislation favorable to their preferred ideological propensities passed in Congress, their state legislatures, or even at the local board of education level. For instance, in many locales around the country, boards of education have in recent years adopted official policies requiring school districts to teach "moral education"--usually meaning indoctrination of traditional core societal values such as "patriotism" or "hard work," or more universal values such as "justice" and "love"--as part of the official curriculum. Somehow, it is believed by these local-level politicians, moral training in schools will make a difference for the better in the future because students will become purer human beings and citizens as a more or less direct result of such indoctrination.

Judges, especially federal judges, and, most significantly, justices of the United States Supreme Court, have played a central role in recent years in molding public opinion about education. In 1897, the Court helped to perpetuate educationally-sponsored racism by its decision in *Plessy v. Ferguson* that separate schools for "colored" children and white children were equal. In 1954, the Supreme Court reversed *Plessy* in the famous "desegregation decision," *Brown v. Board of Education of Topeka*, proclaiming that "separate is inherently unequal." At present, the Reagan-packing of the Supreme Court is expected to lead to decisions which officially sanction prayer in public schools.

Whether that will actually happen is not at issue here. The point is that the courts can be a most powerful influence on popular educational opinion and policy, depending upon who sits on the bench at a given time. Whether that opinion and policy ultimately "causes" schooling to bring about the results desired is, of course, challenged herein; the *Brown* decision of 1954 is yet to demonstrate having had a benign effect on either race relations generally or the opportunities of blacks and other severely disadvantaged minorities to succeed in American life.

In regard to opinion molding by leaders of special interest groups, there are so many of the latter that it is not feasible to discuss them all in any detail.[22] There are, for instance, teachers unions (e.g., the American Federation of Teachers [AFT] and the National Education Association [NEA]). Together, they claim to represent some two and one half million American teachers at all levels. There are a variety of educationally interested religious interest groups (e.g., the aforementioned Moral Majority, the Catholic Church, the Anti-Defamation League of B'Nai B'rith, etc.) There are women's groups (e.g., the PTA, the League of Women Voters). There are organizations of school administrators (e.g., the National Association of School Administrators), whose members occasionally side with teachers unions (as when both teacher and administrator interests, such as salaries, are at stake) and more often oppose them (as when teachers unions resist bureau-technocratic mandates supported by administrators, such as state or national testing of already credentialed teachers). And, there are various ethnic minority interests seeking to equalize economic and social opportunity for their underprivileged constituents via compensatory education, ethnic and multicultural curricula, bilingual education, affirmative action hiring of school personnel, and a variety of other social, educational, and political initiatives.

To take only one of the great variety of interest groups interested in what schools may do for society, let us look briefly at the two major teachers unions in the United States, the AFT and the NEA. The NEA, with approximately 1.8 million members, has traditionally been the more conservative of the two, but in recent years--prodded by the smaller, more militant AFT--it has become defiantly "liberal" in most of its areas of interest. It supports the Democratic Party ticket at all levels, and has been only lukewarm on the back-to-basics issue; it has, in fact, developed a controversial model program for nuclear disarmament studies in secondary schools. On the other hand, the once "radical" AFT has seemingly turned conservative in the last few years in regard to its support of "nation at risk"-type educational ideology, if not of Republican political candidates.

Albert Shanker, the long-term AFT President, has written numerous pieces for newspapers and magazines on the imperative for educational reform of a conservative character--most recently advocating a national licensing test for teachers comparable in difficulty to the Bar Examination for attorneys. This pleases educational and other American conservatives enormously. His message is that only by restoring educational "excellence" to our schools--a euphemism for back-to-basics policies, programs, and teaching methods--will our society get back on track as a great nation which provides genuine equality of opportunity for all races, classes, and creeds. He has been opposed to the NEA's Nuclear Disarmament studies program on the grounds that it is not value-free, but rather biased toward a particularistic conception of the good not shared by most Americans. He is also opposed to what he considers excessive preoccupation with such out-of-the-mainstream panaceas as bilingual education. (Conversely, the NEA has until quite recently been opposed to the kind of tough testing of teachers that Shanker and the AFT advocate on the grounds that such testing would single out teachers from among other professionals for a simplistic assessment of their competence.)

Lest this abrupt reversal of ideological preferences seem ironical, it should be observed that the NEA has historically represented the largely middle-class educational establishment in general and is consistent in continuing to side with the forces of new (government interventionist) liberalism. On the other hand, the labor-oriented AFT--connected as it is with the AFL-CIO--has been faced with the dual challenge of trying to represent the more militant economic demands of its historically working-class oriented constituency, while simultaneously responding positively to the latters' essentially conservative notions of the purposes of schooling and pedagogical methodology (application of human engineering and neo-fundamentalist ideology and behavioristic learning theory). One must remember that today's working-class includes many "new ethnics" who desire equality for themselves and their children, yet are more typically conservative in curricular and pedagogical values. The AFT cannot, Shanker realizes, afford to portray itself as the left/liberal organization it once was, while the basically middle-class NEA suddenly emerges as the natural ally of mainstream liberal, or welfare state, educational utilitarianism.

C. Non-Affiliated Opinion Molders:

Another segment of the population is involved in developing and retaining faith in the ameliorative properties of schooling, primarily by helping opinion leaders to widely disseminate currently fashionable educational ideologies. Especially significant in this regard are the great majority of teachers of teachers (as distinguished from cosmopolite educational intellectuals), independent pollsters, and journalistic editorial writers and talkshow hosts on radio and television.

These people typically are not true intellectuals psychologically driven by their precarious marginality to create new conceptions of educational efficacy. Nor are they leaders of special interest groups seeking to manipulate public opinion favorable to their chosen cause. Nonetheless, they possess varying degrees of influence over educationally related opinion by helping to mold it on the basis of either personal predilection or commitment to publicize ("advertize") collected data. They are essentially intermediaries and translators whose job is to interpret the content of ideological creations so that it becomes available to the broader public in a simplified form.

For instance, the average teacher of teachers, including most administrators of teacher education schools and departments, is not an original creator of complex ideologies of educational efficacy. He or she may occasionally contribute to the ongoing scholarly debate about "competency-based teacher education," "measurement-driven instruction," "effective schools," and so on; but their primary role is as an ordinary classroom instructor in a college or university which trains school teachers and other professional educators for jobs with salaries. Since there are tens of thousands of such ordinary teachers of teachers working with hundreds of thousands of prospective and practicing schoolpeople, their influence as molders of professional opinion cannot be discounted. These teacher educators hold more or less well-thought out opinions about what the functions of public schools ought to be; their values are transmitted to their students, not infrequently producing some role-conflict in the latter once they leave the training program to enter the so-called "real world" of the classroom with its contradictory ideological pressures on school personnel.[23]

To illustrate: As of this writing, large numbers of future teachers and school administrators are being influenced by their Education professors to believe that educational excellence means returning to a highly structured program of traditional subject matter taught by adult-centered methods that were generally discredited by the teacher education establishment only ten or fifteen years ago when "neo-progressive" educational ideology with its more student-centered and humanistic classroom prescriptions was in vogue. Where did their professors receive their own sense of what is currently in style ideologically? In large part, from several heavily advertized national reports damning the alleged mediocrity of the United States educational system and blaming this system for producing "losers" in the competitive world market as well as in domestic affairs. These reports have been followed by bestselling reactionary and conservative tracts, such as Allan Bloom's *The Closing of the American Mind* and E. O. Hirsch, Jr.'s *Cultural Literacy*. With noteworthy exceptions (e.g., modest current interest in "whole language" approaches to teaching reading, in promoting "critical thinking" by students, etc.), the climate of teacher education in American society is rapidly turning to the "essentialist" right, partly as a result of the favorable attention such tradition-oriented reports have obtained from the mass media.[24]

State education departments everywhere have urged new legislation requiring a revival of fundamentalist as well as human engineering ideology in the formal education domain; in turn, this legislation is acquiesced to readily by nervous university-level officials and bureaucrats fearful of losing professional accreditation for their programs and possibly their jobs. The essentialist new order insidiously infects classroom instructors in their teacher preparation institutions, most of whom are not wiling or able to resist neo-fundamentalist/human engineering rhetoric even when they recognize its pervasive influence on their own and their students' thinking. Students who take classes from the majority of teachers of teachers, then, are surprised to learn from the intellectual maverick among their professors that there actually is more than one way of envisioning the mission of public schools and the professional roles of public school workers. It is not an exaggeration to assert that most prospective teachers today are being indoctrinated by the essentialist "hidden curriculum" of the new teacher education, in much the same way as ten years ago they would have been by that of neo-progressivism.

Another public opinion molding group is that of independent pollsters, especially the Gallup organization which annually surveys the American public on its attitudes about public education. The pollsters sample public and professional opinion about what are conceived to be the problems of public education and what the schools ought to be doing to improve their quality. The results of such surveys are then published in professional journals and textbooks and, in abbreviated form, in newspapers and glossy magazines all across the United States.

Once they are widely disseminated, such survey results are picked up by newspaper and magazine editorial writers and, in the few remaining public affairs programs, by radio and television talkshow hosts as fuel for their typically polemical efforts to sway the minds of mass America.

As in the case of teachers of teachers, a question of chicken or egg can be raised with regard to both the pollsters and the journalist/entertainers. Do the polls and editorials **reflect** true public opinion or help **mold** it? I suggest that they do both. However, as molders of public opinion about education, their role, whether they are cognizant of it or not, is essentially to help coalesce disparate ideological propensities that were lying dormant prior to the publication of explicit arguments on behalf of the propensity gathering strength in a given era. At present, the pollsters and journalists/entertainers are playing a role in helping to **unify** American educational opinion in support of essentialist and perennialist educational ideology by widely diffusing the impression that everyone ought to be getting on the bandwagon of conservative/reactionary educational reform.

Such advertizing can be very effective. Once the movement toward retrogressive reform has gathered sufficient force for the pollsters, journalists, and entertainers to become significantly involved, it is nearly impossible for today's average, "other-directed" American to ignore the ideological prodding of these non-affiliated significant reference figures; and the momentum toward universalizing a singular messianic conception of schooling throughout the entire culture becomes practically irresistible. Faith in the capacity of our schools to "save" American society by completely institutionalizing the new ideological fashion in policy and practice sweeps the country and is virtually total. All other once-competitive ideologies are swept aside by the tidal wave of current educational fashion--i.e., neo-fundamentalism and human engineering--or safely contained for the time being.

D. Interactive Adopters of the Faith:

In the light of the above, it may be fairly evident what parts classroom teachers, parents of school children, and other concerned citizens play in the EMC drama; nonetheless, a few short comments are in order.

American school teachers, for the most part, do what they are told to do to obtain and retain their somewhat thankless jobs. They learn some, although not enough of, what is expected of them during their university training from their professors and from their experiences as student teachers; and, once on the job, from their principals and other district administrators. The latter typically can be counted on to appease prevailing ideological trends by demanding that teachers dutifully carry out in their daily classroom practice the mandates of those ideological interests in power at any given time. Furthermore, they are placed under direct pressure from parents of the children in their classes and indirect pressure from all the media sources utilized by taxpayer groups and other citizens interested in having their views on schooling implemented.

If teachers do attempt to resist the considerable ideological pressures from all sides on their roles, they do so discreetly. Otherwise, they are called to task and sanctioned for failing to follow orders from above or for displaying lack of appropriate role deference to those they are expected to serve. Thus, the job may entail considerable role strain and produce abnormally high rates of burnout during a period of universal messianic faith in formal education, factionalized by ideological conflict. Such strain cannot be avoided without either convincing oneself of the validity of the prevailing ideological fashion (which many teachers try unsuccessfully to do), developing a genuine **philosophy** of education strong enough to combat the centripetal role pressures from conflicting alters (which teachers historically have been discouraged for doing by the forces of economic expediency and anti-intellectualism that have dominated the institutions of schooling in American culture), or resigning from their positions (which has been the last resort of innumerable teachers disillusioned with their working conditions). Psychocultural therapy utilizing intensive group dynamics and role-playing applied to problems of occupational survival may help somewhat to avert and mitigate the effects of strain and burnout; but not many teachers as yet have access to such therapy, nor does it strike at the roots of contemporary teacher role strain, which are **sociocultural** in nature, not individual.[25]

The irony is that since ideological fashions in education tend to change every few years, by the time a new corps of loyalists to the current main ideology has been trained, recruited, and tenured and the older teacher corps has burned out or retired, ideological fashions may have changed once again. Thus, when contemporary right-wing style educational messianism is eventually unmasked, as it is already beginning to be, intellectuals, opinion leaders and molders waiting in the wings will seek to revise the ideological bases of the EMC accordingly, most likely returning, pendulum-like, to one or more variations of progressivist conceptions of the public schools' social efficacy.

As America moves gradually toward the left again in its educational thinking, the conservative teaching corps that has largely replaced the previous more liberally oriented corps will itself become fatigued by conflicting ideological pressures from parents, administrators, taxpayers, professors, etc.; and many of them will burn out or retire prematurely. In short, the "ironic cycle" will probably repeat itself, other things being equal. As Roelofs has put it in terms of government: "American government [substitute education] is destined to go on forever just as it is."[26]

Other possibilities are, of course, conceivable; albeit, not predictable. An especially provocative one is that large numbers of parents of school children may decided that they have had enough to unkept promises from the representatives of tax-supported state schools. With greater or lesser reluctance, those parents may turn to the private educational sector. Some have already done so. But, with the recently reinvigorated hope that public schools will redeem society via implementation of neo-fundamentalist/human engineering reforms stressing the New Basics, the momentum toward private schooling has eased at least temporarily. Formerly disenchanted parents are once again pinning their hopes on this public school revival by enrolling their children in them instead of fighting strenuously for vouchers and tuition-tax credits for private schools. However, the climate for private schooling has warmed sufficiently so that when new right educational ideology eventually does fail to achieve its avowed purpose of renewing America, that may be the final blow for vast numbers of the previously faithful. If public school-disaffected intellectuals and other leading educational ideologues on both the left and the right are prepared to seize that moment, and are able to unite politically to revive their proposals for vouchers and tax credits, we are likely to then see a massive shift in the public's allegiance from the public to the private educational sector.

That would not necessarily mean that parents who in the next ten years enroll their children in private schools will have, thereby, lost their faith in the messianic potential of formal education; on the contrary. It would mean that America will have finally reneged on its century and a half "contract" with Horace Mann, Henry Barnard, John Dewey, and the other great historic public school proponents. It will have decided that public schools, as we have come to know them, are not able to shoulder the immense burden of salvaging an endangered society, and have simply transferred its citizens' faith and allegiance to the private educational sector. Should that occur, the term "private school" will, for all intents and purposes, become obsolete in hopes that a new conception of public educational messianism will justify itself.

Conclusion

More than fifty years ago sociologist Willard Waller pointed out that, as social organizations, schools are "little societies" in their own right.[27] So are hospitals, prisons, and the other "total" or "semi-total" institutions about which Erving Goffman[28] has written so penetratingly. Nonetheless, schools are embedded in larger, more inclusive communities. They are only one, albeit an important institution of their communities and of American society as a whole.

The American people appear to have ignored this third fact in their zeal to attribute messianic properties to the school for reasons discussed at length herein. But, Americans can be forgiven for their eagerness to be "saved" by the formal education institution on the grounds that community at every level is itself in disarray; and few intellectuals, politicians, and other public figures have had the insightfulness and courage demanded to take on the immense problem of redesigning and reordering societal life in America. In a manner of speaking, our leaders have "defaulted" on their responsibilities to their constituencies, the citizenry of this nation.

What is the confused, civically uncommitted public to do under such circumstances? As things stand, what it has done increasingly up to the present; namely, rely on the avoidance techniques of trying to ignore the basic social problems giving rise to general cultural community collapse, while projecting or displacing its anxieties thereby generated onto the one institution besides advanced corporate capitalism (which promises partial escape from this worldly insecurity for those fortunate enough to become wealthy) that is most easily rationalized as a universal panacea, the public school.

In the end, such rationalization will prove self-defeating. Only genuine truth, not rationalized emotive idealism, will set us free. The truth about schools is that, as **one** component of the comprehensive community/societal structure, they can provide knowledge, viewed in its broadest sense, to the interested and capable; not a small or unimportant task in and of itself. But, the kind of **massive social change** required to reintegrate cultural community life in an increasingly fragmented America entails a full-blown commitment on the parts of virtually everyone to analyzing what has gone awry, and then working **together** to rebuild America. **Social self-reliance**, then, is the key to interlinked individual and societal salvation.

The school will have a significant, primarily mind-expanding role to play in this massive reconstruction project; let there be no misunderstanding about that. However, regardless of its importance, such a role will necessarily be highly limited.

Chapter 7

Blaming the Victim: The Teacher as Scapegoat in the EMC Drama

The Teacher as Scapegoat

In the last analysis, it is the school's **teachers** who are affected most directly by the collective self-denial of responsibility for undertaking resolution of America's manifold social problems. They are the ones held most immediately and fully accountable for the inevitable failure of the schooling messiah to fulfill its exaggerated promises. Of course, school administrators and especially university teachers of teachers receive a share of the blame, the former for allegedly failing to lead sufficiently well for their teachers to teach effectively and the latter for failing to prepare teachers to be competent professionals in the first place.[1]

Although the classroom teacher is most acutely touched by the EMC, all three groups of professional players are targeted for negative sanctions when the schooling messiah is unable to achieve the goals expected of it by a disabled society. Nonetheless, the fact is that great administrators and brilliant teachers of teachers everywhere will not make a significant dent in the problem of "poor" teaching, because, at its core, the problem is not a professional one, as we have been led to believe. It is a basic social problem. It is a problem of displacement of broad societal responsibility for decision making and action onto, ultimately, the principal formal educators of contemporary children and youth: the schoolteacher.

As employed in the present chapter, then, the concept of displacement is extended to mean that one specialized group in the society, classroom teachers, singled out to directly implement the reforms assigned the schooling system, cannot do for the American people as a whole what only the latter in concert must accept responsibility for doing themselves; no more than teachers can be expected to love a parent's child under their tutelage because that child is not loved at home. That which teachers **can** do, if they are effective, is help receptive students **learn** whatever it is that schools determine is normatively appropriate and pragmatically feasible to incorporate in specialized curricula--no more, no less.

So, when American teachers do necessarily fail to fulfill the impossible "meta-teaching" expectations which have been demanded of them by the American people, the public, in a pharisaical effort to "save face" for its failure of nerve, makes of them a **scapegoat**; that is, opportunistically blames teachers for its own [displaced] "mistakes and crimes." In the words of Daniel Duke:

> Teachers have the sometimes dubious distinction of being the symbol of the public school. When student achievement declines, it is the teacher who has failed to teach basic skills. When unemployment and juvenile delinquency climb, it is the teacher who has neglected career education, good work habits, and student self-esteem. Low teacher expectations for minority students are regarded as a subtle form of racism. Lack of classroom control and teachers' reluctance to model appropriate behavior are cited as reasons why young people lack discipline and respect for authority. The waste of public resources on questionable educational innovations and teacher pressure--through collective bargaining--for higher salaries are cited as contributions to fiscal crisis....[2]

Duke confounds the issue by adding the following:

> Ironically teachers are partially to blame for this situation. They did their job too well. By educating the vast majority of the nation's youth, American teachers helped create a situation in which public schooling ceased to be a special or privileged experience....[3]

If anyone, then, is selected as the chief victim for the scapegoating public and its spokespeople representing various educational interest groups, it is the hapless teacher isolated and alone in his or her classroom with twenty to forty-plus children struggling sometimes quite desperately to stay alive professionally, much less creatively facilitating learning and, moreover, saving a troubled America.

Who Are America's Real Teachers?

Imagine a representative, or "average" American elementary or secondary school teacher today. Such a teacher is moderately to highly intelligent, although SAT, IQ, and other misleading standardized test scores[4] might not reflect their true ability; in no small part because, increasingly, teachers are members of some disadvantaged ethnic minority--Hispanic or black especially. Furthermore, the partial institutionalization of feminist ideology has fostered a move away from teaching and other once "female" careers by more advantaged--hence, test-wise--white Anglo Saxon Protestant women who were formerly the mainstay of the profession. The latter are now majoring in law and medicine, which pay considerably higher salaries and command profoundly greater respect from clients and social status from the public in general.[5]

She (most teachers continue to be women, especially, of course, at the elementary level; this despite almost heroic efforts to bring in more men since the late 1950s) works in an urban or semi-urban setting with ethnic minority children of poverty or working-class backgrounds, who, on the average, perform unspectacularly on their own state-mandated standardized tests; and, as a result of an unfavorable ecological imbalance in the social class structure, have relatively little underlying incentive to be in school in the first place. In 1982 she earned a substandard wage of about $12,000 if a beginner and about $24,000 after thirty years for a 45-60 hour work week, after about five years of university preparation (some of which went to union dues to prevent salary and working conditions from eroding even further[6]). Lest it be countered that salaries for beginning teachers had nearly doubled by 1989 as a result of several national reports condemning the plight of formal education and of teachers, I should remind readers that they are still far less than those paid for equally qualified and less committed workers in business and other professional occupations at the outset of their careers and thereafter. Professional organization leaders are now talking seriously about appropriate teacher salaries ranging from $30-60 thousand dollars or more per academic year, comparable to the average salaries of college and university professors.

The parents of these representative teachers' students are generally "a-cooperative"--caught up in their own personal struggles (e.g., consider the plight of the new working single-parent mother), if not utterly antagonistic or superciliously overbearing. The principal, essentially a business manager in the United States--on orders from the central administrative bureaucracy above, which is frequently tied into state and federal policy and funding requirements--is bearing down on teachers harder than ever before to "produce" in the classroom. (Such productivity today includes "attractive" bulletin boards as well as annually increasing pupil achievement test scores in all curriculum areas.) Unfortunately, the typical highly pressured American teacher has perhaps twenty minutes a day in which to teach social studies, fifteen minutes for science, and two hours for reading at the elementary school level; if an academic secondary teacher with five sections of a class, she or he may have 125-150 papers to grade in front of the television set several nights each week. And, the spouses and children of the teachers portrayed not infrequently complain that the latter are "always tired" and unavailable to give them the attention they deserve.

If we study American teachers more closely, we find that the details of their occupational and personal lives vary, although most are expected to carry inordinate career-related burdens. For example, if one is employed by an upper middle-class suburban school district with "mainline" students from professional homes, one might enjoy a greater latitude in what and how they teach and more consistently positive reactions from administrators after their highly achievement-motivated students have been tested in the now-ubiquitous regional and state-wide annual academic competitions. But arrogant parents with advanced degrees, nowadays including "liberated fathers," may persistently interfere with the teacher's professional discretion or may even occasionally threaten to drive the teacher from the school if disappointed in some way by the latter; for instance, by the teacher's insisting upon standards of pupil behavior--discipline--with which the affluent suburban parent disagrees. Beginning teachers are not infrequently shocked and dismayed to learn that working in wealthy "country club" schools may be equally harrowing, in its way, as working in the most socioeconomically depressed inner-city school.

Carolyn Mahalko-Bakinow, a teacher interviewed on public television not long ago, had the following to say about the growing stresses of the position:

> I think, in any school, there are three areas that I feel that teachers need more support from the administration. They must be firm and consistent. I am firm and consistent in my [eighth grade] classroom, and I don't feel that administrators always are. But then, sometimes too, they're hampered by legal restraints and then, underlying it all, is a growing lack of parental concern or cooperation. When you get a note from a parent that says, "My child will not stay after school for you. **I told my child they do not have to listen to you.**"[7] (Emphases added.)

If employed by a small town or country school district, one is likely to enjoy a more nearly ideal work situation in one sense. Such teachers typically were born and raised in the area and have returned there to work and raise their own families after graduating college and getting married--the main reason they were probably hired or at least stayed on after the first year or two. Everyone in the community knows and basically trusts such a teacher, because she is one of their own. She is a respected and even influential member of a supportive community. On the other hand, the rural teacher is not as likely as the more typical urban or suburban teacher to have sufficient financial or professional assistance to purchase needed supplies and to keep updated via workshops and university courses on technical and other advances made in the field. Frequently she must be a super-generalist--a teacher of several grade levels and subject areas. Super-generalists under these conditions, trying to work with diverse youngsters growing up in an age of high technology and unprecedented social complexity, have an increasingly frustrating challenge.[8]

To reiterate, I am speaking of averages, not exceptions. There are almost three million teachers in the United States today. Like people in every other line of work, the great majority are, by definition, average for the occupation in ways depicted above, including ability, incentive, working conditions, salary, and so forth. Occasionally--rarely--an exceptional teacher slips through the selecting and sorting net which recruits, trains, and retains teachers. Thus, a small proportion of uniquely talented teachers work under the rather depressing circumstances outlined above--even in the worst urban or rural slums imaginable--and are brilliantly effective for at least a few years. Everyone who comes into contact with him or her--students, parents, principal, colleagues, recognizes and acknowledges this rare teacher's great giftedness. She or he is a genuine **artist** of the classroom, whose efforts to reach students are, indeed, wonderful to behold.

Seymour Sarason may be at least partially correct in his judgment that the simple secret of this exceptional teacher's success is a unique ability to bring the **outside** world into the classroom; which, he claims, is what excites students and adults alike.[9] I think the matter is more complex, having known highly gifted teachers who were not philosophical Realists such as those admired by Sarason. Certainly, one of the significant factors separating out excellent teachers from the rest, regardless of philosophy, is what social psychologists like to call "personal sense of efficacy." Ample research findings are now available to demonstrate that "there is a relationship between teachers' sense of efficacy and student achievement."[10] The researchers cited, Patricia Ashton and Rodman Webb, go on to say:

> ....Teachers with a strong sense of efficacy believe that they are capable of having a positive effect on student performance. They choose challenging activities and are motivated to try harder when obstacles confront them. They become engrossed in the teaching situation itself, are not easily diverted, and experience pride in their accomplishments when the work is done.[11]

Not infrequently, their students are in awe of them and enjoy going to school solely to be under their graceful tutelage. In short, they teach superlatively, and their students almost invariably learn a great deal in their classes.

But, we should not lose perspective. Most teachers, like the majority in every other walk of life, are average people whose influence on their students will be moderate; no amount of wishful thinking can alter this reality. Furthermore, even the most rarely gifted teachers frequently lose their passion, becoming disillusioned nowadays after a few years of such total dedication to their calling. In fact, the most highly gifted ones understandably burn out earlier than their less committed colleagues, as a rule.[12] After they resign, they usually enter a more financially rewarding and less morally and intellectually demanding occupation, such as selling stocks and bonds. If they do not quit the field of education entirely, they are often drafted into the ranks of more honored and highly paid educational administration; or, if unusually scholarly in bent, some become college professors, teachers of teachers. In either case, they are lost to the children so deeply in direct need of superior teachers. Under extremely stressful conditions, some become mentally ill or alcoholic, or drug abusers as a result of their immoderate exertions. This is a fact that has gone virtually unnoticed in the literature.[13]

Few stay on in sustained and uninterrupted brilliance for an entire career as classroom teachers, to be emulated by all the other less gifted teachers; and the ranks of those few are declining rapidly as new career opportunities open up for women and as working/ professional conditions continue to worsen. So, it is important to bear in mind that the great majority of public school teachers in the United States as everywhere else are **ordinarily** gifted people. As such, they are destined to disappoint the public which has displaced responsibility for changing society onto the schools in which they labor.

Moreover, it is unrealistic to expect that American society will **ever** have at its disposal more than a relatively small number of such brilliantly creative artist-teachers as pictured above, even if someday we should manage to make teaching the fine artistic endeavor it intrinsically is. Why not? Because genuine greatness in **any** field of endeavor, including the arts, is always an extraordinarily rare commodity. One giant out of one hundred more or less ordinarily talented professional teaching artists is, therefore, nothing to sneer at, ever.

So, in sum, not possessing an unusual sense of efficacy, a surfeit of talent, most teachers are not and cannot fairly be expected to be superiorly effective in the classroom with their students, regardless of their philosophies or their dedicated efforts. As Harry N. Chandler, a public school teacher and head of the Department of Exceptional Student Services in McMnneville School District, Oregon, sagely observes:

> I do think public school teachers **should** be better. They **should** be the best possible people for their jobs. They **should** be willing and be able to work successfully with any child who comes down the pike. They **should** be, but they are not, and there is no reason to think that they ever will be.[14]

Thus, while it is useful for scholars to study exemplary teachers in order to better understand the possibilities and limitations of educational efficacy; and while the large majority of ordinary teachers can, with certainty, learn from their dazzling example how to become substantially more proficient as artists of the classroom, it is futile to expect that most of the three million teachers in this society will ever be strikingly accomplished themselves. Talented and acceptably proficient at their demanding art, yes; great, no. And, that is as it is in every other field. The difference is that the American people do not expect all lawyers to be Clarence Darrows nor all physicians to be Albert Schweitzers. All architects are not expected to be Frank Lloyd Wrights nor all painters Picasso. The public, including their clients, expects most professionals to be averagely proficient; and considers itself fortunate, indeed, if ever attended to by an authentic genius in his or her work. Americans do, however, expect and even demand that the majority of their children's teachers be committed, effective redeemers of American society, the working disciples of the schooling messiah. Such expectations are the more incredible when one considers how shabbily Americans treat their teachers socially and economically. Nonetheless, such expectations prevail as the norm.

Even, however, if, as has been suggested recently, the public and school officials were to acknowledge their frankly deplorable treatment of the nation's teachers, and, accordingly, helped them to work in enjoyable and professionally respectable environments on a far more collegial basis involving greatly expanded individual autonomy, the people of this society still would not obtain the results they seem to want. We would, unquestionably, have an incomparably better educational system in this society with vastly increased and improved learning occurring in our schools, a feat to be very proud of. But, our deep-seated faith and displaced hope for cultural redemption via schooling would continue to remain frustrated. The reason? Schooling is a false messiah. It is not a miracle-working panacea. It is at most a process whereby limited aspirations for self-fulfillment and cultural humanization may be fostered over the long term. There are no guarantees even of that, as the historical record has shown repeatedly down to the present.

Thus, assuming the very best as an achievable goal, teachers as the missionaries of educational messianism cannot save America. To continue to expect them to do so is to selectively attend to ideologically induced emotion while ignoring logic inferred from factual evidence. And, at present, the American teaching corps are far from being the best that they might someday become. Still, the American people fantasize about being salvaged as a society by these mostly ordinary, hardworking, and variously talented teachers, and are troubled when the latter disappoint them repeatedly, as inevitably they must.

America's teachers are under attack incessantly from every side. Teachers of teachers, themselves a constant butt of ridicule from outside, are the least brutal in their attacks, because they know more than do most others about the actual work of teachers. Nonetheless, many of them fall into the trap of mimicking the majority by essentially "blaming the victim." They tirelessly invent "new" methods and strategies designed to enable teachers to become more "competent," on the undocumented presumption that improvement in learning will occur as a direct result of increased technical proficiency. However, methods and competencies are not at issue, as they seem to believe. Most teachers **are** already reasonably competent, and have all the methods they will ever need.

Competence is what H. H. Morris calls "a red herring."[15] Displacement of responsibility for socially self-reliant **community** decision-making and action onto already impossibly burdened professionals in classrooms is the real issue. Educational scholarship which concentrated on the broader, more overarching question of institutional efficacy in a holistic ecological context would yield a refreshingly productive spinoff in terms of preparing teachers as highly creative, hence effective, classroom artists instead of merely competent functionaries.

The other reference groups attacking teachers today for their failure to solve the problems of American society--non-educational scholars, parents, administrators, journalists, local and state educational officials, politicians, religious leaders, and so on-- vary in the harshness of their criticisms of the teaching profession. Some are less narrow-minded and unkindly than others; but, taken together, we find a relatively unsympathetic, unempathic view of public schoolteachers by the majority. The general consensus is that teachers are at the root of the failure of the American dream, because teachers are woefully inadequate as human beings and service workers.

This negative conception of the profession holds teachers, the victims, accountable for the inadequacy of the schools and, by extension, of the society. Teachers are considered at fault for supposedly not trying harder with their students, not being dedicated enough to their calling, not really wanting to teach while doing so either as a last resort or for pin money, not being better students in college, not being willing to work around the clock and the year for substandard pay, and so on, *ad infinitum*. There is a strong element of moral outrage in such unqualified claims, as if teachers have let society down in their agreed upon role as the conscience of the world. A graduate student put it well not long ago, when he said: "Teachers are the monks of modern America." The metaphor is apt, but not entirely fitting; for, unlike those who have taken vows of penance, most teachers want only to live in this world, and contribute to it modestly by performing their art with children and youth. They do not want their unsought role as monks. And, unlike the latter, they at least have the meaningful option of leaving the profession to do less socially significant work in the private sector, work that is respected and decently paid, albeit not necessarily personally satisfying.

Indeed, teachers **are** leaving in sizeable numbers--the finest reluctantly; or, if close to retirement, are holding on as best they can. Those who do stay are increasingly behaving in the manner depicted by the stereotypes of them--a self-fulfilling prophecy. Ploddingly and disinterestedly, growing numbers "put in their time," talk snidely about administrators and parents among those whom they trust (fellow teachers, as a rule), and go home (or, increasingly, to cocktail lounges) at the end of the workday and week to socialize with other adults and watch TV; basically, to forget their burdensome jobs for awhile.[16]

Conclusion

It has become a commonplace to assert that teaching can be considered almost a disaster area in contemporary American society. If that is true, it is because teachers have been ordered to perform virtual feats of wizardry with children, to convert universal ignorance into knowledge-based culturally redemptive power. And, when it becomes evident that teachers are not magicians but just ordinarily competent and hardworking people like everyone else, instead of modifying its exorbitant expectations of teachers to more realistic proportions while offering them a kindly helping hand, the public and its representative educational officials call on teachers to do more of the same, better, with little or no additional support.

It should hardly be surprising, under the circumstances, that many teachers become dispirited, and their classroom performances actually deteriorate instead of improving. Thus, the scapegoat fulfills the prophesy. The victim becomes objectifiably blamable. The critics of schooling find their ever-escalating attacks on American teachers ironically justified. An end to the dilemma of educational messianism seems nowhere in sight, from the perspective of the reflected dilemma of most contemporary teachers.

Chapter 8

Four Undesirable Scenarios of Future Messianic Faith in Schooling

A Venture in Futuristic Forecasting

What can reasonably be expected of the American people in the foreseeable future? Will they continue to evade collective responsibilities while placing inordinate faith in the school's social efficacy, as they have been doing for the last thirty years? Alternately, will messianic faith in the schooling institution be transferred to another single social institution? A third prospect is that the American people will become severely disenchanted with **all** of their central institutions and allow the society to collapse of its own weight from internal normative disintegration and external exploitation of its people's weaknesses. As one writer says of the American socioeconomic system:

> ....In my more negative moments, I am almost persuaded that liberal capitalism has indeed been an historical oddity that, like an earlier experiment in democracy (Athens at the height of its glory), always carried within it the seeds of its own decay.[1]

It is also conceivable that the American people will proceed to muddle along with greater uncertainty that even the EMC phenomenon has signified without establishing any set course, whether beneficial or detrimental to our character as a society. Perhaps such a "muddling along" state of affairs should be considered still another scenario in itself, making a total of four worthy of serious discussion.[2] In summary, they are:

1. Persistance of the EMC;
2. Replacement of schooling by a new messiah complex;
3. Disillusionment, surrender, and sociocultural demise;
4. Muddling along.

Let me emphasize at the outset that each scenario to be discussed is a more or less undesirable[3] image of the future, including a worst case scenario (number 3). Nonetheless, one or another may come to pass if the American people do not take substantial steps to move beyond their present passivity and dependency in the face of the future. It should also be observed that they are constructed ideal types. Hence, whichever one (or more), if any, does come to pass, the actual outcome is likely to diverge somewhat from the models presented.

In the concluding chapter, still a fifth scenario will be presented, one that I believe offers plausible hope for the future--partly because it can be achieved without sacrificing our most commonly cherished core values as a society. That preferred scenario will deal with the restoration of significant social self-reliance on the part of the American people. And, therein, I will attempt to articulate a less immoderate conception of the appropriate role of formal education in the overall social ecology.

Four Undesirable Scenarios of the Future

Scenario #1: Persistence of the EMC

In this first scenario, little changes in the fundamental way most Americans think about their schooling system. Despite growing skepticism regarding its social efficacy by sociologists and a handful of truly objective educational intellectuals, most Americans, including the majority of professional educators in the field continue to anoint the formal education institution with messianic attributes as they simultaneously elude the challenge of becoming self-reliant as a unified people. In this scenario, the particular expectations demanded of the schools may change with the shifting sands of ideological preference in the culture at large--as in recent years the ideological climate has become increasingly conservative; but the overriding **faith** in their social power is still maintained. Thus, perhaps there will be a return to a more liberal or even radical conception of schooling efficacy, reminiscent of the 1960s and early 1970s before educational liberalism was contained by the forces of socioeducational reaction.

For instance, in the 1996 Presidential election, the Democratic candidate wins following sixteen years of a strong Republican bias influencing the mass public's conception of the functional role of public schools. Regardless of which particular Democratic candidate actually becomes the next President, his or her election encourages newly energized educational spokespeople and the leading organizations of teachers--always at bottom more liberally inclined than the general public--to begin pushing once again for such policies as stricter enforcement of desegregation laws, increased federal expenditures for poverty programs, reinvigorated stress in the core curriculums of elementary and secondary schools on social studies which focus on reducing political apathy and increasing participation in the democratic process, and so on. What the educational right likes to call the "frills and fads" (subjects such as art, music, drivers training, etc.) will be restored to the curriculum of the public schools in hopes of building a more balanced and well-rounded citizenry prepared for a future of expanded leisure as well as income-producing occupational endeavor. Less stress than at present will be placed on educating youngsters for "traditional" values such as patriotism, competitiveness, rugged individualism, the work-success ethic, and so on. More will be placed on the virtues of public service, social welfare, internationalism, relativistic moral attitudes, aesthetic appreciation, and the like.[4]

But, to repeat, this first scenario postulates that the EMC will remain basically intact, regardless of which operational ideology is in sway at any designated time in the foreseeable future. The point is that, above and beyond particularistic ideological claims, and despite growing warnings by intellectuals and educational researchers, most modern people simply continue to believe self-delusively in the secularly salvationary power of the schooling process for the improvement of everyday life on this continent, much in the way that the Puritan colonists believed in the spiritually redemptive power of hard work for the afterlife. Not to so believe is viewed by the great majority as a sacrilege--a heresy. To publicly suggest that schools have far less utilitarian efficacy than most of us are accustomed to believing will continue to be distressing to the average educational true believer, even though he or she can point to no significant evidence that their sustained faith in the transcending powers of public schooling is warranted.

There are great numbers of Americans, including powerful professional bureaucrats involved directly with formal education--hence a group with genuine vested interests in perpetuating the EMC under what Arthur Wise terms their increasingly "hyperrationalized" control[5]--who now place enormous faith in the social capacity of schooling. There is no obvious reason to assume that they will not continue to selectively inattend to the accumulating evidence that they have been tilting at windmills in their ongoing efforts to harness the presumed prepotency of formal education.

This deeply ingrained is the historic American propensity for imagining a powerfully utilitarian significance for the institution. Both the professional bureaucrats and the average man or woman in the street are encouraged in such futile fantasizing by educational "celebrities" who insist on oversimplifying the issues involved. In this regard, it is edifying to reread the inflammatory words of William Bennett, former Secretary of the Department of Education:

> Our national security is no less at risk from a poor school than from a poor army or navy.[6]

The messianic faith on the majority of people will be continually buoyed up by the undeniable fact that in postindustrial America schooling at increasingly advanced levels **is**, indeed, required by more and more people in order to **understand** the complexities of modern life in and of itself, as well as to learn some of the technical skills required of many (not all, as is frequently claimed) workers in such a complex society. More than ever, schools are cultural essentials for teaching the next generation how to **think clearly and critically**. Schooling may indirectly **assist** in the overall process of improving the human condition--no small contribution. To acknowledge such a fact is, however, emphatically not to give credibility to the far-fetched notion that schooling can directly resolve the difficult social problems of modern America, which is what great numbers of Americans do and will continue to believe if the first scenario proves to be accurate.

So, scenario number 1 is, unquestionably, a provocative image of the future, albeit not a hopeful one. It postulates the persistence of a dangerous cultural tendency to escape from reality by displacing necessary responsibility for facing reality squarely onto an institution which was never meant to do more than help actualize and humanize those who would find the necessary incentive to overcome the inevitable obstacles on the road to the future, principally from sources outside the school; that is, from sustained human interaction with each other in the crucible of the living community.[7]

Scenario #2: Replacement of Schooling by a New Messiah Complex

Since this book is directed centrally at schooling, I have not felt obliged in earlier chapters to enter into more than cursory discussion of other forms of dysfunctional displacement of responsibility for confronting life's challenges to which Americans have become increasingly addicted in recent years. For example, I have not concentrated on escapism into excessive television watching, spectator sports, use of alcohol and hard drugs, delinquency and crime, religious cults, workaholism, exorbitant material consumption, obsession with pornography, adulation of celebrities, and so forth. Such forms of unhealthy escapism abound today. The fact that I have treated them more as symptoms of deeper underlying problems rather than as forms of escapism does not mean that I do not acknowledge their function in the latter regard.

Others have spoken of this generalized tendency toward escapism *en masse* for a number of years. A recent story in the *Los Angeles Times* covering the American Psychological Association's convention there in 1985 summed up the opinions of psychologists from around the country about our escapist-prone society:

> The psychologists see a population in which many, if not most, are almost adamantly avoiding looming personal, domestic, and international troubles in favor of instant gratification and self-deception.
> Drugs, drink, denial and the single-minded pursuit of career or money have become major means for many Americans attempting to insulate themselves from the world at large, they add. And, some conclude, rampant concern for self is ripping up the social fabric, tearing hardest at minorities and the poor.
> "People are kind of frightened and they're covering it up with a quick fix," said Stanley Graham, a New York psychologist who listed cocaine and alcohol as

two of the most worrisome forms of escapism....[8]

In sociologist Orrin Klapp's terms, most of the above forms of escape from responsibility can be placed in the category of "kicks"--quick fixes to calm deeply troubled Americans for a short time so that they can bear going on with life in the unstable and disconnected society which is the root source of most of their troubles.[9]

These escape mechanisms provide only temporary relief, which is why so many Americans turn to the schooling messiah, and cling to it all the more tenaciously. Schooling offers the illusion of a "permanent fix," because so much money and time is invested in this ongoing institutionalized activity, and Americans have always liked to see their major investments pay off with big, concretely measurable return within a stipulated timeframe. As a highly utilitarian culture, America has difficulty accepting more nebulous, personally significant, and long-ranged returns on its educational dollar, although it has been my contention throughout that such comparatively non-utilitarian returns are nearly all anyone has the right to expect from the schooling process.[10]

At any rate, there is one candidate for serious competition with schooling as the secular messiah of the future, a candidate claiming to offer more than mere kicks and quick fixes. I refer to the rapidly developing **institution** of scientific psychotherapy.

Our second scenario envisages the mental health movement in all its scientific paraphernalia **replacing** schooling as the principal agency of cultural redemption in American society. The psychiatrist, psychologist, psychiatric social worker, *et al.*, become to the average American what the teacher has been, the psychological society's right arm.

Instead of educating the young *en masse* for their future roles in a rapidly changing society according to the dictates of the power groups whose concrete ideologies prevail at a given time, in this psychotherapeutic scenario of the future, we see adults (primarily) being "**reeducated**."[11] The purpose of such reeducation is not to heal a sick society, but rather to adjust people emotionally as increasingly **privatized individuals** to the society's pathologies, whatever they happen to be at any given moment.

Such a scenario implies that most Americans will have given up their obsession with schooling as a panacea for major social ills, recognizing at last that the institution has been a false messiah. But, instead of taking the logical next step in their thinking--a realization that true hope for cultural redemption lies in a restoration of social self-reliance, these same Americans **transfer** their displaced faith from teachers to mental health counselors. They continue to seek escape from stressful reality rather than struggling for ways to openly confront and tame reality. The therapist supposedly helps them grapple with their confused personal lives, but ignores the **collective root** of their confusion.

For example, if one's marriage is about to end in painful divorce, then the therapist will guide the victim in rebuilding their personal life so s/he can risk remarriage or learn ways to bear the loneliness of remaining single after the separation. There is little serious concern in the psychological society for the common underlying causes of the skyrocketing divorce rate of the last two decades; and, accordingly, for the search for community/cultural strategies for curbing the incidence of divorce and improving marriages in general.[12]

Another illustration: One may be unhappily dislocated from his or her ethnic, class, and/or geographical roots, as a result of socioeconomic mobility. The prevailing cultural mythology maintains that one has the right, indeed, obligation, or moving "up" and away from one's roots, even though after a few years of novelty, one may feel as trapped as though one had never left home. Rather than carefully analyzing the underlying sociological forces and the interpersonal dynamics that influence vast numbers of Americans today to place themselves voluntarily in uncontrollable circumstances far from their subcultural roots, circumstances which are necessarily alienating because of their disorienting character, the dislocated mobile person is, instead, exhorted to seek professional help in ameliorating his or her supposedly personal problems. Because such assistance focuses on the individual almost exclusively, rather than on that individual's location in the social order, it can normally be only temporarily palliative.

In thinking about the enormity of the problems that therapists now presumptuously claim to be able to treat, the reader will begin to have some idea of what the future will be like should this second scenario be acted out on the cultural stage of American life. I mentioned divorce and existential anomie. Those problems are at the tip of the mental health iceberg. There is virtually nothing that most modern professional therapists, in their conceit, do not claim to be able to treat: social isolation of the aged; career burnout; loss of a loved one through death; fear of heights; alcoholism; compulsive gambling; the after-effects of rape; a tyrannical boss; the consequences of serious racial, ethnic, or religious discrimination; and so on and on in a catalog of contemporary human misery.

Psychotherapy can be relied upon, so this scenario suggests, to make everyday existence in a pathological society bearable by helping the individual victim of the societal disease believe, falsely, that he or she is truly capable of controlling their own fate by personal effort, regardless of the larger structural forces that contributed most profoundly to loss of fate control. The model paraded is that of the **rugged individualist**, dressed up in contemporary scientific clothes, overcoming the ever-present dangers of life in a rapidly changing society by sheer dint of appropriate thinking (acquired by means of reeducation) and by **personally** self-reliant effort functionally connected to such thinking. That is to say, if one thinks correctly (whether the term "thinking" is defined by humanistic, gestalt, interactionist, neo-Freudian, or any other school of psychotherapy, it nearly always refers to some version of culturally relativistic thought **not** embedded in historically rooted values, norms, and concepts), one can conquer the world unaided--except by his or her psychiatrist. Otherwise, one is to blame for being unwilling to place their **faith** in the therapist and, thereby, benefit from the process.

The psychotherapeutic scenario is not implausible. If American society is not about to reclaim its sense of social self-reliance, and if enough Americans eventually lose faith in the culturally redemptive power of schooling, the educational apostate who is personally lost will necessarily seek the most well-advertised and available alternative to sustained anomie. The therapeutic messiah promises salvation in the hallowed tradition of American individualism. That is not enough, as Robert Bellah and his colleagues has demonstrated in their provocative social psychological study *Habits of the Heart.*[13] All people need to belong; they need bonding; they need community. But, like music, therapy **can**, perhaps, temporarily assuage our sorrows.

Therapy can be one form of modest aid to individuals who have been wounded by the relentless pressures of living in a highly unstable secular society. In such a society, skeptical of priests, rabbis, and ministers, it has a useful, if limited, role to play in actualizing and humanizing some of its receptive members, as formal education does in its own way. The error lies, as in the case of the EMC, in **exaggerating** its efficacy and endowing psychotherapy with quasi-divine healing power for everyone collectively.[14]

However, it is conceivable that we are, in fact, moving in that direction. A time not too far in the future can be envisioned when every American will claim the right to a free or inexpensive mental health counselor at the taxpayer's expense, as we presently claim the right to a public school education. As our structural problems mount without resolution, psychotherapy will cease to be a luxury serving primarily the wealthy. The great middle-class mainstream and the underclass generally will also demand to consult with these modern high priests of the mind.

The day can be envisioned when, instead of schools of education being held accountable for producing three million competent teachers for our nation's public schools, the social reform literature will be bolding calling for university production of an equivalent number of competent psychotherapists, so that every adult and child in the country may have an "equal opportunity" to secure good mental health.

Scenario #3: Disillusionment, Surrender, and Sociocultural Demise

In contrast with the first two scenarios presented, the idea of an imminent "fall of the American empire" seems less plausible, but yet not impossible. It is no exaggeration to assert that, despite outward pretensions to the contrary, many people from all walks of life, including the privileged as well as the less fortunate, are close to the raw edge of despair as we near the close of the twentieth century. Disillusioned with the fabled American dream, whether they have become "success stories" supportive of that dream, are still seeking the dangling carrot held out incessantly before them, or have given up any pretense of hope for its achievement, these people search desperately for human meaning in an increasingly "meaningless" world.

When, in 1983, I lived for a time in Israel in order to examine the concept of messiahism in its diverse forms, both sacred and secular, I saw a nation of pioneers working together for the conceived purpose of building a new society amidst surrounding enemies. Whatever knowledgeable non-Israelis may think of the Zionist ideal and whatever other "faults" the Israeli people may have, at least they imputed meaning to their lives. They emphatically did not then suffer ennui, anomie, or alienation as so many modern Americans do. They had a common goal, to construct a Zionist homeland; and utilized all of their institutional resources--including the schooling system--in striving to achieve it.

I returned to the United States and was able, by contrast, to clearly see what I had previously suspected but dared not fully acknowledge: a society in process of losing its direction, going in several directions at once confusedly but with no central course set for the year 2000 and beyond. I also saw widespread denial of the seriousness of the society's problems by its people, strongly abetted by a political administration in Washington that insisted upon looking only at the "sunny side" of things. (Former President Reagan called it "morning in America.") The reform reports of the 1980s clearly represented a massive displacement of socially self-reliant effort to restore a sense of societal purpose onto the formal education system. Denial and displacement continue as we move into the 1990s. Awareness of such escapism is tolerable, if not comforting.

But, suppose we envision a time in the next several years when that displaced faith in formal education becomes substantially eroded as a result of sustained and no longer deniable failure by the schooling system to fulfill its role as a secular messiah. Some scholars believe that time has already arrived. For instance, Michael Bakalis, writing in the *Phi Delta Kappan* recently, said:

> This is a time of high anxiety with a widespread sense that things are out of control....In such a time people project blame and disavow responsibility; since the education establishment has occupied such a revered place in terms of what the public believed it could do, it is not surprising that it has increasingly become the national scapegoat. If our schools are not viewed as the cause of all of our problems, they are too often blamed for failing to solve those problems. **Americans' attitudes toward their schools is analogous to the disappointment we feel when someone we trust, respect, or revere lets us down.**[15] (Emphases added.)

If and when the public schooling system is abandoned, not only by the affluent but by the majority of American parents, their messianic dependency needs may be transferred to a different focal institution; especially psychotherapy, as suggested earlier. That is possible. However, if that should happen, if the institution of psychotherapy itself should then fall short in its greatly expanded function of adjusting ever-increasing numbers of troubled Americans to their lot in life, at that juncture where can the people turn for help? Organized religion, including televangelism, has declined to the point of being little more than a comforting source of ritual to be paid courteous lip service by all but the most out-of-touch. Nostrums such as commercial television, drugs and alcohol, hedonistic consumption, enforced leisure, militaristic buildups and posturing, the cult of celebrity, and other escape mechanisms are likely to grow tiresome and boring after a time.

It may be argued that neo-conservatives will be unable to restore the ailing Work Ethic as a central value in an increasingly technocratic society, and that vast numbers of Americans will become world-weary of their increasingly fast-paced, high-pressured, and materialistic lifestyles. It is doubtful that such lifestyles will indefinitely compensate for underlying feelings of anomie and cultural estrangement.

History informs us that without either a central purpose in life to live for on a sustained basis, whether it be to build a family dynasty, break down the frontiers of civilization, create beautiful works of art (or at least the illusion of such a purpose, such as the EMC has been supplying to date), people cannot long endure as vital and compassionate human beings. Few Americans today do, in fact, possess such a central purpose to organize their lives. Those who are devoting their lives to something more than accumulating wealth and associated prestige are rare enough so as to occasionally be claimed as cultural heroes; one singularly impressive example being crusader for the homeless, Mitch Snyder; another, consumer advocate Ralph Nader.

But, when even the heroes have become world-weary, when an entire nation including all its principal institutions is seen as having lost its sense of guiding purpose or is unmasked, we no longer have a **society**, but rather a very large collection of human organisms operating on cue according to Skinnerian behavior modification principles.

American society is now in serious trouble both internally and as a participant in world affairs. There can hardly be serious argument about that assertion. Even the authors of the *A Nation at Risk* report,[16] which exemplified educational messianism at its conservative apex, agree, although they failed to pinpoint the cultural sources of America's major problems and prescribed the wrong remedy. The nation's social and economic problems are not going away, despite the rhetoric of trusted authority figures such as Ronald Reagan, who cast an eight-year spell over most people in the absence of real widespread central purpose and commitment any longer. The poor are still with us, although increasingly invisible throughout the 1980s;

they seem to be growing in number, while the rich grow increasingly self-absorbed.[17] Social Security is in potential danger of being gradually curtailed as the last vestige of financial aid to millions of elderly Americans who had paid into it for years and who believe that its minimal benefits are owed them for their lifetimes of hard work.

In spite of recent federal legislation, the entire health care system in this country is in peril of falling increasingly behind those of other advanced industrial and post-industrial societies in terms of costs and attendant quality of care for all but the affluent. Crime is rampant despite the building of new prisons everywhere, stiffer penalties for felonies, and a decline in the number of males under twenty-five years of age. According even to proponents of serial marriage as an emergent norm, the family is in near shambles; although the divorce rate may, belatedly, be starting to level off slightly.

In short, the fabric of American culture is already disintegrating, however much politicians and other institutional guardians attempt to disguise this fact in order to keep public morale from plummeting precipitously. But, to date, the public has willingly cooperated with the politicians by trying to deny this truth, using a protective psychological mechanism known as displacement--particularly displacement onto schools--of responsibility for bringing about recovery.

The scenario under consideration, then, is that continued denial of collective responsibility for reclaiming the American dream must sooner or later culminate perforce in a collective dispiritedness.

Should that happen, the people of the United States will become a depressed agglomerate of self-absorbed individuals, hardly able to function on a day-to-day personal basis unless constantly reinforced by positive stimuli from above, much less contribute thoughtfully and assertively to a revival of democracy in its Jeffersonian/Deweyan sense. Whether by default we are then taken over by alien intruders on the left, as the paranoid right fears, or are transformed from within into what some contemptuously call a "third world" country or, given the contemporary crisis of capitalism here, more likely, in the opinion of a number of scholars, a late modern version of a fascist state,[18] we will, in effect, have surrendered as a people to the forces that we failed to confront in unison. Accordingly, we will have gone the way of other once-vital societies that were unable to heed the increasingly signs of demoralization and loss of cultural commitment by the people to a central, guiding vision.

Disillusionment, surrender, and sociocultural demise is possible, unless the American people stop avoiding reality and begin, instead, to experiment with new forms of social self-reliance.[19] If such a scenario does come to pass, a singularly impressive experiment in organized human being and becoming will have been forfeited.

Scenario #4: Muddling Along

Although current trends are not encouraging, such a total cultural demise probably will not happen--if one of the first two or the fifth scenario eventuates instead or if we continue to muddle along as we have been doing for many years now.

Indeed, the nation has been muddling along. Whether it continues to rely on schools as its principle panacea in the future or turns to some other form of cultural escapism, there is good reason to predict that instead of setting itself on a more true, long-term course and taking responsibility as a whole people for reaching clearly defined societal goals in the face of inevitable obstacles which are, nonetheless, surmountable, the nation will continue to drift along "mindlessly"--to use educational critic Charles Silberman's term made famous in his 1970 best-seller *Crisis in the Classroom*.[20] It will drift along into the future hoping that, somehow, things will work themselves out satisfyingly in the end.

My late friend and colleague Maurice Hunt said it well ten years ago:

> ....There is the possibility that the nation will continue muddling along with its present major institutional structures and general confusion and inconsistency in values and beliefs. This is not to suggest that institutional structures will not change...But the change we have been experiencing...is change in which clear-cur long-range goals are absent. It is change based upon accident, impulse, or the continuation of diverse and contradictory trends now operating.
>
> Our national distaste for long-range planning, though quite harmonious with our widely held belief that laissez-faire and advanced industrialism are compatible, suggests the very strong likelihood that the nation will continue as long as it can in a course of drift and muddle, using a band-aid approach to solving the most pressing

> social problems of any particular year....[21] (Emphases added.)

Hunt was careful to emphasize that prevailing institutional changes might well take place during this muddling along process.

Similarly, I have acknowledged that our extraordinary faith in the culturally redemptive power of schooling might be transferred to that of psychotherapy or some other exploitable institution. But we both agree on the possibility of continued cultural drift into the foreseeable future as an alternative scenario worth considering. Hunt justifies this possibility on the basis of "our national distaste for long-range planning" which is consistent with a national "belief that laissez-faire and advanced industrialism are compatible."[22] To this harmonious alliance of distaste for social planning and sustained belief in laissez-faire individualism, I would merely add the following caveat: As a result of the enormous toll upon us taken by the massive and heretofore uncontrolled social changes occurring in this society in the past thirty years, Americans have become an increasingly timid and anxious people, compared to their forebears who experienced change on a smaller, hence more directly and personally governable scale. They are disinclined to experiment with initially distasteful new models of living founded upon unfamiliar beliefs and values, particularly in the fast-receding and ever-more-abstract public sphere.

In its inhibiting concern that the future will bring more of the same--sustained social upheaval and cultural fragmentation--the nation may very well continue to blunder its way into that kind of dismaying future by default.

On the other hand, as in the past, it may be argued that Americans are uniquely well-suited to muddling along, because their social and cultural superstructure has built-in mechanisms for correction if and when things get too far off track. This is commonly referred to as the "pendulum swing" phenomenon, pleasing to modern conservatives and liberals alike, including professional educators.[23]

But the cultural pendulum seems to be swinging in a larger and larger arc; the corrections needed in economic and social affairs are becoming increasingly major as the scope of real social change widens and deepens unremittingly--witness the continuing governmental manipulations of the economy in a desperate attempt to repair the fiscal damage wrought in 1987 by "Black Monday" at the stock market. At some point, the correction mechanisms built into the social system may cease to function as they are supposed to, because they were originally designed for a less demanding, more culturally cohesive, more slowly changing epoch. That point may already have been reached, as the skyrocketing national debt suggests. It may now be too great to ever be paid off.

More directly related to the immediate problems of the schools, the United States has, in the opinions of many social scientists, become a nation of suburban sprawl since the end of World War II. The new demographics of America are based on laissez-faire marketplace considerations, with minimal governmental intervention and planning. People leave the decaying central cities *en masse* to purchase homes in the kind of suburban tract that they believe will best fit their particularistic socioeconomic, ideological, and lifestyle needs--uncaringly abandoning the more highly structured central cities to the racially and ethnically new arrivals to America and the economically disenfranchised, especially blacks, Hispanics, and Southeast Asians. These new demographics have been cogently summarized by political scientist Ira Katznelson and historian Margaret Weir in their erudite new study[24] of the decline of schooling and the democratic ideal in American society:

> The expansion and development of post-war suburbia has created brand-new regions that have become increasingly independent of adjacent central cities. More and more the new suburbs have been penetrated by national, rather than local, economic institutions. Their massive consumer markets are controlled largely by national retail chains, grouped at strips alongside major highways. Fast-food restaurants, gas stations, supermarkets, automobile dealerships, and massive department stores integrated into the national corporate economy and new, often mammoth factories and company headquarters are the dominant economic institutions. Spread out in a low-density sprawl, these regions have an economic role quite different from the traditional functions of bedroom communities.
>
> The physical form of modern suburban America has been shaped by market processes operating relatively unconstrained by government and public planning...Investors, developers, speculators, bankers, politicians, and planners have joined together to make what appears to be an unplanned environ-

ment, but disciplined by markets and profits.... The result of this process is easy to see: the creation of massive residential and commercial areas lacking in history, communal foci, and other boundaries. Land-use patterns in these spaces even more rigidly divide work and off-work sections from each other than has been the case in central cities; and, further, these new spaces starkly segment living and shopping quarters. Each function is in its own, clearly demarcated place.

....Families who purchase homes at the same time purchase homogeneous residential communities, which are tailored to and protected by existing zoning arrangements. To buy a house is to purchase a community identity, social standing, neighbors with similar incomes and tastes, and a neighborhood all at once.

In the big city, diversity in the social character, uses, and organization of space is tempered by shared government and a politics of the city as a whole. In the suburbs, political fragmentation overlaps social segregation. Lacking serious metropolitan or regional governments, political authority tends to be used to reinforce regional differentiation and segregation. The divisions between political communities, magnified by the desire to protect favorable property values, create a much more complex and fragmented social order than the old-fashioned portrait of a homogenous middle-class suburbia.

....Schools continue to be subject in a formal way to public oversight. The politics of education, however, has been overtaken as a result of weak and fragmented governments as a determining factor by private housing markets protected by defensive zoning. The neighborhood basis of schooling has long challenged the ideal of the common school. But the combination of residential segregation and the fragmentation of political boundaries is unprecedented.[25]

Katznelson and Weir conclude that the new suburban demographics described above are making almost imminent the ending of the vision of the public schooling system as Americans have known it for over one hundred and fifty years, and the increasing privatization of American life. They are concerned, and with good reason. For such muddling along into the future is extraordinarily risky, given the high stakes involved today--the nation's very survival as a viable, coherent democratic society. Still, scenario 4 is quite plausible, because, in their bewilderment at what has befallen them as a function of massive sociocultural change in recent years and their self-centered loss of interest in the public good, most Americans have not yet come to appreciate the stakes involved in this risky game.

If they did, they might decide to stop muddling along; and, as an alternative, begin to assess their plight, and decide rationally upon strategic courses of action to ameliorate it in the short as well as long term. Finally, they might tentatively take some first halting steps to reconstruct the seriously faulty social structure they have kept in disrepair, regardless of how difficult or distasteful.

Discussion

The point of developing alternative scenarios of the future is to postulate two or more images which may be extrapolated from past and present trends, but which cannot be held with any certainty. That is, they are no more or less than educated guesses. In that spirit of speculation and tentativeness, no claim herein is made to having any uncanny sense of which, if any, of the four scenarios projected in this chapter has the greatest likelihood of actually coming to pass. That posture is supported by futurist Lloyd Williams' critique of the forecasting enterprise when he comments aridly:

> ....Certitude, although a necessary quality of the successful revolutionary, is not a characteristic of the civilized mind. Since futurists are not disposed to storm the barricades of orthodoxy with guns, certitude in the face of critics is unbecoming.[26]

The most I am willing to conjecture is that, extrapolating from past and present cultural tendencies and social trends, it does seem more likely that scenarios number 1, 2, or 4 (or some combination of these) will come to pass than number 3--at least for the immediately foreseeable future, say the next thirty years.

I think the dystopian view--that American society will collapse entirely under the weight of internal and external pressures--is farfetched, although not to be ruled out entirely. With all its glaring weaknesses, the American social structure nonetheless appears to yet retain sufficient strength and elasticity to counteract the growing trend toward withdrawal from public involvement into alienated and disillusioned privatism before we have become a national of behaviorally modifiable organisms. Prior to that stage, sufficient warning signals are likely to have been sent out by intellectuals and politicians via the mass media to rekindle the waning American spirit enough to keep us going, albeit if only barely so.

What is more important to say at this time is that one can only hope that all four are highly improbable scenarios, that **none** of them is fated to come about. They are all, more or less, pessimistic scenarios offering little hope for vibrantly and progressively improving living and coping with the nation's major social problems.

If the third scenario--disillusionment, surrender, and sociocultural demise--is the most gloomy to contemplate, the belief that it is the least likely to be actualized is small comfort to those who want more out of life in America than bare survival as the year 2000 comes into view. None of the other three scenarios warrants popular enthusiasm. Indeed, each depicts a forlorn future of ongoing boredom relieved only by ritualized worship of secular messiahs whose promises of miracle cures are rarely kept, or by intermittent little explosions of faddish ideological fervency.

A not inconceivable future of continued messianic faith in public schooling (scenario number 1) conjures up images of busy educational functionaries developing and refining "innovations" without end to appease every powerful interest group that newly emerges to self-righteously exhort the schools and their overburdened teachers to end poverty, reduce crime and drug abuse, increase worker productivity, or resurrect a general feeling of blind love-it-or-leave-it patriotism in the apathetic citizenry. No major societal problems ever become resolved, but the schooling process, with its priests and prophets goes on forever as a ceremonial ritual without substance.[27]

The scenario of a transference of messianic faith from schooling to psychotherapy proffers the imagery of equally busy psychological caseworkers tirelessly treating huge numbers of emotionally burdened and anxious clients from every walk of life on a weekly appointment basis. After several weeks or months of such treatment, the clients leave therapy feeling cleansed and perhaps affectively "reborn," their psychic aches and pains gone for awhile. But, once on their own again in the stress-producing structures of their purposeless lives and work, they become emotionally disabled anew, and return to the therapists' offices. There they receive additional solace from the secular high priests of a society perpetually out of kilter, one which psychically bruises all of its members in one way or another, but rarely tries to locate the deep-lying **roots** of their problems or takes decisive collective steps to eradicate them once and for all by reconstructive social surgery.

There is a bare shred of hope that this scenario may not be a strong contender in the marketplace of probable futures. That hope is based on the fact that some psychologists themselves are beginning to warn each other, if not the general public, not to become entranced with their self-importance as professionals. They are calling for less ideological fervor and more modesty and thirst for theoretical understanding of the **social** character of emotional disorders than they have displayed heretofore. A discerning few are admitting that their discipline has considerably less to offer than most of its practitioners from Freud on down to the present have led the world to believe.[28] Their candidness is a significant, if faltering, step in the right direction of discouraging simplistic overdependency upon the curative effects of a single institutional sector in our multi-institutional society.

Finally, a future of incessant muddling along evokes a picture of everyman and everywoman tilting at windmills in their endlessly quixotic struggle to impute meaning to an existentially barren life course in the new suburbia so cogently described by Katznelson and Weir.[29] At times, the windmill seems to respond, and the nation's leaders take credit for cultural renewal. When such renewal is short-lived, the leaders have nothing to say. Once in a while, a comparatively minor problem such as excessive interest rates in home mortgages actually is temporarily resolved, thereby keeping alive hope and faith in the American predilection for muddling along; so that, to quote Hunt again, "the nation will continue as long as it can in a course of drift and muddle, using a band-aid approach to solving the most pressing social problems of any particular year."[30] How long can that be?

I would be overly sanguine in hypothesizing an end to muddling along by the end of this century. It is best not to be explicit. It is impossible to say when a major cultural crisis provoked by powerful intrusive forces colliding with internal structural weaknesses will eventuate to bring an end to the prevailing American lassitude in regard to becoming involved in planning and rebuilding our ailing society.

But, if three of the four scenarios presented in this chapter are hollow and depressing to envision, and the fourth abysmal, there is yet a slim chance for something more encouraging. There is still a fifth image of the future to consider, one of an entirely different, more optimistic cast.

The concluding chapter will examine the possibility of significant social change in America, and of the school's special--if limited--role in a socially self-reliant society based on the sense of healthy belongingness in integrative community.

Chapter 9

Instead of Educational Messianism: A More Balanced Image of the Education Ecology

Recapitulation

In this concluding chapter, consideration will be given to what I conceive as a viable alternative to avoiding the difficult problems of modern life by deflecting them onto an artificially separated and idealized institution. Before turning to that alternative, it will be useful to briefly restate my overall thesis and reiterate my position on the prospects envisioned in Chapter 8.

First, I have been contending that since the end of World War II, and especially in the decade of the 1950s, the majority of Americans have singled out and become increasingly dependent on the institution of public schooling for help in overcoming massive dislocations of a rapidly changing social order. Examples given of such dislocations have ranged from declining economic competitiveness in the international marketplace to fundamental sociological problems, including the veritable destruction of the nuclear family and rampant crime in the streets.

I have argued that the level and extent of dependency upon public schools for social problem solving is becoming so great as to now constitute what can be considered a near-universal faith--quasi-religious in nature--in their culturally redemptive capabilities. That faith is shared by the public and most professional educators alike.

In regard to the latter group, Larry Cuban is less benign than I have been throughout, claiming that professionals may knowingly be exploiting the national dependency on formal education:

> In this national exercise in buck-passing, the education community has not been blameless. Sensing the potential for money and recognition, school boards, superintendents, and school staffs swore that they could do whatever needed to be done. Few public officials turned down the chance to solve a national problem (even when they had no idea of how to go about it) or stopped to consider the adverse consequences of promising something that they could not deliver.
>
> Once the responsibility for solving a national problem has been shifted to the schools, other methods of solving the problem tend to be ignored.[1]

This historically unprecedented faith in the salvationary capacity of schooling has been herein termed the "Educational Messiah Complex." That metaphor has been employed both in an anthropological sense to connote the ascendancy of a new cultural universal as well as in its psychopathological origins and implications. I have argued that schooling is a "false messiah," lacking the social efficacy attributed it by true-believing Americans.

I have discussed the major ideological manifestations of educational messianism in recent years, and shown how the central actors on the stage of all formal educational endeavor, school teachers, have been heavily burdened by conflicting and unremitting ideological pressures from outsiders who use teachers as scapegoats for their displaced confusions, frustrations, anxieties, and even personal career ambitions.

Such ubiquitous displacement of self-regard and perceived locus of fate control is at the core of the EMC phenomenon. The American people have become increasingly unable to face squarely the manifold problems that beset them as members of a civilization undergoing basic transformation from the industrial age, with its emphasis on material productivity, to an age of post-industrialism, and its attendant stress on human services and advanced information technology.

In their incapacity they have learned from each other interpersonally and through such institutions as the mass and electronic media to collectively displace their growing failure of nerve onto the relatively safe institution of schooling. The latter conveniently symbolizes successful transition into the future that most Americans are unprepared to deal with forthrightly and in their own generation. They neatly rationalize that more and more schooling for their children will, by converting knowledge into utilitarian social power, cause the latter to grow up to be adults armed with problem-solving skills and the will to implement those skills. From this perspective, they will then do what their parents' generation failed to do; namely, tackle gamely the monumental problems of their own day--which will be largely hand-me-downs from the present day.

Thus, the children of this society, even more than their overburdened teachers, ultimately suffer the major consequences of their elders' escapist tendencies, as America's problems continue to worsen. Yet, intellectuals and opinion leaders rarely consider the potentially explosive power of the social dynamite being stored up for the future when America's children grow up to realize that they have been led astray by their parents.

Four scenarios of the educational future have been postulated. Although undesirable, they are, nonetheless, plausible:

1. The persistence of the EMC well into the foreseeable future (with the social dynamite implications alluded to above);
2. Loss of displaced faith in the culturally redemptive power of schooling as it is increasingly seen to be a false messiah; accompanied by transference of such displaced faith onto some other major institution which emerges as a source of redemptive promise--most likely, the increasingly influential institution of psychotherapy;
3. Cultural decay, erosion, and annihilation as a worst case scenario should the American people eventually unmask the false messiah of schooling, as well as the other panaceas which arise to take its place; while yet remaining inert in the face of their impotence;
4. Running in place indefinitely or, otherwise expressed, "muddling along," patching up the cracks in the sociocultural plaster as they regularly recur, with or without sustained faith in the schooling messiah or its possible replacements.

This is not the appropriate forum to describe in elaborate detail precisely how the American people ought to proceed once they have, optimistically, achieved genuine insight into their collective dilemma and, accordingly, reclaimed their civic responsibilities. Within the compass of the present project, it is enough that the outline of a better way to envision our collective challenge be sketched; and that an undoubtedly oversimplified way to begin looking elsewhere than to our schools for cultural salvation be suggested.

A More Balanced Image of the Socioeducational Ecology

The conception of the American future that I should like to propose is one of renewed social self-reliance in a framework of restored, or reconstructed, cultural community encompassing local, regional, and national levels of civic participation and reordered conceptions of institutional efficacy and purpose. Such a vision is not at all utopian. However, achieving it will be far from easy.

A. Renewed Social Self-Reliance:

The first point to be made about the scenario under consideration is that in order to begin effectively coping with its enormously complex problems, the growing sociopsychological atomization of American society will have to end. The distorting and ultimately nihilistic mythology of rugged, self-reliant, privatistic individualism will, necessarily, be replaced by an eroded cultural universal, newly restored, which stresses working together for the common good--without abandoning aesthetically pleasing, energizing, contributory, and self-affirming individualism in the process.

This is the essence of democracy, as understood both by some of the founding fathers of this nation (e.g., Thomas Jefferson) and its most insightful social and educational philosopher, John Dewey. To employ political theorist Benjamin Barber's term, this society needs "**strong democracy**":

> ....The real choice we face in the coming years is not between Republicans and Democrats, or between the supply-side and the welfare state, or between hawks and doves; it is between an even more meaningless and weak form of democracy in which we periodically rubber-stamp the bureaucrats and

> politicians who govern for us and over us and in our stead, and a strong democracy in which we reassume the responsibilities of self-government.[2]

At present, it is essentially everyone for themselves in America. To the extent that any self-reliance still remains, it is **individual** self-reliance, looking out for number one and perhaps his or her family exclusively and increasingly narcissistically.[3] Whatever social self-reliance exists tends to be found in the increasingly forgotten slums of our large cities, where local neighborhood adolescent gangs have been sanctioned to defend their one-block or one-apartment turf from outsiders considered dangerous, largely because our ruggedly individualistic traditions still operate to minimize public police protection, particularly where it is most needed.[4]

For all intents and purposes, the rest of us are becoming even more separate from each other and alienated from the depersonalized social system which treats us as if we count for little more than to fuel the economic machinery which incessantly exploits us. Even the rare so-called "self-actualized" individuals glowingly described by humanist psychologist Abraham Maslow and others appear to be characterized by a certain relationship to the alienating conditions of modern American life. Theirs is a relationship in which they have managed to survive "well" (in Maslow's view) by becoming more or less successfully **aloof** from the impersonal forces which traumatize the great majority of ordinary mortals to a greater or lesser extent.[5]

The well-known fact is that the big problems of today's America, as distinguished from those of the frontier, are supra **collective**, not individual or even single interest group in character (even in the past, most were collective in nature, according to social historians): institutionalized divorce patterns; widespread substance abuse; paranoia about Cuba and the U.S.S.R.; institutionalized racism and sexism; increasing poverty and underemployment; overcrowded prisons everywhere; shoddy automobiles and other American-made products; preoccupation with money, sex, and violence; destruction of the natural environment; "AIDS;" and so on.

These are not problems amenable to quick treatment by ruggedly self-reliant individuals or temporarily cohesive members of inspired minority groups, much less passive dependency upon miraculous outputs from bureaucratized agencies such as schools, assigned to perform meta-institutional functions. They require unified behavioral commitment by every citizen, regardless of otherwise particularistic interests, loyalties, and lifestyles. These are transcending social problems amenable only to treatment by the cultural collective viewed universally; which, therefore, must be sufficiently self-reliant as an integrated whole to bring **shared** individual, or interpersonal, wisdom and power to bear to resolve them--in the now nearly extinct tradition of civic responsibility.

The old and tired mythology of the ruggedly self-reliant, if jaded, cowboy or detective hero perhaps best exemplified in Clint Eastwood and Charles Bronson movies, needs to be replaced with a perspective that recognizes that each individual member of American society is, nonetheless, in the same leaking lifeboat together. Everyone must actively cooperate or surely all shall drown! In Robert Bellah's words, "The time may be approaching when we will either reform our republic or fall into the hands of despotism, as many republics have done before us."[6]

B. A Framework of Restored Cultural Community with a Balanced Socioeducational Ecology:

Social self-reliance and the rebuilding of cultural community necessarily go hand-in-hand; there cannot be one without the other. In order for the American people to throw off their long-ingrained penchant for going it alone--which has led them down the primrose path to inevitable over-dependency on the spurious messiah of schooling--it is incumbent upon them to simultaneously reconstruct the society's eroding base of cultural community at all levels of human interaction, from the local community grassroots through the state or regional subcultural network to the societal (and, indeed, global[7]) civic culture which binds the entire social structure together.

"Human beings are community animals," asserted the distinguished social and educational philosopher Kenneth Benne in his 1981 DeGarmo Lecture for the Society for Professors of Education.[8] Benne was correct. The sense of true belongingness to community gives the only authentic purpose there is in living in this world. One might surmise that its lack in a modernized society such as the United States motivates great numbers of Americans, as contrasted with the inhabitants of most other "secular" societies, to seek after evangelical religious movements and cults promising salvation in heaven after they have left the world. Certainly, as has been argued herein, it is behind the displacement of responsibility onto public schools known as educational messianism.

This sense of belongingness to a real community of fellow mortals lends vital purpose to life, because community is the natural milieu of human beings, to which all of its individual members (including the most nonconformist and privatistically inclined) extract fellow feeling and return it unstingily by their unselfconscious desire to contribute their various talents for the purely primordial joy of being--with and for each other. One need not artificially force oneself to a life of "altruism" in the genuine cultural community, as do some of us, in our unnatural state of anomie, in order to manufacture a reason for existence in the vacuum.

Philosopher Alan Watts lucidly clarifies what I am trying to convey in the following words:

> Where there is to be creative action, it is quite beside the point to discuss what we should or should not do in order to be right or good. A mind that is single and sincere is not interested in being good, in conducting relations with other people so as to live up to a rule. Nor, on the other hand, is it interested in being free, in acting perversely just to prove its independence. Its interest is not in itself, but in the people and problems of which it is aware; these are itself. It acts not according to the rule, but according to the circumstances of the moment, and the "well" it wishes to others is not security but liberty.[9]

When I speak of community, I am referring to an idea not easy to define, since I am concerned with more than just the conventional, understood, local, organic, or *gemeinshaft* symbolism; hence, it may be more appropriate to allude to it as Watts does in the above-quoted passage. His allusion is to the notion of communion with all others with whom an individual might identify in his or her humanness, regardless of territorial imperatives. Such a communion conception of community is akin to Martin Buber's notion of the I and the Thou; therefore, it implies a dialogical relationship between human beings, or what John Dewey envisioned as one of shared experience in nurturing significant communication.[10]

In their controversial 1985 study contrasting the two major competing cultural themes in American life, "Individualism" and "Community," sociologist Robert Bellah and his associates at the University of California, Berkeley defined community by contrasting it with the term "lifestyle," with which it is often mistaken today:

> The term "lifestyle"...is linked most closely to leisure and consumption and is usually unrelated to the world of work. It brings together those who are socially, economically, or culturally similar, and one of its chief aims is the enjoyment of being with those who "share one's lifestyle."
>
> Though the term "community" is widely and loosely used by Americans, and often in connection with lifestyle, we would like to reserve it for a more specific meaning. Whereas **a community attempts to be a inclusive whole, celebrating the interdependence of public and private life and the different callings of all**, lifestyle is fundamentally segmental and celebrates the narcissism of similarity. It usually explicitly involves a contrast with others who "do not share one's lifestyle." For this reason, we speak not of lifestyle communities, but of lifestyle enclaves. Such enclaves are segmental in two senses.
>
> ....We might consider the lifestyle enclave an appropriate form of collective support in an otherwise radically individualizing society...or, to put it somewhat differently...perhaps the lifestyle enclave is the necessary social form of **private** life in a society such as ours.[11] (Emphases added.)

"A community attempts to be an inclusive whole, celebrating the interdependence of [both] public and private life and the different callings [or, as Dewey would say, 'interests'] of all." This idea is perhaps most vividly--and often sentimentally--portrayed in the old-fashioned small town of agrarian America, where members of the community are said to have known the names of their grocer and druggist, where walking the streets (even at night) they might say hello to acquaintances from different social classes than their own or eat at the same table with persons holding different "lifestyles" at the annual 4th of July town picnic. Public and private life do converge in such traditional American communities. But, for all practical purposes, as educational ethnographer Alan Peshkin in his study of the Midwestern village of "Mansfield" informs us, such autonomous communities are gone in contemporary America, where the majority of people now live in large and quite depersonalized metropolitan cities and their sprawling suburbs.[12]

Not many corporation executives today acknowledge the existence of the "invisible" laborers in the plants they manage, even in the work place itself, much less on the streets--partly because they hardly walk streets any longer; but drive everywhere they go. Not many women or men know their grocer's name, since practically everyone shops at the huge chain supermarket. (Some learn the names of the checkers, however, by reading them on their namecards.) Few members of the upper-middle and upper classes attend the annual county fair, even in those cities that still have such public celebrations. They either consider it too dangerous to mingle with the lower-classes from whom they have become estranged, or they have become "too sophisticated" to appreciate the local homespun flavor of such galas.

In one city with which I am familiar, the "better class" of citizens who feel obligated morally or for reasons of career advancement to do good works for the poor now are taken on bus tours around the "worst parts of town" so that they can learn about the depressed conditions in which the underclass live out their lives; they would never consider walking in the toured neighborhoods or even of doing business there.

At most, "community" for the majority is the immediate neighborhood, where everyone lives in the same model of tract house or condominium with "people they can trust" because of their similarity (as they trust the fast food franchise outlets and motel chains they prefer to independent food and lodging services). In brief, they live in lifestyle enclaves, not communities.

The point here is that we cannot realistically hope to return to older forms of *gemeinshaft* territorial community, such as that imagined in the small town of the Midwest. "We can't go home again," in that sense at least. Most people would not want to even if they could; "home" was, in fact, too stultifying even at its best, contrary to what wistful idealists would sometimes have us believe.

"The problem is," to quote Thomas Brindley, "How can we have communities and still maintain the modern world!"[13] Americans can try to rebuild integral community in contemporary *gesellshaft* society in the terms of the new by keeping in mind that the **essence** of community--whatever its outward form--remains "the interdependence of public and private life and the different callings of all."

Attempting to rebuild community in fast-disintegrating America will obviously be a distinctive challenge, since, as noted, it is neither possible nor desirable to return to the localistic style of the "sacred" past. That entails wishing for moral reintegration as a secular nation without slighting the enormous diversity uniquely inherent in this pluralistic society, both subcultural and individual. Failure to maintain the delicate balance between the societal whole and its people will result in a more or less bungling national-level central bureaucracy interfering increasingly with the private lives of the people against their wishes. (In Peshkin's language, "A banal national ideology would descend like a pall to smother heterodoxy."[14]) That eventuality can be precluded by building a self-renewing, or "ultrastable" **strong democratic** version of overarching community from the grassroots through the state/regional levels to the supersocietal level.

R. Freeman Butts' call for a "new civism,"[15] with its acknowledged conservative bias, may, nonetheless, be applicable here insofar as he recognizes that restored civic responsibility has to be founded both on the micro as well as the macro and intermediate levels of social organization without ignoring the importance of determined interpersonal communication at any one of them. The new civism may, in fact, be a better term for our purposes than the narrower term, "new federalism," coined recently by democratic political theorists such as Barber.

One trusts that, as in the case of another diminished cause involving children, racial desegregation of schools, such a challenge appears not so forbidding that it is added to the list of tasks diverted to the institution via conventionally ritualistic high school classes in "civics." Advocates of the new civism must carefully guard against dilution and ceremonial coaptation, as in the case of desegregation.

Yet, the challenge must be faced, if confidence in the American future is to be restored. The development of interdependent primary and secondary communities of democratically involved, socially self-reliant members is the *sine qua non* of ending the dangerous illusion that someone else can save us from ourselves. I am not alone in what I say. Peshkin, Benne, Brindley, and Bellah are only a representative few deeply concerned about the loss of genuine community to atomized, fractionated, overly individualistic American society today, and of the imperative need for reformative, even reconstructive social surgery to replace this loss, as the latter phrases it:

> ....Though the processes of separation and individuation were necessary to free us from the tyrannical structures of the past, they must be balanced by a

renewal of commitment and community, if they are not to end in self-destruction or turn into their opposites.[16]

The above words speak eloquently to the very issues that have been raised and addressed in this book on the special relation of secularized messianic faith to the actual meaning and function of the schooling endeavor: issues such as displacement of responsibility, alienation, searching for panaceas, and the need for recommitment to the social self-reliance that is engendered only by authentic community at every level of the human enterprise and that reciprocally returns authentic personhood to each individual member of the socially self-reliant community.

The ideas contained in this fifth scenario are not utopian ideas; on the contrary, they are eminently practical. Truly utopian are the so-called practical man's and woman's willingness to overly objectify to the point of abstraction those other men and women in our disconnected society who have elected to work with children in centers of learning. It is utopian to depersonalize and dehumanize the formal educational endeavor by imputing godlike power to human effort, as if it were a Platonic or Hegelian Absolute Ideal operating "out there." To realize this is to have a chance, however, slim, at regaining control over our lives by reuniting ourselves with each other in common struggle to achieve the ends of the disappearing American dream of gradual progress toward self-perfection, regardless of whether those ends are ever fully achieved or not.

But, there also remains to be considered one final and overarching idea embedded in the organizing concept of socially self-reliant community as a preferred image, or scenario of America's future. I refer to the idea of thinking about life in the reconstructed cultural community from the perspective of **a more balanced social ecology**.

More specifically, in relation to education, I propose that the place of schooling in the overall social ecology be envisioned in a radically different way than most Americans have been doing for the past thirty years. I suggest that we reorder the balance of the social ecology of the cultural community postulated so that, again, as in the past, there is organic harmony between the properly understood influence and efficacy of the institutional schooling process and the influence and efficacy of all other components of a reconstituted social order.

From the ecological perspective, borrowed from the natural

sciences, the different elements of the sociocultural environment all have their unique and important roles to play in the scheme of things. If every element of the ecological whole finds its proper "fit" in that superstructure--in this instance, the reconstituted cultural community--social life is likely to proceed harmoniously, albeit not always consensually. Conflict is also an integral aspect of interdependent relationships, whether in animal collectivities or human communities.[17] This is the position of cultural pluralism in its most encompassing sense. It differs dramatically from cultural determinism, the model depicted by the EMC.

From the latter perspective, when economic determinists, whether they are classical liberals or Marxists, erroneously posit the "natural" prime moving influence of the marketplace in the life of a society and downplay the equally important role of "non-material" aspects of organized social life such as health care, family relations, the arts, formal education, etc., they contribute to the general confusion of the populace. They do so by exaggerating the importance to the community and its members of work, accumulation of wealth, and material consumption in the scheme of human affairs; thus distorting the direction of a society's individual and collective efforts, and making people less authentically human and less able to attack their real individual and group problems effectively.

In the case of education, the EMC signifies an extremely serious and wrongheaded deterministic belief of modern times that "going to school" has become the prime mover of societal health and happiness, even more so than the marketplace which some influential educational messianists want the institution to serve slavishly. As the true believers in contemporary educational determinism imagine, by putting most of our societal eggs in the basket of more and more years of schooling, knowledge will become the "cultural capital" of an efficient and orderly industrial society--or perhaps of an equally efficient and well-ordered post-industrial society (a contradiction in terms, since a post-industrial society is, by definition, a person-centered, service-oriented one in which efficiency and order may not always be guaranteed with the precision demanded of an industrial society).

Ethical and logical questions aside, however, such anointing of the schooling institution with prime moving capabilities once reserved--mistakenly--for the marketplace and factory alone is bound to be mischievous. For, as we have seen, it debases those who place exaggerated faith in a relatively inefficacious institution in cost-benefit terms, certainly one which can never hope to achieve the narrowly utilitarian goals expected of it by the faithful who confuse the school with a factory; it leads to disenchantment with schools and teachers when it is discovered that they cannot possibly perform the extra functions demanded of them; and it distracts the public from directly confronting those basic problems which the faithful have displaced onto the schooling messiah.

In a more ecologically balanced society, in which socially self-reliant members of the cultural community confronted their collective problems steadily with directness instead of delegating them to schoolteachers, formal education (like earning a living and building a family) would come to be seen as **one** among many institutional sectors, each of which plays its **individually unique, important, yet distinctively limited** role in humanizing life for those who belong. Such a pluralistic, as opposed to deterministic, conception of the role of schooling does not detract from the significance of that role; but, it more realistically comprehends its possibilities and its limitations. Hence, it permits schools to become singularly efficient in what **they** are capable of doing best, seeking and transmitting knowledge and knowledge-acquiring skills to students, in the broadest sense of facilitating development of increasingly complex thinking abilities, not trying to convert them to a currently fashionable, narrowly ideological point of view.

I agree with Joshua Meyrowitz when he speaks of the necessity for the school to maintain a "knowledge edge" by teaching its students **more** than they can learn elsewhere. He is probably correct when he suggests that "reading remains the school's trump card."[18] But, he is even more accurate when he points to its role in fostering skills and experiences nowhere else to be inculcated, "including systematic acquisition of knowledge, interpretation, criticism, and the methodologies of learning and thinking. Another key example of such a skill is the ability to interact with other people--**to speak, listen, argue, and discuss.**[19] For a socially self-reliant people, the school can make no greater contribution than to instill those four requirements of effective interpersonal interaction.

As centers of excellence in their unique function, then, schools, both tax-supported as well as privately funded, will most assuredly serve a general public citizenry again appreciative of their important but acknowledgedly limited contribution to the local, regional, and national community. Teachers in such schools are no longer perceived of as the right arm of the anointed one, so they feel comfortable in expressing themselves as the **artists** of the classroom that teachers are intrinsically meant to be.[20] Freed from the untenable myth that the schools they work in are public utilities like the telephone company, with verifiable practical outputs guaranteed in the short term through the supposedly "advanced technology of teaching," schoolteachers are liberated from the ideological and political pressures imposed by a multiplicity of disparate special interest groups which currently perplex them. They are emancipated from the formal accountability requirements beloved of the modern technocratic mentality to ply their unique art of, in Ignacio Gotz's words, "unconcealing the truth"[21] to those of their students who wish to have the truth unconcealed and are able to appreciate the art of teaching involved.

In this ecologically balanced view of schooling, teachers are freed to **create** their own special learning environments, consonant with their personal vision of their integral relationship to their multi-layered communities. The duality of "I" (the teacher) against "them" (the public, including students) is gone, replaced with the dialogical spirit of "I with Thou." In Arthur Wirth's language, the interests of the teacher's mind "is not in itself, but in the people and problems of which it is aware; **these are itself**." Or, to be more prosaic:

> Reflection on the subtle complexities of significant learning gives the lie to the simplistic notion that we can get effective education by "making school hard and flunking a lot of them." What we need is an education that **challenges** all of them. That can happen only if we have teachers who find fulfillment and challenge in their own work. The creative ones won't remain if they are offered only technocratic straight-jackets that stifle their personal enthusiasms.[22]

It needs to be recognized, then, that schools in the ecologically balanced, socially self-reliant community are one of many important components of society writ large, and that they have a highly distinctive yet limited role to play in community/societal development; however, it is a mostly **indirect** role as touchstones of long-term cultural renewal rather than a direct role as agents of short-term cultural redemption. The function of American schools should be altered, but they yet remain significant forces for progressive social change.

Of course schools should have units on the environment, because it is intrinsically good to understand how fragile it is, and there **may** even be some positive long-term spinoff; no guarantees--guarantees are for public utilities, not formal education institutions. Both conservative and liberal educational thinkers can agree about that, if they are willing to set aside their ideological blinders.

Certainly, schools should be desegregated, because simple justice and decency demand it, even if greater racial tolerance and raised academic achievement scores for minorities do not result immediately; they **might**--optimistically--in the due course of time. Desegregation, at any rate, is educationally sound.

On the other hand, it is neither good nor useful for schools to try to indoctrinate students with the "right" values, such as "patriotism," even in the most reconnected of cultural communities. Such indoctrination simply does not work; moreover, it is not educative, and, therefore, detracts from the principal functions of a highly specialized social institution. The way to develop patriotic loyalties, honesty, or any other values deemed appropriate for a person-centered post-industrial democracy is to create more organic, more participatory, more dynamic primary as well as secondary arrangements in the overall social ecology (including arrangements within the school and classroom community themselves as integral parts of the overall ecology) promotive of fellow feeling and the loyalty and "patriotism" it engenders; i.e., arrangements in which young and older, ethnically minority and majority, ideologically left- and right-wing members alike feel free to voice their honest convictions and to display their personal distinctiveness, however "outrageous."

Only such interpersonal and intergroup **informal educational** arrangements on a community basis, whether at the grassroots or the national level, will generate a sense of civic cohesiveness and loyalty of consenting as well as, especially, dissenting[23] members to each other. Their primal human need to **belong** and to offer their diverse talents and ideas to the corporate whole will guarantee desirable moral development, not some superficial program of "correct" values imposed externally by a self-righteous, disconnected group of zealots who have sanctified the school with messianic attributes in their naivete, confusion, and distrust of opposing outlooks. Broad-based **educative** democracy, not totalitarian fascism, is the appropriate road to moral reintegration of the American sociocultural system.

That which I am trying to convey has elsewhere been expressed articulately from a "political" perspective:

> Democratic politics is an **encounter** among people with differing interests, perspectives, and opinions; an encounter in which they reconsider and mutually revise opinions and interests, both individual and common. It happens always in a context of **conflict, imperfect knowledge, and uncertainty, but where community action is necessary**. The resolutions achieved are always more or less temporary, subject to reconsideration, and rarely unanimous. What matters is not unanimity but discourse. The substantive common interest is only discovered or created in democratic political struggle, and it remains contested as much as shared. Far from being inimical to democracy, conflict--handled in democratic ways, with openness and persuasion--is what makes democracy work, what makes for the mutual revision of opinions and interests.[24] (Emphases added.)

In sum, schools simply cannot by themselves eradicate the alienating and other dysfunctional conditions of modern mass society, as they have been asked to do during the epoch of educational messianism. They are not a prime mover of desired changes in basic values and behavioral norms (e.g., increased respect for racial, ethnic, religious, and gender preference) nor even a very effective device for implementing secondary reforms of a technological character (e.g., increasing the potential productivity of industrial workers in a post-industrial age).

Schools are not public utilities, guaranteeing access to the good life, as most Americans have become accustomed to believe in their confused separateness. Once this is understood, the American people will have one less crutch available to justify refusal to join together and become socially self-reliant again as interactive members of learning communities working for the welfare of each other via the process of authentic civic encounter. There is no other desirable alternative in this society.

Throughout this analysis, I have been somewhat critical of the tendency of modern psychology to ape the educational establishment by exploiting growing American faith in the redemptive power of psychotherapy. But, like Garth Wood,[25] an iconoclastic psychiatrist who believes that, while its benefits have been overblown, therapy **is** called for in a rather small percentage of emotionally deeply troubled individuals, I too have considerable respect for a select few of its theorists and practitioners. One of them, Rollo May, not long ago articulated the "educational American dilemma" very eloquently without, perhaps, realizing it. He said:

> We are living at a time when one age is dying and the new age is not yet born....
>
> A choice confronts us. Shall we, as we feel our foundations shaking, withdraw in anxiety and panic? Frightened by the loss of our familiar mooring places, shall we become paralyzed and cover our inaction with apathy?....
>
> Or shall we seize the courage necessary to perceive our sensitivity, awareness, and responsibility in the face of radical change? Shall we consciously participate, on however small the scale, in the forming of the new society?....
>
> We are called upon to do something new, to confront a no man's land, to push into a forest where there are no well-worn paths and from which no one has returned to guide us...To live into the future means to leap into the unknown, and this requires a degree of courage for which there is no immediate precedent and which few people realize.[26]

As May's words clearly recommend, the one thing Americans who want to be "saved" from the onslaught of the emerging new age must stop doing is waiting for the false messiah of schooling or, for that matter, psychotherapy or any other **single social institution** to do it for them.

The school cannot redeem society. That is an unhealthy expectation which can only lead to disaster by default. The most the school can do for society is to help **energize**, **humanize**, and **civilize**--i.e., **actualize**--its members; no small assignment, since the humane and civil interests and capabilities of an actualizing people writ large must form the **base** of all serious efforts to reconstruct society and the community.[27]

That is precisely what all genuine art does. Its inclusive function is to risk the possibility of civilizing people, of trying without assurance of success to help those who may be receptive to respond authentically to the humanizing influence of the work of the artist.

Schools in the ecologically balanced community postulated are

centers of artistic activity instead of the incarnation of society's displacement of responsibility for steadfastly working out its problems of massive social change and the future. As such, they do no more **nor less** than help create and preserve the truth which contributes in a most important and ongoing way to the energizing, humanizing, and civilizing of the people. And, in the final analysis, the very idea of schooling itself comes down to its teachers, who are the artists of the classrooms of the cultural community(ies) envisioned. In the words of Gotz:

> What lets teacher and pupil fulfill their own roles authentically is art. Art...is the creation and the preservation of truth. This is what teaching and learning set out to do when they are authentic.[28]

That which prevents this society from releasing the potential inherent in authentic schooling and teaching is the American people's failure of nerve, their unduly anxious propensity for evading their common burdens by transferring them instead to the nation's schoolteachers, who neither want their unsought role as societal redeemers nor have the slightest hope of carrying out such a role successfully. The great majority of teachers correctly want and are capable of being "only" artists, not missionaries. And, as I have argued elsewhere,[29] most **can** be artists, despite what skeptics may believe--if cultural community can be developed along the lines suggested.

Conclusion:
A Specific Policy Recommendation for Change

Before school became the almost exclusive agency of life preparation in the minds of most Americans, our predecessors received the bulk of their education for life in living communities. They learned from schoolteachers, to be sure; but, more importantly, they learned from each other--from their extended families, their neighbors, local merchants and craftspeople, religious affiliations, and meaningful participation in community recreational and civic organizations. The public school movement culminating in today's overtaxed monolith was, more than anything else, the ideological manifestation of the **collapse** of such organic community and the well-intentioned, if misguided, efforts of influential reformers to replace it with a single social institution.

As indicated earlier, we cannot return to the "sacred" social order of the crude and simple past--most Americans would not want to, if they could. For better or for worse, the United States has become an enormously complex secular civilization. But, it is yet possible to internally reorganize this depersonalizing post-industrial society into smaller, more cohesive units that are conductive to active, productive, trustful, healthy day-to-day living arrangements for people who acknowledge once again that they need each other, not as commodities, but as fellows. The future of American society as an extraordinarily complex affair that is optimally sustainable rests upon our ability to decentralize human relationships while retaining the connective tissue of the whole cultural cloth. In short, the American people need to become serious about building a person-centered civilization along modern lines.

Anticipating the future, Dewey directed his seminal efforts at such a reasonable goal many years ago, focusing upon the unique role of education, both formal and informal, in the transactional give and take of the community building process. Unfortunately, his temperate transactionalism gave way to impassioned ideological faith in the efficacy of schooling as a prime mover of cultural revitalization--today attributed to the institution by both liberals and conservatives alike.

Dewey would have approved of returning to a conception of society based upon interpersonal, intergroup, and inter-institutional give and take. He would, were he with us today, agree that in the modern age, as always before, a **variety** of educative influences, both formal and especially informal, are called for in the making of an individual and the remaking of the world. I think he would insist that the schools of the person-centered society cease to be seen as the only source of significant education and social change, regardless of their potentially valuable contribution in both respects.

In this fifth scenario, schools no longer are perceived as the secular messiah designed to eradicate poverty, crime, and mental illness, and in other ways to save a society in crisis unaided. The schools of such a society become one very important component of a **broader** community effort, founded on the recognition that democratic problem solving, formation of acceptable social self-concepts and long-term personal identity, and positive movement into the future are interrelated essentials of a total community endeavor.

Tax- and tuition-supported schools in the broader "educative community" postulated offer young people an opportunity to learn some of what they may need to know in order to participate meaningfully and self-fulfillingly as private individuals and public citizens in society at all levels. Note that I am visualizing not "community schools" (i.e., centers of all community activity), but "schools of the community" (unique components of the broader sociocultural ecology). In that regard, Dewey and I might disagree slightly; he envisioning schools as taking a greater and more directly focussed leadership role in community and societal life than I do.

The current reactionary belief of neo-fundamentalists that schools should confine their function to teaching the rudiments of reading, writing, arithmetic, American history, and patriotism in an authoritarian manner is as untenable as the reformist visions of the social re-engineers they have replaced since the early 1970s. It is to be hoped that this phase in our continuing ideological struggle over the ends and means of education will pass quickly, and that, regardless of where they attend school, all American children can soon be exposed to a broadening and enriching comprehensive program of liberal educational studies taught by creative, free teachers committed to their intellectual growth as full human beings and full-fledged participants in a modern democratic society.

Notwithstanding that hope, we may find that all that most schools, public or private, can do best in actual practice is to teach the young to be intellectually self-sufficient through efficient and effective employment of the printed word; and that other heretofore untapped teaching institutions and resources of a broader educative community (including not least the electronic mass media) can do a far better job of facilitating their in-depth learning about contemporary politics and economics, careers, multicultural exploration and human relations, leisure and artistic options and skills, the effective use of the newer high technologies, and the search for worthwhile individual and common values.

If, in exploring the possibilities of school-related teaching and learning, the American people should find that their ambitions continue to outstrip that institution's capabilities, we should be prepared--not to deschool society as has been suggested in recent years by educational anarchists such as Ivan Illich and John Holt, which is like throwing the baby out with the bath water--but, more sanely and without rancor, to concede unproductive educational territory to other community resources, both public and private, that they acknowledge can do a better job than schools of promoting learning in those areas. Schools permitted and willing to make such concessions will be appreciated for their singular ability to perform necessary, but not sufficient, community/culture support functions dependably instead of haphazardly as at present, whether those functions be broadly conceived or limited strictly to print-related intellectual development of young people.

Thus, the time has come to reevaluate the unique role of both schools and other institutions of learning and human liberation within an interlinked cultural community context that is holistically educative.

In alluding to Israel earlier, I took pains to stress that society's unique commitment, as a garrison state, to the conception of community espoused herein. Israel is a nation of necessary heroes. Undoubtedly, conditions that require necessary heroism facilitate the development and nurturing of social self-reliance. Such conditions are apparently not manifest in American society at present. Nonetheless, the great humanistic scholar Ernest Becker in his Pulitzer prize-winning book *The Denial of Death*, suggests a justification for perhaps **creating** them:

> When we appreciate how natural it is for man to strive and be a hero, how deeply it goes in his evolutionary and organismic constitutions, how openly he shows it as a child, then it is all the most curious how ignorant most of us are, consciously, of what we really want and need. In our culture anyway, especially in modern times, the heroic seems too big for us, or we too small for it...The urge to heroism is natural, and to admit it honest....
>
> ....If everyone honestly admitted his urge to be a hero, it would be a devastating release of truth. It would make men demand that culture give them their due--a primary sense of human value as unique contributors to cosmic life....[30]

Notwithstanding those inspiring words by Becker, perhaps only perceived threat to the very survival of a collectivity can motivate people sufficiently to unite them and bond them together to work concretely for a cause greater than their individual self-interests. As sociological theorists of a "functionalist" orientation like to believe, perhaps only a major "intrusive force," exploiting extreme organizational weaknesses, can bring about significant social change on a temporary or permanent basis.

If so, America may be destined to go on indefinitely into the future denying its persistent major and minor problems as a society, while its people displace their fears of "heroically" confronting those problems onto the schools--or some other convenient substitute for direct action. Waiting for a crisis brought about intrusively from outside is like waiting for the onslaught of cancer before quitting smoking.

As observed in the previous chapter, there is no guarantee that one of the four gloomy scenarios of America's destiny ventured therein will not come to pass. We may, indeed, have ahead of us a rather joyless and troubled long-term future at best and a disemboweled one at worst if we continue to foolishly attempt, in the words of Erich Fromm, to "escape from our freedom."[31]

But, it need not inevitably be that way. If, instead of continuing to displace faith onto the false secular messiah of schooling, or some other single institution such as psychotherapy, the American people somehow regain faith in themselves, they may yet become enabled to find themselves; and, not just temporarily during wartime or following a natural catastrophe such as a flood or major earthquake (e.g., the San Francisco quake of 1989), or in the wake of a major depression, as the functionalist position suggests.

To do so, the American people must, indeed, "seize the courage necessary to live into the future." And they must do so in the name of **this** society's unique sociocultural structure, not in the name of any other nation's ideological orientation, regardless of how apparently successful other nations may be as a result of their experiments with new and unfamiliar social and political ideologies. In taking this position, I am rejecting both the functionalist conception of social change, which essentially supports passivity by members of a society until the society has become seriously weakened structurally--to the point of crisis--as well as the conflict theory of change, which urges taking concrete steps to actively promote or even create "dysfunctional" social conditions which can then be exploited by intrusive forces. If the functionalists are overly passive, the adherents of conflict theory are unduly anxious to demolish a social order which, however flawed, is potentially restorable.

The great majority of Americans would prefer to have their damaged social structure repaired and restored rather than rebuilt *en toto* from the foundation. That being the case, necessary social reconstruction should not be taken either too lightly, in the manner of the minor reform-minded functionalists, nor too literally, as the revolutionary-oriented proponents of conflict theory are prone to do. Social reconstruction, as herein espoused, means restoration of a badly damaged society in **its** cultural/historical and developmental terms of uniqueness, nothing less and nothing more.

From the perspective espoused, then, the American people are well-advised to "lower" their educational expectations to warrantable proportions. The school must cease to be viewed as a primarily instrumental institution and, instead, be reconceived of as a major agency of **diffuse** and **non-guaranteeable** learning for the sake of learning and becoming fully human as unique individuals and as participating members of the cultural community undergoing reconstruction; i.e., of intellectual, existential, and civil self-realization.

The first step, then, toward actualizing the authentically educative potential lying dormant in our nation's schools and schoolteachers is the ending of the school's cultural hegemony as a directly accountable and indispensible social utility set apart from the other institutional elements of the sociocultural ecology.

Simultaneously, its vital significance within the overarching framework of socially self-reliant cultural community redevelopment as a center for experimentation on the intellectual emancipation of the human spirit in the **indirect** service of long-term progressive cultural renewal must be restored.

Such a tradeoff is justified in terms of what the school's institutional capabilities and purposes are in fact, rather than fantasy. Furthermore, the tradeoff is long overdue, although I am not sanguine about its taking place in the near future without a far more superior understanding of human ecology and more enlightened moral leadership by educational statespeople, elected officials, and other persons in positions of public influence than we have become accustomed to since the end of World War II and our concomitant national preoccupation with returning to the cocoon of irresponsible individualism.

After all, a social movement of the magnitude proposed is unlikely to get off the ground and sustain its momentum without committed men and women of broad and deep vision to guide the rest of the citizenry toward their collective dream of "living in a society that would really be worth living in."[32] If we cannot depend upon the emergence of such superior leadership, we will perforce need to think in terms of other alternatives.

Are we likely to obtain that level of leadership in the near future? I do not think so. Let us be candid. Those who are in positions of sociopolitical and educational power at the present time are, as Cuban pointed out earlier, not likely to either stop passing the buck nor to return it to those who passed it. Most have become captives of the EMC either for sincere reasons of faith and conviction--however misguided--or as a result of unenlightened self-interest.

Certainly, school officials and other professional educational power figures **should** know better than to continue to sustain a cultural mythology as corrosive as the EMC--and some of them do, as I have suggested above. But, we cannot, realistically, expect the educational establishment as a whole to lead in a movement to put themselves and their special interests out of business. They simply have too much at stake, whether they are consciously aware of their ulterior motives or not.

An alternative might be to ask the educational intellectuals and scholars who teach teachers to lead in a massive project to begin preparing prospective teachers and retraining experienced practitioners to reconceptualize their professional mission; i.e., to make them aware of their unwitting acceptance of the hegemony of educational messianism, and then to alter their assumptions of their roles so that, in the future, teachers reject such conceptions, and think of themselves instead of free artists of the classroom. Unfortunately, this alternative, appealing as if may be to pedagogical purists, is probably not feasible either. For, even if enough teachers of teachers can be found to take on the monumental project of fostering consciousness raising and reconceptualization of teaching (which is highly improbably, because they too are caught up in the tentacles of educational messianism), once the newly awakened cadres of teachers obtained positions in the public schools, most would be forced to seriously compromise their art or lose their jobs. Teaching is a highly politicized occupation in American society, even for the merely competent role-centered majority, much less the artistically creative minority who seek self-actualization via the classroom.

I do, however, believe that American teacher educators as an occupational group possess sufficient academic freedom to utilize their positions, if they wish, to make a modest contribution to the ending of educational messianism and the rebalancing of the socioeducational ecology. They can make a contribution by taking the notion of teaching as a genuine art form seriously; and, accordingly, by attempting to influence their students to reconceptualize their mission and role along those lines, knowing in advance full well that a considerable part of their effort will probably be fruitless. Still, perhaps a small percentage of teachers thus trained as artists rather than organizational role incumbents would persist in acting as if they were artists once out in the field, even if they were required to moderate their preferred behavior in conformity with external pressures directly related to their survival as professionals. If even a small minority of teachers could think like artists of the classroom and yet retain their positions (largely through skillful micropolitical strategic interaction), other teachers coming up in future years would at least have desirable "role models" to emulate. Small beginnings can sometimes lead to greater outcomes in the long term.[33]

For now, perhaps the best prospect of reducing American overdependency upon the schooling system for resolving major social problems will come not from politicians, educational leaders, and teachers, but rather from the lay public itself. Such an unspectacular movement to eradicate educational messianism and restore cultural community must originate at the grassroots, with **parents** of schoolchildren, although proffered support and assistance from well-placed and influential statespeople, public officials, and policy makers should not be cavalierly rejected.

Parents must finally secure the longstanding and highly touted right to send their children to the schools of their own choice, "public" or "private," rather than continue to be forced, unless wealthy, to have them attend the nearest tax-supported state school assigned. Accordingly, parents must be granted vouchers of tuition-tax credits, or whatever it takes financially, to send their children to schools that are required to compete in a relatively "free market." They must be permitted to translate their messianic faith into concrete action that allows them to risk **making mistakes** in the choice of their children's formal educational according to their ideological biases, right, left, or in between.

At present, such mistakes are being made for them, thus perpetuating the very public passivity and irresponsibility that I have been deploring. Given the right to make such "mistakes," they will, thereby, destroy the hegemony of the monolithic "public" schooling system which, because of its very basic premise of integrative commonality,[34] helps considerably to perpetuate the overriding mythology that schools have **non-educational** benefits of great significance to confer on society at large.

Once the prevailing state public school monopoly is broken up, the American people will have no recourse other than to look elsewhere than to formal education for solutions to their manifold problem--even if all they find is an equally untenable messianic replacement such a psychotherapy. As least the **schools**, with which the present analysis is focally concerned, will have ceased contributing to a hurtful cultural illusion; and, large numbers of people may be stimulated to think seriously about becoming socially self-reliant as activists in the broad-based social reconstruction project espoused herein.

If all American parents were enabled to send their children to the schools of their choice, many adventuresome teachers and other educational professionals currently forced to work for the state in bureaucratically stifling and authoritarian contexts would have a new incentive to open their own schools or seek employment in newly opened schools in hopes of becoming relatively freer to teach what they wished to and more nearly in their own preferred way. Parents would, in effect, choose schools and teachers by reputation, as they now choose hospitals and physicians--surely a comparably critical choice. They would have the financial resources to do so because the government would subsidize them with vouchers or some other form of tuition credit instead of requiring them to pay expensive fees in addition to their taxes in order to have their children attend the schools of their own choosing.

I submit that, given such a newly available opportunity, many American parents, in particular working single parents and the disadvantaged who are currently estranged from public institutions to a greater extent than others in American society, would elect to take advantage of it. They would send their children to "private" schools in the belief that the latter would serve them and their children more effectively, ideologically and educationally, than available state monopoly schools.

In turn, however, it should be stressed that having finally begun losing sizable numbers of their disenchanted clientele, the conventional public schools would either take substantial steps to become more appealing to parents--in part by providing more alternatives themselves (as some are already beginning to do)--or eventually close their doors. Ironically, I doubt that enough people would actually defect to the private sector to cause the latter to happen; the very knowledge that they **could** close, at any time, would appease most parents, and keep the remaining state schools in line.

In any case, **both** public and private schools would benefit by the inevitably greater cooperation of those parents who enrolled their children voluntarily in them. That would be in great contrast to the situation today in which, consciously or insensibly, most parents are alienated from the schools and teachers of their children because they realize that they have little or no voice in selecting them.

I wish to strongly reiterate that under such a plan as proposed, both private and public schools would fail to satisfy parents' **ideological** demands for non-educational (messianic) outcomes. But, parents and their children would receive greater **educational** benefits, as described earlier in this chapter, than have heretofore been available for most. At the minimum, they would **believe** they have a psychological consequence of having made a personal commitment to the schooling service of their choice. In this regard, it is helpful to quote Donald Erickson, a highly regarded authority on private schools and parent choice:

> The history of private schools suggests that when government does not interfere, schools tend to appear and die, grow and decline, in response to variegated, constantly changing preferences of citizens. Citizens who actively choose the schools which their children attend, from among a variety of available options, seem far more satisfied with their schools than are parents who simply do the "normal" thing, with little thought. Moreover, the active choosers appear to be more concerned, informed, and sophisticated.[35]

In short, by opening up significant options for schooling to parents--i.e., options that are not merely within the prevailing public sector (to which the dominant public school interest groups have, thus far, been successful in limiting the political debate), but that do not exclude them either--the EMC will be unmasked, because **no** school, public or private, can perform the impossible. All that **any** school ought to be expected to achieve is educational in character. Schools are benign educational services, not beneficent public welfare agencies. To finally realize this, the American people will, in my considered opinion, have to be offered the chance to have their illusions about the non-educational benefits of schooling dispelled by the only means possible; possessing the right to test their assumptions about institutional efficacy in schools that they, not the state, have selected.

Once those freely chosen schools have demonstrated their incapacity to accomplish the superfluous functions that they were naively presumed to be able to perform, the American public may then at last concede that its faith in formal education's culturally redemptive power was displaced; it will then have no alternative other than to look elsewhere for "miracles."

Or, more hopefully, to cease waiting passively for miracles altogether; and, instead, begin the arduous process of working together democratically as members of restorative cultural communities to resolve common problems of living in the new age that is opening up. Then, the American people will begin to realize that education for social and cultural "salvation," including reintegration of a dangerously fragmented social order, does not occur in highly specialized places called schools. The improvement of human conditions occurs from working together actively on problems of mutual concern in less rigidly structured socioeducational organizations called communities--of which schools are only **one** component whose distinguishing function is to help receptive youngsters learn how to **think** clearly and profoundly so that they may fulfill their own destinies as individuals and make responsible contributions to the broader community development process envisioned.

All elements of American society who thoroughly distrust radical overhauling of formal education, including the ending of the state "public" schooling monopoly, will resist these recommendations: i.e., state socialists who will consider it regressively supportive of the "contradictions of corporate capitalism;" corporate capitalist who seek a malleable lower working force to insure the perpetuation of their ever-increasing acquisitive needs (while, increasingly, they send their own children to exclusive private schools); upper echelon professional educators who have powerful career-related vested interests at stake; progressive liberal educational intellectuals who have internalized the myth of the public school's messianic functions and are distrustful of the capabilities of the "masses" while also being unjustifiably paranoid about the educational right's alleged long-term agenda to "displace democratic public education;"[36] and politicians eager to appease influential state school monopoly interests in order to insure their votes at election time.

On the other hand, those who are likely to accept or at least seriously consider such recommendations include the thoughtful minority of public policy makers, citizens, and scholars who seek a **stronger** democracy brought about in part via considerably expanded parental power in the educational decision-making process, the overwhelming majority of schoolteachers who want simply to be sufficiently unrestrained to inspire their students to learn what they have to teach within reasonably flexible legal and policy parameters, and virtually all of the so-called "little Americans" who want a greater say so about the education of their own children, even though their excessive faith in schooling's messianic attributes may be wrong-headed.

Why not permit these great numbers of ordinary American parents to have their way, wrongheaded though they may be? Grant them the opportunity to learn from their mistakes, from trial and error. That is the democratic way, particularly in a culturally pluralistic society, because it demonstrates genuine trust in individual citizens of every socioeconomic rank (especially of the poor) and ethnic commitment. The most they can lose is their naivete about what schools are for; but, in exchange, they may gain a genuine **education** for their children, principally because the schools and their teachers selected will be far more "accountable" to their clients than is typically the case at present in rigid school bureaucracies operated under state monopoly conditions.

Even more importantly, they will receive a second chance at recapturing the essence of the real American dream, i.e., the challenge of working together again with other public spirited citizens of a strongly democratic community in the pursuit of--if not vulgar "happiness"--certainly a **meaningful** existence as we push forward onto the frontiers of our emerging post-industrial civilization.

I fully appreciate, but do not concur with, strong democracy advocate Barber's fear when he cautions that:

> there are great dangers in the libertarian spirit of the voucher scheme, which is inimical to the very idea of a public good and of public judgments politically generated. The voucher system would mobilize individuals, but it would mobilize them via private incentives; it speaks exclusively to their private interests as parents and thus as consumers of parental goods.[37]

He worries that "vouchers would seem then to serve activity but to corrupt community."[38] But, interestingly, after discussing the possible dangers to strong democracy of a free-choice schooling system, Barber--certainly no ultra-conservative--concludes by **endorsing** such a system, nonetheless. That is to say, aware of its potential abuses, **he proposes that we take the risk anyway**:

> The strong democrat cannot endorse the voucher

> idea with enthusiasm, but he may nonetheless feel persuaded to agree with a dean of the Harvard School of Education, who has written: "Given the condition of the schools that serve poor youngsters, it takes a depressing amount of paranoia to suggest that we should not even give the voucher plan a reasonable trial."[39]

It can hardly be denied that there **are**, indeed, risks in what I am proposing and what Barber can only lukewarmly endorse--obviously everything of any value involves risks. But, I might add, Barber is, in my opinion, a **true** utopian in terms of practically every one of his own proposals for instituting strong democracy in practice in the United States, with the singular exception of the voucher system that even he grudgingly supports in the final analysis.

If the question is **how** to achieve the restoration of social self-reliance that Barber and I both agree is so crucial to America's collective future health and well-being, then, I submit that his anxieties about vouchers are based on his undue stress on the "libertarian" aspects of such a system coupled with an intuitive belief that parent educational choice as an alternative to entrenched state school monopolization has a uniquely high probability of being actualized in the foreseeable future, unlike most of his other, more esoteric proposals; e.g., weekly neighborhood "talk sessions," "TV town meetings," a "Civic Communications Cooperative," "office-holding by lot," "universal citizen service," and most other aspects of his interrelated program for constructing a strong democracy by the year 2000.[40] Barber's overall program is premature, at the very least.

Conversely, parent choice of schooling by vouchers or other fiscal means has a **realistic** chance of being approved as general public policy by the year 2000 or shortly thereafter, ironically **because** there are, indeed, risks that it may be abused by what Barber terms self-interested, non-public spirited "free riders." In other words, it alone among his plethora of policy speculations can appeal to a wide enough spectrum of the American people in the foreseeable future to be considered a pragmatically workable prospect for democratically reforming public education, and, indirectly, American society writ large. Thus, it is a **practical** idea whose time has come rather than a utopian chimera. **After** parent choice of schooling has begun to be implemented in American society, **then**, perhaps, will programs such as that offered by Barber be worthy of serious consideration. In the meantime, they are, to repeat, premature. All things considered, then, parent choice of schooling has a strong probability of succeeding, although it does admittedly involve risk.

But, that is the entire point. My reason for writing this book has been to demonstrate why the American people **must** begin to take risks again. We must stop hoping for "guaranteeable" results from our efforts, or, more precisely, the efforts of "miracle-working" others; and, instead, start gambling on our **own** practical resources as a socially self-reliant people, Nothing ventured, nothing gained. Let us, indeed, take a chance for a change.

Let us take risks, while building in the best possible safeguards against so-called "libertarian" excesses in any parent free choice initiative developed; for example, anti-discrimination clauses for schools accepting vouchers; mixtures of "private" **and** "public" schools permitted to accept vouchers; supplementary tuition allowances for poor parents who wish to send their children to exceptionally expensive private schools; excusal from religious practices by non-believing, non-practicing students voluntarily attending Catholic or other parochial schools (as is today the case in many urban areas where, for instance, Jewish children attend Catholic high schools in order to obtain what their parents and they consider a better education); and so on.

Even the enemies of vouchers and tuition tax-credits admit that major protections against libertarian excesses can and already have been built into parent choice proposals. Political theorist Amy Gutman, for example, candidly acknowledges the following:

> ....Most sophisticated voucher plans...make substantial concessions to the democratic purposes of primary education by conditioning certification of voucher schools upon their meeting a set of minimal standards. The most carefully designed and defended voucher plan would constrain all schools that accepted vouchers (a) not to discriminate in their admissions policies against children on grounds of race, socio-economic status, or intelligence, (b) not to require or accept tuition payments above the level set by the voucher, (c) not to expel students except under certain specified circumstances and then only with due process, (d) to supply a governmental information agency with detailed reports of their governance procedures and the academic

> achievement, socio-economic status, and racial composition of their student body, and (e) to require a minimum number of hours of instruction with a significant portion devoted to reading and mathematics. **This list is meant to be suggestive rather than exhaustive.**[41] (Emphases added.)

Barber and Gutmann make my case: A well-regulated or "constrained" system of parent choice **can** be developed in the United States within a **Constitutionally acceptable framework** and on the basis of **democratically agreed upon normative principles** translated into policy and practice. For reasons discussed at length in this, as well as earlier chapters, such a constrained choice system **should** be developed.

When should the American people get started on such a venture? When shall public-spirited sociopolitical realists across the land in teachers colleges, legislative chambers, media editorial offices, and on the streets of the nation's cities and towns begin mobilizing for basic reforms of the financing of public education, so that every parent may send their children to the schools of their choice in the interests of ending the hegemony of the Educational Messiah Complex, and restoring our democratic social self-reliance as we press forward into the enigmatic future?

There is no better time than the **present**, with its barely concealed but as yet largely contained societal turbulence coupled with a special national accent on major educational reform of both the ends and means of the schooling enterprise. Now is the time to begin sowing the seeds of such a plausible and **genuinely** redemptive, albeit admittedly heretical idea. Let us hope they take root in the ever-optimistic American mind while conditions for undertaking fundamental change are both palpably recognizable as well as feasible.

Indeed, a start in the direction proposed is already underway as we move into the 1990s. Greatly expanded parent choice of schooling appears to be strongly endorsed by influential figures at all levels of the civic/political/professional structure in this society. But, this endorsement is, as yet, limited to choice **within** the "public" school sector, excluding private schools and vouchers or tuition tax-credits. While, from the perspective of the present analysis of cultural denial, such a limitation is hardly surprising, the growing momentum for substantially greater choice by clients of institutionalized education is a beginning. And, that is ground for optimism.

Notes

Chapter 1

1. David P. Gardner and the National Commission on Excellence in Education, *A Nation at Risk: The Imperative for Educational Reform* (Washington, D.C.; U.S. Department of Education, 1983).
2. Charles R. Morris, "The Coming Global Boom," *The Atlantic Monthly* 264 (October 1989), pp. 55-56.
3. Peter Drucker, "The Worst Thing Is to Modernize," *U.S. News and World Report* (February 2, 1987), p. 23.
4. Paul Hawken, *The Next Economy* (New York: Ballantine Books, 1983), p. 106.
5. While not absolutely essential, a disclaimer is in order at the outset; namely, that boarding schools are excluded from the present analysis. Boarding schools are far more than schools; they are quasi-families and communities in miniature. That is, they are what may be termed "total institutions." As such, they may wield substantially greater influence over their clientele (at least during their period of residence) than may day schools. The key fact to remember, always, is that with extremely rare exceptions--certain wealthy parents, parents of severely handicapped children, and custodians of some serious juvenile offenders--the American people simply find the idea of boarding schools obnoxious. This aversion is in contrast with the attitudes commonly held by parents in many other nations throughout the world.
6. See, especially, Benjamin R. Barber, *Strong Democracy: Participatory*

Politics for a New Age (Berkeley and Los Angeles: University of California Press, 1984).

Chapter 2

1. Martin Gross, *The Psychological Society: A Critical Analysis of Psychiatry, Psychotherapy, and the Psychological Revolution* (New York: Random House, 1978).
2. Jack Gratus, *The False Messiahs* (New York: Taplinger Publishing Company, 1975), p. 25.
3. *Ibid.*, p. 7.
4. See Yonine Talmon, "Millenarianism," in *International Encyclopedia of the Social Sciences* 10, edited by David L. Sills (New York: Crowell Collier and Macmillan, 1968), pp. 349-62.
5. See Morris S. Schwartz and Charlotte G. Schwartz, "Mental Health: The Concept," in *International Encyclopedia of the Social Sciences* 10, p. 220.
6. See Kenneth M. Dolbeare and Patricia Dolbeare, *American Ideologies: The Competing Political Beliefs of the 1970s*, 3rd edition (Chicago: Rand McNally, 1976), pp. 225-28.
7. David Tyack and Elizabeth Hanson, "Hard Times, Hard Choices: The Case for Coherence in Public School Leadership," *Phi Delta Kappan* 63 (April 1982), p. 514.
8. Theodore Brameld, *Education as Power* (New York: Holt, Rinehart, and Winston, 1965), p. 1.
9. The major studies confirming this distressing fact are too numerous to detail. In 1983 alone major research-based reports identifying the disparities were released by The College Board, the Twentieth Century Fund, the National Science Foundation, the Educational Commission of the States, and The National Commission on Excellence in Education.
10. See Richard Pratte, *Ideology and Education* (New York: David McKay, 1977), pp. 137-52. See also David Nyberg and Kieran Egan, *The Erosion of Education: Socialization and the Schools* (New York: Teachers College Press, 1981).
11. Martin Buber, *I and Thou*, translated by Ronald G. Smith (New York: Charles Scribner's Sons, 1958).
12. The women in Israel have complaints comparable to women in the United States about gender inequality, with the exception of their participation in the military. For example, both men and women soldiers patrol the streets of Jerusalem with rifles and submachine guns; and female teachers may sometimes be seen carrying weapons as they shepherd their classes on field trips.
13. David H. Kamens, "Education ad Democracy: A Comparative Interna-

tional Analysis," *Sociology of Education* 61 (April 1988), p. 116.
14. Michael S. Kimmel, "A Prejudice against Prejudice," *Psychology Today* 20 (December 1986), pp. 47-52.
15. For a thorough review of Pettigrew's thoughts in this area, see: Thomas F. Pettigrew, *Racially Separate or Together?* (New York: McGraw-Hill, 1971); Thomas F. Pettigrew, *Racial Discrimination in the United States* (New York: Harper & Row, 1975); and Thomas F. Pettigrew, *The Sociology of Race Relations: Reflection and Reform* (New York: Free Press, 1980).

Chapter 3

1. Robert E. Mason, *Educational Ideals in American Society* (Boston: Allyn and Bacon, 1960), p. 100.
2. Richard J. Whalen, "America's Identity Crisis," *Social Science and Modern Society* 20 (November/December 1982), p. 61.
3. Henri Desroche, *The Sociology of Hope* (London: Routledge and Kegan Paul, 1979), p. 61.
4. Henry J. Perkinson, *The Imperfect Panacea: American Faith in Education, 1865-1965* (New York: Random House, 1968), p. 3.
5. *Ibid.*
6. Merle Curti, *The Social Ideas of American Educators* (Totowa, N.J.: Littlefield, Adams and Company, 1978), p. 582.
7. Mary Anne Raywid, *The Axe-Grinders: Critics of Our Public Schools* (New York: Macmillan, 1962).
8. R. Freeman Butts, *Public Education in the United States: From Revolution to Reform* (New York: Holt, Rinehart and Winston, 1978), pp. 9-12.
9. See Francisco O. Ramirez and John Boli, "The Political Construction of Mass Schooling: European Origins and Worldwide Institutionalization," *Sociology of Education* 60 (January 1987), pp. 2-17.
10. Butts, *Public Education*, pp. 364-95.
11. *Ibid.*, p. 10.
12. Horace Mann, *Twelfth Annual Report to the [Massachusetts] Board of Education* (Boston: Dutton and Wentworth, State Printers, 1848), p. 55.
13. Michael B. Katz, *Class, Bureaucracy, and Schools: The Illusion of Educational Change in America* (New York: Praeger Publishers, 1971).
14. Diane Ravitch, *The Troubled Crusade: American Education 1945-1980* (New York: Basic Books, 1983), p. 43.
15. John Dewey, *My Pedagogic Creed* (Washington, D.C.: Progressive Education Association, 1929), p. 17.
16. See Curti, *Social Ideas*, p. 507.
17. Sanford W. Reitman, *Education, Society, and Change* (Boston: Allyn

and Bacon, 1981), pp. 488-89.

18. See Barry M. Franklin, *Building the American Community: The School Curriculum and the Search for Social Control* (London and Philadelphia: The Falmer Press, 1986), pp. 119-37.
19. Ravitch, *Troubled Crusade*, pp. 44-5.
20. George S. Counts, *Dare the School Build a New Social Order?* (New York: John Day Company, 1932).
21. Ravitch, *Troubled Crusade*, pp. 85-6.
22. David P. Gardner and the National Commission on Excellence in Education, *A Nation at Risk: The Imperative for Educational Reform* (Washington, D.C.: United States Department of Education, 1983).
23. Diane Ravitch, "The Educational Pendulum," *Psychology Today* 17 (October 1983), p. 64.
24. Curti, *Social Ideas*, p. 585.

Chapter 4

1. Some representative works included Mortimer Smith, *And Madly Teach: A Layman Looks at Public School Education* (Chicago: Henry Regner, 1949); Albert Lynd, *Quackery in the Public Schools* (Boston: Little Brown, 1953); Arthur Bestor, *Educational Wastelands: The Retreat from Learning in Our Public Schools* (Urbana: University of Illinois Press, 1953); Paul Woodring, *Let's Talk Sense About Our Schools* (New York: McGraw-Hill, 1953); Robert Hutchins, *The Conflict in Education in a Democratic Society* (New York: Harper and Brothers, 1953): C. Winfield Scott and Clyde M. Hill, eds., *Public Education Under Criticism* (New York: Prentice-Hall, 1954); James B. Conant, *The American High School Today* (New York: McGraw-Hill, 1959): Hyman G. Rickover, *Education and Freedom* (New York: E.P. Dutton Company, 1959); James D. Koerner, *The Miseducation of American Teachers* (Boston: Houghton Mifflin Company, 1963); Mortimer J. Adler and Milton Mayer, *The Revolution in Education* (Chicago: University of Chicago Press, 1958); Max Rafferty, *Suffer Little Children* (New York: Devin-Adair Company, 1962).
2. Diane Ravitch, *The Troubled Crusade: American Education 1945-1980* (New York: Basic Books, 1983), p. 142.
3. James L. Sundquist, *Politics and Policy: The Eisenhower, Kennedy, and Johnson Years* (Washington, D.C.: The Brookings Institution, 1968), pp. 216-17.
4. For instance, see Kenneth Kenniston, *The Uncommitted: Alienated Youth in American Society* (New York, Harcourt, Brace and World, 1965); Theodore Roszak, *The Making of a Counter Culture: Reflections on the Technocratic Society and its Youthful Opposition* (Garden City, N.J.: Doubleday and Company, 1969); Charles Reich, *The*

Greening of America: How the Youth Revolution is Trying to Make America Livable (New York: Random House, 1970).

5. See Arthur E. Wise, *Legislated Learning: The Bureaucratization of the American Classroom* (Berkeley: University of California Press, 1979).
6. Ivan Illich, "After Deschooling, What?" in *After Deschooling, What?*, edited by Alan Gartner, Colin Greer, and Frank Riessman (New York: Social Policy, 1973), pp. 5-6. See also, Illich, *Deschooling Society* (New York: Harper and Row, 1971).
7. See A. S. Neill, *Summerhill: A Radical Approach to Child Rearing* (New York: Hart Publishing Company, 1960).
8. See Vernon H. Smith, *Alternative Schools: The Development of Options in Public Education* (Lincoln, NE: Professional Educators Publication, 1974); and Mario D. Fantini, *Public Schools of Choice* (New York: Simon and Schuster, 1973).
9. Alvin Toffler, *Future Shock* (New York: Bantam Books, 1970).

Chapter 5

1. Henri Desroche, *The Sociology of Hope* (London: Routledge and Kegan Paul, 1979), p. 4.
2. Francisco O. Ramirez and John Boli, "The Political Construction of Mass Schooling: European Origins and Worldwide Institutionalization," *Sociology of Education* 60 (January 1987), p. 11.
3. William F. O'Neill, *Educational Ideologies: Contemporary Expressions of Educational Philosophy* (Santa Monica, CA: Goodyear Publishing Company, 1981).
4. John Palmer, "Who Should Define the Meaning of Citizenship?" *Journal of Teacher Education* 34 (November-December 1983), p. 51.
5. Quoted in *Teacher Education Reports* 8 (August 29, 1985): p. 3.
6. See, in this regard, Raymond Callahan's classic, *Education and the Cult of Efficiency: A Study of the Social Forces that Have Shaped the Administration of the Public Schools* (Chicago: University of Chicago Press, 1962).
7. Max Rafferty, *Classroom Countdown: Education at the Crossroads* (New York: Hawthorn Books, 1970), p. 67.
8. Henry S. Meyers, Jr., *Fundamentally Speaking* (San Francisco: Strawberry Hill Press, 1977), pp. 18-19.
9. *Ibid.*, pp. 75-76.
10. Ronald Reagan, Weekly Radio Broadcast, 1983. Quoted in the *Fresno Bee* (March 13, 1983).
11. Ben Brodinsky, "The New Right: The Movement and its Impact," *Phi Delta Kappan* 64 (October 1982), p. 87.
12. J. Charles Park, "The New Right: Threat to Democracy in Education," *Educational Leadership* 38 (November 1980), pp. 146-7.

13. James Howard, "The Time for Basic Education," *The Education Digest* 47 (September 1981), p. 8.
14. Meyers, Jr., *Fundamentally Speaking*, p. 86.
15. Rafferty, *Classroom Countdown*, pp. 232, 250.
16. Mortimer J. Adler, *et al.*, *The Paideia Proposal: An Educational Manifesto* (New York: Macmillan, 1982).
17. For an analytical treatment of educational ideologies categorized as having (1) social purposes, or noneducational benefits, (2) individual purposes, or educational benefits, and (3) humanistic purposes, or person-centered benefits, see Richard Pratte, *Ideology and Education* (New York: David McKay, 1977), pp. 124-188.
18. Adler, *Paideia*, p. 79.
19. Hillary Thimmesh, "Education is About Civilization: Lose Sight of That and You Lose Sight of Humanity," *Chronicle of Higher Education* 28 (June 20, 1984), p. 64.
20. Tomas A. Arciniega, "Bilingual Education in the 1980s," *The Education Digest* 48 (September 1982), p. 10.
21. Seymour W. Itzkoff, *A New Public Education* (New York: David McKay, 1976), p. 351.
22. John E. Coons and Stephen D. Sugarman, *Education By Choice: The Case for Family Control* (Berkeley: University of California Press, 1978), p. 98.
23. Daniel Patrick Moynihan, "Government and the Ruin of Private Education," *Harper's* 255 (April 1978), p. 38.
24. Allan C. Carlson, "Religion, the State and the Schools: Reflections on the Deweyan Perspective," *Current Issues in Education* 3 (Fall 1983), p. 30.
25. James Michael Lee, "Religion and the Public Schools: A Pluralistic View," *California Journal of Teacher Education* 9 (Spring 1982), p. 13.
26. Carlson, "Religion and Deweyan Perspective," p. 32.
27. Arthur E. Wise, *Legislated Learning: The Bureaucratization of the American Classroom* (Berkeley: University of California Press, 1979).
28. United States Commission on Civil Rights, *Intimidation and Violence: Racial and Religious Bigotry in America* (Washington, D.C., Clearinghouse Publication 77, January, 1983), pp. 28-9.
29. Publicity brochure, Educators for Social Responsibility (No publication data available).
30. Charles Silberman, *Crisis in the Classroom* (New York: Random House, 1970); Jonathan Kozol, *Death at an Early Age: The Destruction of the Hearts and Minds of Negro Children in the Boston Public Schools* (Boston: Houghton Mifflin, 1976); Neil Postman and Charles Weingartner, *Teaching as a Subversive Activity* (New York: Delacorte Press, 1969); James Herndon, *The Way It Spozed to Be* (New York: Bantam Books, 1969).
31. Morris L. Bigge, *Learning Theories for Teachers*, 3rd edition (New York:

Harper and Row, 1976), p. 33.
32. Daryl Siedentop, "Some Basic Talk about What's Basic," *NAASP Bulletin* 62 (May 1978), p. 2.
33. Zvi Lamm, "The Status of Knowledge in the Radical Concept of Education," in *Curriculum and the Cultural Revolution*, edited by David E. Purpel and Maurice Belanger (Berkeley: McGutchen, 1972), pp. 136, 138.
34. *Ibid.*, p. 139.
35. Lillian S. Stephens, *The Teacher's Guide to Open Education* (New York: Holt, Rinehart and Winston, 1984), p. 29.
36. Alvin Toffler, *Future Shock* (New York: Bantam Books, 1970).
37. Ronald F. Barnes, "An Educator Looks Back from 1996," *The Futurist* 12 (April 1978), pp. 123-26.
38. Michael D. Usdan, "Realities of the 1980s: Implications for Teacher Educators," *Journal of Teacher Education* 32 (July-August 1981), p. 30.
39. Harold Entwistle, "Antonio Gramsci and the School as Hegemonic," *Educational Theory* 28 (Winter 1978), p. 32.
40. George S. Counts, *Dare the School Build a New Social Order?* (New York: The John Day Company, 1932).
41. Theodore Brameld, "Social Frontiers: Retrospective and Prospective," *Phi Delta Kappan* 59 (October 1977), p. 119.
42. Mannheim's actual words were as follows: "Only those orientations transcending reality will be referred to as utopian which, when they pass over into conduct, tend to shatter, either partially or wholly, the order of things prevailing at the time. In limiting the meaning of the term 'utopia' to that type of orientation which transcends reality and which at the same time breaks the bonds of the existing order, a distinction is set up between the utopian and the ideological states of mind" [the latter being the outlook which seeks to preserve "the prevailing order of things"]. Thus, Mannheim's concept of ideology differs from most modern conceptions, including my own, in being a value schema interested in avoiding change. In this book, **any** value orientation directed at active social change--whether retrogressive, progressive, or revolutionary--is considered "ideological," if it is socially embedded and emotionally provocative, controversial, etc. See Karl Mannheim, *Ideology and Utopia: An Introduction to the Sociology of Knowledge* (New York; Harcourt, Brace and World, 1936), p. 192.
43. Vincent Crockenberg and Richard LaBrecque, editors, *Culture as Education* (Dubuque, IA: Kendall/Hunt Publishing Company, 1977), p. x.
44. See, for instance, Elizabeth Cogan, "Individualism, Collectivism, and Radical Educational Reform," *Harvard Educational Review* 48 (May 1978), p. 227-66. Also see, Jonathan Kozol, *The Night is Dark and I am*

Far from Home (Boston: Houghton Mifflin, 1975).

45. As quoted in George H. Wood, "Beyond Radical Cynicism," *Educational Theory* 32 (Spring 1982), p. 68.
46. Ann and Harold Berlak, *Dilemmas of Schooling: Teaching and Social Change* (New York: Methuen and Company, 1981).
47. Henry A. Giroux and Roger I. Simon, *Popular Culture, Schooling and Everyday Life* (Granby, MA: Bergin & Garvey, 1989).
48. As a former teacher who relied fairly successfully upon Meadian social psychology and as a long-time supervisor of student teachers, I confess to being intrigued by the training possibilities of the Berlaks' theory of interpersonal dynamics. However, the question remains as to whether the acknowledged subtle influence on students' values achieved thereby can be retained unless it squares with the students' enculturated values from outside of school. My experience has been that children eventually "tell on teachers"--that is, parents "know everything that goes on" in classrooms. This is particularly true if what goes on is not in fundamental accord with their own values, which they want passed on to their children.
49. Martin Carnoy and Henry Levin, *The Limits of Educational Reform* (New York: David McKay, 1976), pp. 282-83.
50. Thomas F. Green, *et al*, *Predicting the Behavior of the Educational System* (Syracuse, NY: The University Press, 1980).
51. James E. McClellan, review of Green's *Predicting Behavior of Educational System*, *Educational Theory* 30 (Fall 1980), p. 365.
52. *Ibid.*
53. Fred Moore, *Skool Resistance* (Palo Alto, CA: Learning is Living, undated), p. 15.
54. Ivan Illich, "After Deschooling, What?" in *After Deschooling, What?*, edited by Alan Gartner, Colin Greer, and Frank Reissman (New York: Social Policy, 1973), pp. 5-6.
55. Shirley Hale Willis, "The Urgent Need for Education about Cults," *Phi Delta Kappan* 64 (March 1983), p. 502.
56. See, for example, Saul V. Levine, *Radical Departures: Desperate Detours to Growing Up* (New York: Harcourt, Brace and Jovanovich, 1984).
57. Willis, "Urgent Need," 502.
58. *Ibid.*
59. *Ibid.*
60. *Ibid.*
61. *Ibid.*
62. *Ibid.*
63. Levine, *Radical Departures.*
64. Leonard J. Fein, *The Ecology of the Public School: An Inquiry into Community Control* (Indianapolis & New York: Pegasus, 1971), p. 44.

Chapter 6

1. H. Mark Roelofs, *Ideology and Myth in American Politics: A Critique of a National Political Mind* (Boston: Little, Brown and Company, 1976), p. 242.
2. Richard J. Whalen, "America's Identity Crisis," *Social Science and Modern Society* 20 (November/December 1982), p. 62.
3. Martin Pawley, *The Private Future: Causes and Consequences of Community Collapse in the West* (New York: Random House, 1974), p. 211.
4. *Ibid.*
5. Marvin Harris, *America Now: The Anthropology of a Changing Culture* (New York: Simon and Schuster, 1981).
6. See my earlier discussion in Chapter 4 of the antecedents which led up to the near breakdown of American society in the 1960s.
7. Harris, *America Now*, pp. 22-23.
8. Vance Packard, *A Nation of Strangers* (New York: David McKay, 1972).
9. For instance, Louis Zurcher and R.G. Kirkpatrick have studied the salvationary needs of those "status discontents" who join anti-pornography crusades in earnest. They seek to purify a society which has, in their minds, cast them adrift from their traditional moorings and once comfortable positions by attacking changing sexual norms. See Louis A Zurcher, Jr. and R. George Kirkpatrick, *Citizens for Decency: Antipornography Crusades and Status Defense* (Austin and London: University of Texas Press, 1976).
10. See Michael Lerner, "Editorial: The Disastrous Occupation," *Tikkun* 2 (Spring 1987), pp. 51-60.
11. See Charles Horton Cooley, *Human Nature and the Social Order* (New York: Charles Scribner's Sons, 1902).
12. Nelson N. Foote and Leonard S. Cottrell, Jr., *Identity and Interpersonal Competence: A New Direction in Family Research* (Chicago: The University of Chicago Press, 1955).
13. Everett Rogers, *Diffusion of Innovation* (New York: The Free Press of Glencoe, 1962), p. 219.
14. *Ibid.*, p. 99.
15. Julie Evetts, *The Sociology of Educational Ideas* (London: Routledge and Kegan Paul, 1973), p. 147.
16. *Ibid.*, p. 153.
17. *Ibid.*
18. See, for instance, R. Freeman Butts, *Public Education in the United States: From Revolution to Reform* (New York: Holt, Rinehart and Winston, 1978), pp. 381-95.
19. See David P. Gardner and the National Commission on Excellence in Education, *A Nation at Risk: The Imperative for Educational Reform*

(Washington, DC: U.S. Department of Education, 1983).

20. Some scholars believe that behind this kind of simplicity and dogmatism, especially in regard to literacy teaching, is really a desire to prevent the American people from becoming **critical** of the status quo (e.g., phonics teaching is considered letter-by-letter teaching; reading experts claim that its exclusive use as a teaching method produces comprehension without questioning of the author's ideas). See, for example, Dianne Sima Marcus and Curtis K. Carlson, "Political Philosophy and Reading Make a Dangerous Mix," *Education Week* 5 (February 27, 1985), p. 29.
21. Sometimes it is difficult to separate chicken from egg. Here is an instance in which a conservative national leader supposedly "initiated" a process of intellectual development of an educational ideology; however, the ideological **seeds** had actually been planted for several years. Reagan merely helped them to sprout more rapidly than would otherwise have been the case with a less "educationally concerned" President.
22. One of the earliest critical studies of the groups was Mary Anne Raywid's *The Axe-Grinders: Critics of Our Public Schools* (New York: Macmillan, 1962).
23. See George D. Spindler, "Education in a Transforming American Culture," *Harvard Educational Review* 25 (Summer 1955), p. 145-56.
24. This is said with the recognition that the educational climate had been turning to the right for several years prior to the publication of such reports. Nonetheless, the reports have "institutionalized" reactionary neo-conservativism in American education.
25. See, for instance, Sanford W. Reitman, "Role Strain and the American Teacher," *School Review* 79 (August 1971), pp. 543-59.
26. Roelofs, *Ideology and Myth*, pp. 6-7.
27. Willard Waller, *The Sociology of Teaching* (New York: John Wiley and Sons, 1932).
28. See, for instance, Erving Goffman, *Asylums* (Garden City, NY: Doubleday, Anchor Books, 1961).

Chapter 7

1. Cynically, about every 15 to 20 years, hostility to the teacher education establishment becomes particularly pronounced, and the media report dramatic upswings in the public's contempt for professional schools of teacher preparation, frequently accompanied by demands to reduce what little influence they may already have on the training of prospective and practicing teachers. Elitist denigration of teacher education programs by highly prestigious or prestige-seeking universities and academic departments aids and abets the public's disdain

for teacher education at such intervals. The present period is no exception, according to the most current, scholarly, and popular literature. However, it is surprising, and perhaps hopeful, to note that the 1985 Gallup Poll of the public's attitudes toward education may portend a break in the cycle of blame. According to Emily Feistritzer's analysis of this poll, "a majority of Americans oppose overwhelmingly any effort to meet the emerging shortage [of teachers] by diluting certification standards or reducing the number of teacher preparation courses required of prospective teachers." Emily Feistritzer, *Teacher Education Reports* 7 (July 4, 1984), p. 1. For a carefully thought-out and research-based explication of the problems faced by university teacher education programs in attracting top quality candidates for professional study, see Victor S. Vance and Phillip C. Schlechty, "The Distribution of Academic Ability in the Teaching Force: Policy Implications," *Phi Delta Kappan* 64 (September 1982), pp. 22-27. For an excellent historical account of the betrayal of American elementary and secondary school teachers, see Jurgen Herbst, *And Sadly Teach: Teacher Education and Professionalization in American Culture* (Madison, Wi: University of Wisconsin Press, 1989).

2. Daniel L. Duke, *Teaching: The Imperiled Profession* (Albany: State University of New York Press, 1984), p. 59. See also, Seymour B. Sarason, *Schooling In America: Scapegoat and Salvation* (New York: The Free Press, 1983).
3. Duke, *Imperiled Profession*, p. 5.
4. The SAT scores of teachers, if used as a significant criterion of ability (which many thoughtful scholars refuse to do), in fact provide a highly exploitable target for measurement-minded critics of the schools. Assessment after assessment over the past fifteen years shows clearly that college-bound seniors planning to major in education rank at or near the very bottom of all groups taking the test; this finding notwithstanding that until 1982 the SAT scores of **all** students had been declining year by year. In the words of Vance and Schlechty, "Nearly one-third of those initially attracted to teaching and fully one-third of those who intend to teach at age 30 were drawn from the lowest 20 percent. Surely, no one who accepts a presumed link between academic ability, competence with instructional techniques, and teaching effectiveness would argue that this situation is desirable." Vance and Schlechty, "Distribution of Academic Ability," p. 25. See also, W. Timothy Weaver, "The Talent Poll in Teacher Education," *Journal of Teacher Education* 32 (May-June 1981), p. 32-36.
5. See Duke, *Imperiled Profession*, pp. 17-21.
6. *Ibid.*, p. 40. Efforts have been made since 1982 to substantially raise these national averages, but the current prognosis is, at best, highly uncertain.
7. Cited in Seymour B. Sarason, *The Culture of the School and the Problem*

of Change, 2nd ed. (Boston: Allyn and Bacon, 1982), pp. 207-8.

8. Working in a large state university which attracts considerable numbers of students of teaching from both urban and rural communities, I have been kept informed of these problems over the years by students who live and work in small towns. My informal data are amply confirmed by the fascinating small town participant-observational research of Alan Peshkin of the University of Chicago. See his, *Growing Up American: Schooling and the Survival of Community* (Chicago and London: The University of Chicago Press, 1978).
9. Seymour B. Sarason, *Schooling in America: Scapegoat and Salvation* (New York: The Free Press, 1983), p. 70.
10. Patricia T. Ashton and Rodman B. Webb, *Making a Difference: Teachers Sense of Efficacy and Student Achievement* (New York and London: Longman, 1986), p. 145.
11. *Ibid.*, p. 3.
12. See Vance and Schlechty, "Distribution of Academic Ability;" see also, Duke, *Imperiled Profession.*
13. Since some of the most talented teachers who leave teaching do so to become teachers of teachers, it may be instructive to observe that a major recent study of the latter group's overall psychological fitness for their jobs concluded that "about one-fourth of all instructors in teacher education are 'neurotic' and that about the same proportion may be regarded as having 'character disorders' or as being 'socially maladjusted.'" The study, by B. E. Blanchard, professor emeritus of education at DePaul University, was published in 1982 under the formidable title "The Mental Health of College and University Professors Engaged in Teacher Education" by the World Association for Educational Research in Ghent, Belgium. See a summary by Robert L. Jacobson, "Prevalence of Emotional Ills Seen in Teacher Education," *Chronicle of Higher Education* 22 (January 4, 1984), pp. 21-22. With regard to the growth of drinking among teachers, see Edward F. Pajals and Joseph J. Blase, "Teachers in Bars: From Professional to Personal Self," *Sociology of Education* 57 (July 1984), pp. 164-73.
14. Harry N. Chandler, "School Teachers: Average, Fallible Human Beings," *The Education Digest* 47 (September 1981), p. 46.
15. H. H. Morris, "Teacher Competence: A Red Herring," *Phi Delta Kappan* 63 (October 1981), p. 124. See also, Sanford W. Reitman, "The Micropolitics of Teaching," ERIC document ED 190 515 (Washington, D.C.: Education Resources Information Center, 1979); also included in *Research in Education* (December 1980).
16. Pajals and Blase, "Teachers in Bars."

Chapter 8

1. Stanley Rothman, "Capitalism and Its Enemies," in *Capitalism: Sources of Hostility*, edited by Ernest van den Haag (New Rochelle, NY: Epoch Books, 1979), p. 204.
2. A technical note: I have employed a method of developing scenarios adapted from an approach known as "Field Anomaly Relaxation," in which great latitude is permitted in the process of projecting a variety of alternative conceptions of the future, with intentionally few restraints. See Willis W. Harmon, "The Coming Transformation," *The Futurist* 11 (February 1977), p. 5.
3. It has recently been pointed out that most futurists are overly optimistic in their speculations, **hoping** for some idealized future rather than assessing probabilities objectively. See Lloyd P. Williams, "Some Friendly Criticisms of Futurism," *Educational Studies* 12 (Spring 1981), p. XIII.
4. See Nicholas Rescher, "What is Value Change? A Framework for Research," in *Values and the Future: The Impact of Technological Change on American Values*, edited by Kurt Baier and Nicholas Rescher (New York: The Free Press, 1969), pp. 92-95.
5. See Arthur E. Wise, *Legislated Learning: The Bureaucratization of the American Classroom* (Berkeley: University of California Press, 1979).
6. William J. Bennett, from a speech entitled "Education and National Security," delivered in New Orleans the week of August 29, 1985 to the American Legion Auxiliary. Quoted in *Teacher Education Reports* 8 (August 29, 1985), p. 3.
7. See Sanford W. Reitman, "Daring to Make Teaching an Art," *The Educational Forum* 50 (Winter 1986), p. 145, 46.
8. Gary Abrams, *Los Angeles Times* (October 10, 1985).
9. Orrin E. Klapp, *Collective Search for Identity* (New York: Holt, Rinehart and Winston, 1969).
10. Reitman, "Daring to Make Teaching an Art."
11. For an excellent "humanistic" formulation of this concept, see Carl Rogers' classic, *Client-Centered Therapy: Its Current Practice, Implications, and Theory* (Boston: Houghton Mifflin Company, 1951).
12. For a superb explication of this problem of individualism gone amuck, see Robert N. Bellah, *et al.*, *Habits of the Heart: Individualism and Commitment in American Life* (Berkeley: University of California Press, 1985).
13. *Ibid.*
14. Garth Wood, *The Myth of Neurosis: Overcoming the Illness Excuse* (New York: Harper and Row, 1986).
15. Michael J. Bakalis, "American Education and the Meaning of Scarcity," *Phi Delta Kappan* 63 (September 1981), p. 10.

16. David P. Gardner and the National Commission on Excellence in Education, *A Nation at Risk: The Imperative for Educational Reform* (Washington, D.C.: United States Department of Education, 1983).
17. See Michael Harrington, *The New American Poverty* (New York: Penguin Books, 1984), pp. 65-94.
18. Defined by Keneth and Patricia Dolbeare as "a social order in which a coherent combination of culture, ideology, intellectual currents, social movements, and political organizations lend support to a state practicing extensive social control for the principal benefit of big business interests and finance. It is a combination of action and manipulation from above with acquiescence, divisiveness, and/or helplessness from below. Its goal is total management of all aspects of economic and social life, so that a steadily lower standard of living can be enforced on people without promoting unmanageable social unrest." Kenneth M. Dolbeare and Patricia Dolbeare, *American Ideologies: The Competing Political Beliefs of the 1970s*, 3rd edition (Chicago: Rand McNally, 1976), p. 223.
19. *Ibid.*
20. Charles E. Silberman, *Crisis in the Classroom: The Remaking of American Education* (New York: Random House, 1970).
21. Maurice P. Hunt, *Foundations of Education: Social and Cultural Perspectives* (New York: Holt, Rinehart and Winston, 1975), pp. 542, 43.
22. *Ibid.*
23. See Diane Ravitch, "The Educational Pendulum," *Psychology Today* 17 (October 1983), pp. 62-71. In that regard, see also, Jean Dresden Grambs, "Forty Years of Education: Will the Next Forty Be Any Better?" *Educational Leadership* 38 (May 1981), pp. 651-54.
24. Ira Katznelson and Margaret Weir, *Schooling For All: Class, Race, and the Decline of the Democratic Ideal* (New York: Basic Books, 1985).
25. *Ibid.*, pp. 214-20.
26. Williams, "Some Friendly Criticisms," p. XIV.
27. June K. Edwards, "Have Our Public Schools Become an Established Religion?" *Contemporary Education* 49 (Winter 1978), pp. 91-95.
28. Reported by Colleen Corder, "Social Scientists Urged to Resist the Political Bias in their Research," *The Chronicle of Higher Education* 32 (September 10, 1986), pp. 4, 6. One psychologist who is to be commended for criticizing the unduly individualistic focus of conventional psychotherapy is Paul Wachtel. He says: "Social and interpersonal forces both impinge upon us and are the product of our collective action, as we all constantly shape each other's world. Alone each of us is indeed helpless to change very much about our lives. In the practice of psychotherapy much harm has resulted from the efforts of therapists to help their patients achieve 'autonomy.' Being able to stand alone is the false ideal of the culture of Ronald Reagan. Patients

who benefit from psychotherapy are those who learn the lesson of mutuality, who move beyond both helpless dependency and the false ideal of independence. Mutuality and independence are the lessons we must learn on a social level as well. Our fates lie in each other." See Paul L. Wachtel, "Are We Prisoners of the Past?" *Tikkun* 2 (July/August 1987), p. 92.

29. Katznelson and Weir, *Schooling for All.*
30. Hunt, *Foundations of Education.*

Chapter 9

1. Larry Cuban, "Sex and School Reform," *Phi Delta Kappan* 68 (December 1986), p. 320.
2. Benjamin R. Barber, "Voting Is Not Enough," *The Atlantic Monthly* 253 (June 1984), p. 45.
3. See Christopher Lasch, *The Culture of Narcissism: American Life in An Age of Diminishing Expectations* (New York: Warner, 1979).
4. See Gerald D. Suttles, *The Social Construction of Communities* (Chicago: The University of Chicago Press, 1972), pp. 21-43.
5. See Abraham H. Maslow, *Motivation and Personality* (New York: Harper and Row, 1970).
6. Robert N. Bellah, *et al.*, *Habits of the Heart: Individualism and Commitment in American Life* (Berkeley: University of California Press, 1985), p. 294.
7. Recognizing the vital importance to the very survival of the species of bringing the world together in a universal cultural community, nonetheless, in this book, I elect to arbitrarily limit my remarks about community to the admittedly artificial boundaries of the United States.
8. Kenneth D. Benne, *From Pedagogy to Anthropology: A Challenge to the Educational Professoriate* (The 1981 De Garmo Lecture, Society of Professors of Education, February 19, 1981), p. 9.
9. Alan W. Watts, *The Wisdom of Insecurity: A Message for an Age of Anxiety* (New York: Pantheon Books, 1951), p. 132.
10. See Martin Buber, *I and Thou*, translated by Ronald G. Smith (New York: Charles Scribner's Sons, 1958). Also see, John Dewey, *Democracy and Education: An Introduction to the Philosophy of Education* (New York: Macmillan, 1916), pp. 5-7.
11. Bellah, *Habits of the Heart*, p. 72.
12. Although such communities are gone **for the most part**, there are exceptions, of course. Every semester a few of my students preparing to be teachers travel long distances from their isolated farms and villages to attend my night classes. Their written reports of traditional agrarian community life in the otherwise highly urbanized state of

California are sometimes quite astounding to the citified reader. But, for an in-depth portrait of this almost extinct way of life in the Midwest, read Alan Peshkin, *Growing Up American: Schooling and the Survival of Community* (Chicago: The University of Chicago Press, 1978).

13. Thomas A. Brindley, "No Place for Community," in *Education and Social Concern: An Approach to the Social Foundations*, edited by Robert F. Lawson, Val D. Rust, and Susanne M. Shafer (Ann Arbor, MI: Prakken Publications, 1987), p. 71.
14. Peshkin, *Growing Up American*, p. 201.
15. See, for example, the volume credited to him, especially because of his leadership in the movement toward a "new civism," edited by Alan H. Jones, *Civic Learning for Teachers: Capstone for Educational Reform* (Ann Arbor: Prakken Publications, 1985).
16. Bellah, *Habits of the Heart*, p. 277.
17. The vital role of dissent in education as well as community development is commonly misunderstood both by educators and social workers. All too often, they call for "collaboration" as the only appropriate form of behavior for members of democratic organizations, and are critical of ideas which cast dissent and social conflict in a positive light. But conflict theory is not the exclusive property of Marxists. Both collaboration and conflict are functional for all human organizations under specific circumstances. In short, a variable formulation of interpersonal and intergroup dynamics in the context of community development is the key to moral education in school and society. See Sanford W. Reitman, "The Limitations of Consensus as a Model of Educational Reform," *Teachers College Record* 78 (February 1977), pp. 337-43.
18. Joshua Meyrowitz, *No Sense of Place: The Impact of Electronic Medica on Social Behavior* (New York: Oxford University Press, 1985), p. 257.
19. *Ibid.*
20. See Sanford W. Reitman, "Daring to Make Teaching an Art," *The Educational Forum* 50 (Winter 1986), pp. 137-48.
21. Ignacio Gotz, "Heidegger and the Art of Teaching," *Educational Theory* 33 (Winter 1983), p. 9.
22. Arthur G. Wirth, *Productive Work--in Industry and Schools: Becoming Persons Again* (Lanham, MD: University Press of America, 1983), p. 257.
23. Reitman, "Limitations of Consensus."
24. Hanna F. Pitkin and Sara M. Shumer, "On Participation," *Democracy* 2 (1982), pp. 47-48.
25. Garth Wood, *The Myth of Neurosis: Overcoming the Illness Excuse* (New York: Harper and Row, 1986).
26. Rollo May, *The Courage to Create* (New York: W. W. Norton, 1975), pp. 11, 12.
27. See Sanford W. Reitman, "The Reconstructionism of Harold Rugg,"

Educational Theory 22 (Winter 1972).

28. Gotz, "Heidegger and the Art of Teaching," p. 9.
29. Sanford W. Reitman and Faye R. Reitman, "Teacher Education as the Preparation of Professional Artists: A Preliminary Model," *Teacher Education Quarterly* 15 (Summer 1988), pp. 5-15.
30. Ernest Becker, *The Denial of Death* (New York: The Free Press, 1973), pp. 4, 5.
31. Erich Fromm, *Escape from Freedom* (New York: Holt, Rinehart and Winston, 1964).
32. Bellah, *Habits of the Heart*, p. 285.
33. Sanford W. Reitman, "The Micropolitics of Artistic Teaching: Implications for Foundations Instruction," *Educational Foundations* 3:3 (Fall 1989), pp. 101-117.
34. The premise referred to is the influential, if somewhat exaggerated notion of the nineteenth century public school reformers such as Horace Mann--a notion which has persisted over one hundred and fifty years--that aside from a "good education," going to "common school" alongside children from all walks of life, different ethnic and religious groups, etc. is the single most significant force in binding Americans together as a democratic people.
35. Donald A. Erickson, "Choice and Private Schools: Dynamics of Supply and Demand," in *Private Education: Studies in Choice and Public Policy*, edited by Daniel C. Levy (New York: Oxford University Press, 1986), p. 105. Of additional interest to some readers may be a recent study which supports the importance of continuity between family and school normative patterns. See Donald A. Hansen, "Family-School Articulations: The Effects of Interaction Rule Mismatch," *American Educational Research Journal* 23 (Winter 1986), pp. 643-59. Hansen comments as follows: "The data support one fundamental proposition: There is no interactive influence of families and classrooms; children are relatively advantaged in classrooms that are similar to their families in rules of interaction; and relatively disadvantaged in classrooms that are dissimilar." (p. 656). The implications of that data-based assertion for parental freedom of schooling choice seem indisputable. Nonetheless, I recommend to skeptics the latest comprehensive work of one of the great school "heretics" of the day, sociologist James Coleman (with Thomas Hoffer)'s *Public and Private High Schools: The Impact of Communities* (New York: Basic Books, forthcoming).
36. See, for instance, Ann Bastian, Norm Fruchter, Marily Gittell, Colin Greer, and Kenneth Haskins, "Rethinking the Agenda for Democratic Schooling," *Education Week* (February 4, 1987), p. 22.
37. Benjamin R. Barber, *Strong Democracy: Participatory Politics for a New Age* (Berkeley and Los Angeles: University of California Press, 1984), p. 296.

38. *Ibid.*, p. 297.
39. *Ibid.*, p. 298.
40. For a detailed summary of Barber's proposed comprehensive program to bring about a strongly democratic America, see the concluding chapter of *Strong Democracy*, pp. 261-311.
41. Amy Gutmann, *Democratic Education* (New Jersey: Princeton University Press, 1987), p. 66. Such safeguards as described by Gutmann were, in fact, built into voucher initiatives proposed to the people of California in 1979 and 1982 respectively. The leading proponents of the California voucher initiatives (which failed largely because they were ahead of their time) were John E. Coons and Stephen D. Sugarman, authors of the important book *Education By Choice: The Case for Family Control* (Berkeley: University of Califomia Press, 1978).

Bibliography of Works Cited

Abrams, Gary. *Los Angeles Times*, October 10, 1985.

Adler, Mortimer J., *et al. The Paideia Proposal: An Educational Manifesto.* New York: Macmillan, 1982.

Adler, Mortimer J. and Milton Mayer. *The Revolution in Education.* Chicago: University of Chicago Press, 1958.

Arciniega, Tomas A. "Bilingual Education in the 1980s," *The Education Digest* 48 (1982), p. 10.

Ashton, Patricia T. and Rodman B. Webb. *Making a Difference: Teachers Sense of Efficacy and Student Achievement.* New York and London: Longman, 1986.

Bakalis, Michael J. "American Education and the Meaning of Scarcity," *Phi Delta Kappan* 63 (1981), p. 10.

Barber, Benjamin R. *Strong Democracy: Participatory Politics for a New Age.* Berkeley and Los Angeles: University of California Press, 1984.

Barber, Benjamin R. "Voting Is Not Enough," *The Atlantic Monthly* 253 (1984), p. 45.

Barnes, Ronald F. "An Educator Looks Back from 1996," *The Futurist* 12 (1978), pp. 123-126.

Bastain, Ann, Norm Fruchter, Marily Gittell, Colin Greer, and Kenneth Haskins. "Rethinking the Ageda for Democratic Schooling," *Education Week* (February 4, 1987), p. 22.

Becker, Ernest. *The Denial of Death.* New York: The Free Press, 1973.

Bellah, Robert N. *et al. Habits of the Heart: Individualism and Commitment in American Life.* Berkeley: University of California Press, 1985.

Benne, Kenneth D. *From Pedagogy to Anthropology: A Challenge to the Education Professoriate.* The 1981 De Garmo Lecture. Published by the Society of Professors of Education, 1981.

Bennett, William J. "Education and National Security." A speech delivered in New Orleans the week of August 29, 1985 to the American Legion Auxiliary. Quoted in *Teacher Education Reports*, August 29, 1985, p. 3.

Berlak, Ann and Harold Berlak. *Dilemmas of Schooling: Teaching and Social Change*. New York: Methuen and Company, 1981.

Bestor, Arthur. *Educational Wastelands: The Retreat from Learning in Our Public Schools*. Urbana: University of Illinois Press, 1953.

Bigge, Morris L. *Learning Theories for Teachers*. 3rd edition. New York: Harper and Row, 1976.

Brameld, Theodore. *Education as Power*. New York: Holt, Rinehart and Winston, 1965.

Brameld, Theodore. "Social Frontiers: Retrospective and Prospective." *Phi Delta Kappan*, 59 (1977), pp. 118-20.

Brindley, Thomas A. "No Place for Community." In *Education and Social Concern: An Approach to the Social Foundations*. Ann Arbor, MI: Prakken Publications, 1987.

Brodinsky, Ben. "The New Right: The Movement and its Impact." *Phi Delta Kappan*, 64 (1982), pp. 87-94.

Buber, Martin. *I and Thou*. Translated by Ronald G. Smith. New York: Charles Scribner's Sons, 1958.

Butts, R. Freeman. *Public Education in the United States: From Revolution to Reform*. New York: Holt, Rinehart and Winston, 1978.

Callahan, Raymond. *Education and the Cult of Efficiency: A Study of the Social Forces that have Shaped the Administration of the Public Schools*. Chicago: University of Chicago Press, 1962.

Carlson, Allan C. "Religion, the State and the Schools: Reflections on the Deweyan Perspective." *Current Issues in Education*, 3 (1983), pp. 21-35.

Carnoy, Martin and Henry Levin. *The Limits of Educational Reform*. New York: David McKay, 1976.

Chandler, Harry N. "School Teachers: Average, Fallible Human Beings." *The Education Digest*, 47 (1981), pp. 44-46.

Cogan, Elizabeth. "Individualism, Collectivism, and Radical Educational Reform." *Harvard Educational Review*, 48 (1978), pp. 227-66.

Coleman, James with Thomas Hoffer. *Public and Private High Schools: The Impact of Communities*. New York: Basic Books, forthcoming.

Conant, James B. *The American High School Today*. New York: McGraw-Hill, 1959.

Coons, John E. and Stephen D. Sugarman. *Education by Choice: The Case for Family Control*. Berkeley: University of California Press, 1978.

Corder, Colleen. "Social Scientists Urged to Resist Political Bias in their Research." *The Chronicle of Higher Education*, September 10, 1986, pp. 4, 6.

Cooley, Charles Horton. *Human Nature and the Social Order*. New York: Charles Scribner's Sons, 1902.

Coons, John E. and Stephen D. Sugarman. *Education By Choice: The Case for Family Control*. Berkeley: University of California Press, 1978.

Counts, George S. *Dare the School Build a New Social Order?* New York: John Day Company, 1932.

Crockenberg, Vincent and Richard LaBrecque, editors. *Culture As Education*. Dubuque, IA: Kendall/Hunt Publishing Company, 1977.

Cuban, Larry. "Sex and School Reform." *Phi Delta Kappan*, 68 (1986), pp. 319-21.

Curti, Merle. *The Social Ideas of American Educators*. Totowa, NJ: Littlefield, Adams and Company, 1978.

Desroche, Henri. *The Sociology of Hope*. London: Routledge and Kegan Paul, 1979.

Dewey, John. *Democracy and Education: An Introduction to the Philosophy of Education*. New York: Macmillan, 1916.

Dewey, John. *My Pedagogic Creed*. Washington, D.C.: Progressive Education Association, 1929.

Dolbeare, Kenneth M. and Patricia Dolbeare. *American Ideologies: The Competing Political Beliefs of the 1970s*. 3rd edition. Chicago: Rand McNally, 1976.

Drucker, Peter. "The Worst Thing Is to Modernize." *U. S. News and World Report*, February 2, 1987, p. 23.

Duke, Daniel L. *Teaching: The Imperiled Profession*. Albany: State University of New York Press, 1984.

Educators for Social Responsibility. Publicity brochure. No publication date available.

Edwards, June K. "Have Our Public Schools Become an Established Religion?" *Contemporary Education*, 49 (1978), pp. 91-95.

Entwistle, Harold. "Antonio Gramsci and the School as Hegemonic." *Educational Theory*, 28 (1978), pp. 23-33.

Erickson, Donald A. "Choice and Private Schools: Dynamics of Supply and Demand." In *Private Education: Studies in Choice and Public Policy*. Edited by Daniel C. Levy. New York: Oxford University Press, 1986, pp. 82-109.

Evetts, Julie. *The Sociology of Educational Ideas*. London: Routledge and Kegan Paul, 1973.

Fantini, Mario. *Public Schools of Choice*. New York: Simon and Schuster, 1973.

Fein, Leonard J. *The Ecology of the Public School: An Inquiry into Community Control*. Indianapolis and New York: Pegasus, 1971.

Feistritzer, Emily. *Teacher Education Reports*, July 4, 1984, p. 1.

Feistritzer, Emily. *Teacher Education Reports*, August 29, 1985, p. 3.

Franklin, Barry M. *Building the American Community: The School Curriculum and the Search for Social Control*. London: The Falmer Press,

1986.

Foote, Nelson N. and Leonard S. Cottrell, Jr. *Identity and Interpersonal Competence: A New Direction in Family Research.* Chicago: The University of Chicago Press, 1955.

Fromm, Erich. *Escape from Freedom.* New York: Holt, Rinehart and Winston, 1964.

Gardner, David P. and the National Commission on Excellence in Education. *A Nation At Risk: The Imperative for Educational Reform.* Washington, D.C.: United States Department of Education, 1983.

Giroux, Henry, and Roger I. Simon. *Popular Culture, Schooling and Everyday Life.* Granby, MA: Bergin & Garvey, 1989.

Goffman, Erving. *Asylums.* Garden City, NJ: Doubleday, Anchor Books, 1961.

Gotz, Ignacio. "Heidegger and the Art of Teaching." *Educational Theory,* 33 (1983), pp. 1-9.

Grambs, Jean Dresden. "Forty Years of Education: Will the Next Forty Be Any Better?" *Educational Leadership,* 38 (1981), pp. 651-54.

Gratus, Jack. *The False Messiahs.* New York: Taplinger Publishing Company, 1980.

Green, Thomas F. *et al. Predicting the Behavior of the Educational System.* Syracuse, NY: The University Press, 1980.

Gross, Martin. *The Psychological Society: A Critical Analysis of Psychiatry, Psychotherapy, and the Psychological Revolution.* New York: Random House, 1978.

Gutmann, Amy. *Democratic Education.* Princeton, NJ: Princeton University Press, 1987.

Hansen, Donald A. "Family-School Articulations: The Effects of Interaction Rule Mismatch." *American Educational Research Journal,* 23 (1986), pp. 643-59.

Harmon, Willis W. "The Coming Transformation." *The Futurist,* 11 (1977), pp. 5-11.

Harrington, Michael. *The New American Poverty.* New York: Penguin Books, 1984.

Harris, Marvin. *America Now: The Anthropology of a Changing Culture.* New York: Simon and Schuster, 1981.

Hawken, Paul. *The Next Economy.* New York: Ballantine Books, 1983.

Herbst, Jurgen. *And Sadly Teach: Teacher Education and Professionalization in American Culture.* Madison, WI: University of Wisconsin Press, 1989.

Herndon, James. *The Way It Spozed to Be.* New York: Bantam Books, 1969.

Howard, James. "The Time for Basic Education." *The Education Digest,* 47 (1981), pp. 8-9.

Hunt, Maurice P. *Foundations of Education: Social and Cultural Perspectives.* New York: Holt, Rinehart and Winston, 1975.

Hutchins, Robert M. *The Conflict in Education in a Democratic Society.* New York: Harper and Brothers, 1953.

Illich, Ivan. "After Deschooling, What?" In *After Deschooling, What?* Edited by Alan Gartner, Colin Greer and Frank Reissman. New York: Social Policy, 1973, pp. 1-28.

Illich, Ivan. *Deschooling Society.* New York: Harper and Row, 1971.

Itzkoff, Seymour W. *A New Public Education.* New York: David McKay, 1976.

Jacobson, Robert L. "Prevalence of Emotional Ills Seen in Teacher Education." *The Chronicle of Higher Education*, January 4, 1984, pp. 21-22.

Jones, Alan H., editor. *Civic Learning for Teachers: Capstone for Educational Reform.* Ann Arbor: Prakken Publications, 1985.

Kamens, David H. "Education and Democracy: A Comparative International Analysis," *Sociology of Education* 61 (1988), p. 116.

Katz, Michael B. *Class, Bureaucracy, and Schools: The Illusion of Educational Change in America.* New York: Praeger Publishers, 1971.

Katznelson, Ira and Margaret Weir. *Schooling for All: Class, Race, and the Decline of the Democratic Ideal.* New York: Basic Books, 1985.

Kenniston, Kenneth. *The Uncommitted: Alienated Youth in American Society.* New York: Harcourt, Brace and World, 1965.

Kimmel, Michael S. "A Prejudice Against Prejudice." *Psychology Today,* 20 (1986), pp. 47-52.

Klapp, Orrin E. *Collective Search for Identity.* New York: Holt, Rinehart and Winston, 1969.

Koerner, James D. *The Miseducation of American Teachers.* Boston: Houghton Mifflin Company, 1963.

Kozol, Jonathan. *Death at an Early Age: The Destruction of the Hearts and Minds of Negro Children in the Boston Public Schools.* Boston: Houghton Mifflin, 1976.

Kozol, Jonathan. *The Night is Dark and I am Far from Home.* Boston: Houghton Mifflin, 1975.

Lamm, Zvi. "The Status of Knowledge in the Radical Concept of Education." In *Curriculum and the Cultural Revolution.* Editors David E. Purpel and Maurice Belanger. Berkeley, CA: McCutchen, 1972, pp. 124-42.

Lasch, Christopher. *The Culture of Narcissism: American Life in an Age of Diminishing Expectations.* New York: Warner, 1979.

Lee, James Michael. "Religion and the Public Schools: A Pluralistic View." *California Journal of Teacher Education*, 9 (1982), pp. 1-30.

Lerner, Michael. "Editorial: The Disastrous Occupation." *Tikkun*, 2 (1987), pp. 51-60.

Levine, Saul V. *Radical Departures: Desperate Detours to Growing Up.* New York: Harcourt, Brace, and Jovanovich, 1984.

Lynd, Albert. *Quackery in the Public Schools.* Boston: Little Brown, 1953.

McClellan, James E. Review of Thomas Green's *Predicting the Behavior of*

the Educational System. Educational Theory, 30 (1980), pp. 353-66.
Mann, Horace. *Twelfth Annual Report to the [Massachusetts] Board of Education*. Boston: Dutton and Wentworth, State Printers, 1848.
Mannheim, Karl. *Ideology and Utopia: An Introduction to the Sociology of Knowledge*. New York: Harcourt, Brace and World, 1936.
Marcus, Dianne Sirna and Curtis K. Carlson. "Political Philosophy and Reading Make a Dangerous Mix." *Education Week* (February 27, 1985), p. 29.
Maslow, Abraham H. *Motivation and Personality*. New York: Harper and Row, 1970.
Mason, Robert E. *Educational Ideals in American Society*. Boston: Allyn and Bacon, 1960.
May, Rollo. *The Courage to Create*. New York: W. W. Norton, 1975.
Meyers, Henry S., Jr. *Fundamentally Speaking*. San Francisco: Strawberry Hill Press, 1977.
Meyrowitz, Joshua. *No Sense of Place: The Impact of Electronic Media on Social Behavior*. New York: Oxford University Press, 1985.
Moore, Fred. *Skool Resistance*. Palo Alto, CA: Learning is Living, undated.
Morris, Charles R. "The Coming Global Boom," *The Atlantic Monthly* 264 (1989), pp. 55-56.
Morris, H. H. "Teacher Competence: A Red Herring." *Phi Delta Kappan*, 63 (1981), p. 124.
Moynihan, Daniel Patrick. "Government and the Ruin of Private Education." *Harper's*, 255 (1978), pp. 28-38.
Neill, A. S. *Summerhill: A Radical Approach to Child Rearing*. New York: Hart Publishing Company, 1960.
Nyberg, David and Kieran Egan. *The Erosion of Education: Socialization and the Schools*. New York: Teachers College Press, 1981.
O'Neill, William F. *Educational Ideologies: Contemporary Expressions of Educational Philosophy*. Santa Monica, CA: Goodyear Publishing Company, 1981.
Packard, Vance. *A Nation of Strangers*. New York: David McKay, 1972.
Palmer, John. "Who Should Define the Meaning of Citizenship?" *Journal of Teacher Education*, 34 (1983), pp. 51-53.
Pajals, Edward F. and Joseph J. Blase. "Teachers in Bars: From Professional to Personal Self." *Sociology of Education*, 57 (1984), pp. 164-73.
Park, J. Charles. "The New Right: Threat to Democracy in Education." *Educational Leadership*, 38 (1980), pp. 146-49.
Pawley, Martin. *The Private Future: Causes and Consequences of Community Collapse in the West*. New York: Random House, 1974.
Perkinson, Henry J. *The Imperfect Panacea: American Faith in Education, 1865-1965*. New York: Random House, 1968.
Peshkin, Alan. *Growing Up American: Schooling and the Survival of Community*. Chicago: The University of Chicago Press, 1978.
Pettigrew, Thomas F. *Racial Discrimination in the United States*. New York:

Harper & row, 1975.

Pettigrew, Thomas F. *Racially Separate or Together?* New York: McGraw-Hill, 1971.

Pettigrew, Thomas F. *The Sociology of Race Relations: Reflection and Reform.* New York: Free Press, 1980.

Pitkin, Hanna F. and Sara M. Shumer. "On Participation." *Democracy*, 2 (1982), pp. 47-48.

Postman, Neil and Charles Weingartner. *Teaching as a Subversive Activity.* New York: Delacorte Press, 1969.

Pratte, Richard. *Ideology and Education.* New York: David McKay, 1977.

Rafferty, Max. *Classroom Countdown: Education at the Crossroads.* New York: Hawthorn Books, 1970.

Rafferty, Max. *Suffer Little Children.* New York: Devin-Adair Company, 1962.

Ramirez, Francisco O. and John Boli, "The Political Construction of Mass Schooling: European Origins and Worldwide Institutionalization." *Sociology of Education*, 60 (1987), pp. 2-17.

Ravitch, Diane. "The Educational Pendulum." *Psychology Today*, 17 (1983), pp. 62-71.

Ravitch, Diane. *The Troubled Crusade: American Education 1945-1980.* New York: Basic Books, 1983.

Raywid, Mary Anne. *The Axe-Grinders: Critics of Our Public Schools.* New York: Macmillan, 1962.

Reagan, Ronald. From his Weekly Radio Broadcast, 1983. Quoted in the *Fresno Bee*, March 13, 1983.

Reich, Charles. *The Greening of America: How the Youth Revolution is Trying to Make America Livable.* New York: Random House, 1970.

Reitman, Sanford W. "The Micropolitics of Artistic Teaching: Implications for Foundations Instruction," *Educational Foundations* 3 (1989), pp. 101-117.

Reitman, Sanford W. "Daring to Make Teaching an Art." *The Educational Forum*, 50 (1986), pp. 137-48.

Reitman, Sanford W. *Education, Society, and Change.* Boston: Allyn and Bacon, 1981.

Reitman, Sanford W. "The Limitations of Consensus as a Model of Educational Reform." *Teachers College Record*, 78 (1977), pp. 337-43.

Reitman, Sanford W. "The Micropolitics of Teaching." ERIC document ED 190 515. Washington, DC: Education Resources Information Center, 1979. Abstracted in *Research in Education*, 15 (1980), p. 186.

Reitman, Sanford W. "The Reconstructionism of Harold Rugg." *Educational Theory*, 22 (1972), 51.

Reitman, Sanford W. "Role Strain and the American Teacher." *School Review*, 79 (1971), pp. 543-59.

Reitman, Sanford W. and Reitman, Faye R. "Teacher Education as the

Preparation of Professional Artists." *Teacher Education Quarterly*, 15 (1988), pp. 5-15.

Rescher, Nicholas. "What is Value Change? A Framework for Research." In *Values and the Future: The Impact of Technological Change on American Values*. Edited by Kurt Baier and Nicholas Rescher. New York: The Free Press, 1969, pp. 68-109.

Rickover, Hyman G. *Education and Freedom*. New York: E.P. Dutton Company, 1959.

Roelofs, H. Mark. *Ideology and Myth in American Politics: A Critique of a National Political Mind*. Boston: Little, Brown, and Company, 1976.

Rogers, Carl. *Client-Centered Therapy: Its Current Practice, Implications, and Theory*. Boston: Houghton Mifflin Company, 1951.

Rogers, Everett. *Diffusion of Innovation*. New York: The Free Press of Glencoe, 1962.

Rothman, Stanley. "Capitalism and Its Enemies." In *Capitalism: Sources of Hostility*. Edited by Ernest van den Haag. New Rochelle, NY: Epoch Books, 1979, pp. 173-206.

Roszak, Theodore. *The Making of a Counter Culture: Reflections on the Technocratic Society and its Youthful Opposition*. Garden City, NJ: Doubleday and Company, 1969.

Sarason, Seymour B. *The Culture of the School and the Problem of Change*. 2nd edition. Boston: Allyn and Bacon, 1982.

Sarason, Seymour B. *Schooling In America: Scapegoat and Salvation*. New York: The Free Press, 1983.

Schwartz, Morris S. and Charlotte G. Schwartz. "Mental Health: The Concept." In *International Encyclopedia of the Social Sciences*, 10 Edited by David L. Sills. New York: Crowell Collier and Macmillan, 1968, pp. 215-21.

Scott, Winfield and Clyde M. Hills, editors. *Public Education Under Criticism*. New York: Prentice-Hall, 1954.

Siedentop, Daryl. "Some Basic Talk about What's Basic." *NAASP Bulletin*, 62 (1978), pp. 1-4.

Silberman, Charles E. *Crisis in the Classroom: The Remaking of American Education*. New York: Random House, 1970.

Smith, Mortimer. *And Madly Teach: A Layman Looks at Public School Education*. Chicago: Henry Regner, 1949.

Smith, Vernon H. *Alternative Schools: The Development of Options in Public Education*. Lincoln, NE: Professional Educators Publications, 1974.

Spindler, George D. "Education in a Transforming American Culture." *Harvard Educational Review*, 25 (1955), pp. 145-56.

Stephens, Lillian S. *The Teacher's Guide to Open Education*. New York: Holt, Rinehart and Winston, 1974.

Sundquist, James L. *Politics and Policy: The Eisenhower, Kennedy, and Johnson Years*. Washington, DC: The Brookings Institution, 1968.

Suttles, Gerald D. *The Social Construction of Communities*. Chicago: The University of Chicago Press, 1972.

Talmon, Yonine. "Millenarianism." In *International Encyclopedia of the Social Sciences*, 10. Edited by David L. Sills. New York: Crowell Collier and Macmillan, 1968, pp. 349-62.

Thimmesh, Hillary. "Education is About Civilization: Lose Sight of That and You Lose Sight of Humanity." *The Chronicle of Higher Education* (June 20, 1984), p. 64.

Toffler, Alvin. *Future Shock*. New York: Bantam Books, 1970.

Tyack, David and Elizabeth Hanson. "Hard Times, Hard Choices: The Case for Coherence in Public School Leadership." *Phi Delta Kappan*, 63 (1982), pp. 511-15.

United States Commission on Civil Rights. *Intimidation and Violence: Racial and Religious Bigotry in America*. Washington, DC: Clearinghouse Publication 77, January 1983.

Usdan, Michael D. "Realities of the 1980s: Implications for Teacher Educators." *Journal of Teacher Education*, 32 (1981), pp. 24-30.

Vance, Victor S. and Phillip C. Schlechty. "The Distribution of Academic Ability in the Teaching Force: Policy Implications." *Phi Delta Kappan*, 64 (1982), pp. 22-27.

Wachtel, Paul L. "Are We Prisoners of the Past?" *Tikkun*, 2 (1987), pp. 24-27; 90-92.

Waller, Willard. *The Sociology of Teaching*. New York: John Wiley and Sons, 1932.

Watts, Alan W. *The Wisdom of Insecurity: A Message for an Age of Anxiety*. New York: Pantheon Books, 1951.

Weaver, W. Timothy. "The Talent Pool in Teacher Education." *Journal of Teacher Education*, 32 (1981), pp. 32-36.

Whalen, Richard J. "America's Identity Crisis." *Social Science and Modern Society*, 20 (1982), pp. 59-63.

Williams Lloyd P. "Some Friendly Criticisms of Futurism." *Educational Studies*, 12 (1981), pp. V-XV.

Willis, Shirley Hale. "The Urgent Need for Education about Cults." *Phi Delta Kappan*, 64 (1983), pp. 500-502.

Wirth, Arthur G. *Productive Work--in Industry and Schools: Becoming Persons Again*. Lanham, MD: University Press of America, 1983.

Wise, Arthur E. *Legislated Learning: The Bureaucratization of the American Classroom*. Berkeley, CA: University of California Press, 1979.

Wood, Garth. *The Myth of Neurosis: Overcoming the Illness Excuse*. New York: Harper and Row, 1986.

Wood, George H. "Beyond Radical Cynicism." *Educational Theory*, 32 (1982), pp. 55-71.

Woodring, Paul. *Let's Talk Sense About Our Schools*. New York: McGraw-Hill, 1953.

Zurcher, Jr., Louis A. and R. George Kirkpatrick. *Citizens for Decency:*

Antipornography Crusades as Status Defense. Austin, TX: University of Texas Press, 1976.

Index

About the Author

Sanford W. Reitman was a professor of educational foundations with the School of Education at California State University, Fresno, at the time of his death in 1989 at age 54. He had been a member of the faculty there since 1966, teaching in the fields of educational foundations, elementary education, and clinical supervision, while also serving from 1980 to 1983 as chair of the Department of Teacher Education.

Previously, Reitman was a public and private school teacher at the elementary and secondary levels in Los Angeles, California, and Cleveland, Ohio. He received a B.A. degree in political science and sociology from Ohio University in 1957, an M.A. degree in educational psychology and elementary education from Case Western Reserve University in 1959, and an Ed.D. degree in the social and philosophical foundations of education, also from Case Western Reserve University, in 1969.

He is the author of two previous books, *Foundations of Education for Prospective Teachers* and *Education, Society, and Change*, both published by Allyn and Bacon in, respectively, 1977 and 1981. He is also the author of several dozen educational articles and papers, appearing in such journals as *The Educational Forum, Educational Foundations, Educational Studies, Educational Theory, The Journal of Teacher Education, School Review, Teachers College Record*, and *Teacher Education Quarterly*. He was frequently a presenter at educational conferences, including the American Educational Studies Association (AESA), the Far Western Philosophy of Education Society, the National Council for the Social Studies, and the Philosophy of Education Society, among others. At the time of his death, Reitman was involved in analysis and development of theory and practice around the concept of the teacher as artist, as discussed in his "The Micropolitics of Artistic Teaching: Implications for Foundations Instruction," which was first presented at the AESA annual convention in Toronto in 1988 and later published in the Fall 1989 issue of *Educational Foundations.*

Reitman served on the Executive Council of the American Educational Studies Association (AESA) from 1988 until his death, and had previously served as a member and chair of the AESA Committee on Academic Standards and Accreditation, as well as on that Association's Program Committee and R. Freeman Butts Lecture Committee. He was also a member of Alpha Delta Kappa, the American Educational Research Association, the John Dewey Society, Phi Delta Kappa, the Philosophy of Education Society, the Society of Professors of Education, and the Sociology of Education Society.

Reitman is survived by his wife, Faye Rochelle Reitman, an artist and psychotherapist, who resides in Fresno, California, and their three children, Mitchell Reitman of Fresno, Sharon Lynne Reitman of Seattle, Washington, and Melanie Reitman-Wuest of Hayward, California.